The Pictorial History of
AIR WARFARE

The Pictorial History of
AIR WARFARE
Chris Chant

Foreword by Ira C. Eaker
Lt.-Gen., USAF (Ret.)

OCTOPUS

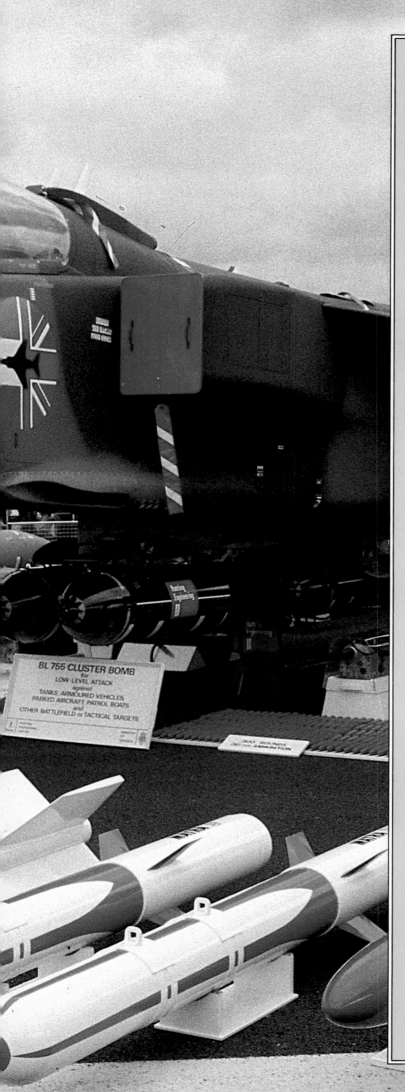

Contents

First published 1979 by Octopus Books Limited
59 Grosvenor Street London W1

©1979 Octopus Books Limited ISBN 0 7064 0977 9

Produced by Mandarin Publishers Limited
22a Westlands Road, Quarry Bay, Hong Kong

Printed in Italy
Nuova Grafica Moderna S.p.A. - Verona

Foreword
by Ira C. Eaker

The Pictorial History of Air Warfare by Chris Chant, published by Octopus, is the best book on this subject I have seen. The photographs are extensive, covering the entire history of air warfare, from mythological times to the present, with accurate captions and descriptions.

But it is the manuscript of this monumental work which I found most rewarding.

There are chapters devoted to the earliest days in aviation, to the years between the two world wars, and especially to air warfare in World War II, both in Europe, against Hitler's Luftwaffe, and in the Pacific against the Japanese war lords – all of which are in general accurate historical summaries, well worth the price of this memorable book.

The chapters on Modern Air Warfare, including Korea and Vietnam and the Arab-Israeli conflicts, are significant summaries.

The chapter devoted to the invention of air weapons, balloons, dirigibles, planes and auxiliary equipment: guns, bombs, cameras and electronic equipment are thorough, superb, and again well illustrated.

There are also chapters devoted to the evolution of tactics and strategy which are generally authoritative and well stated.

Not all the air leaders and combat crews who participated in the air campaigns described in this book will concur in all the author's statements and conclusions. For example, Chant calls any mission of the RAF or the US 8th Air Force which suffered heavy looses a 'defeat'. I agree only if these missions did not accomplish their purpose. It was a series of these 'defeats' which enabled us to destroy the Luftwaffe and much of Germany's war-making potential.

However, this book deserves a prominent place in every aviation library. All combat veterans of the Second World War will find it intensely interesting and students of air warfare in the future will be well rewarded by the great store of fact it discloses and illustrates superbly.

I commend and congratulate Mr Chant and Octopus for this significant contribution to the history of air warfare.

Pioneer Days

Man has long dreamed of flight, and with the dream of emulating the birds there has always been the possible nightmare of air warfare, in which the two dimensions of land and sea warfare would be supplemented by the three-dimensional aspects of air warfare. But despite grandiose schemes for the use of airpower in military ventures, the realization of such notions was denied by the impossibility of flight until the late 18th century.

In 1783 the Montgolfier brothers, papermakers of Lyons, made the world's first flight, in a balloon using the lift of hot air. Shortly after this, the limitations of hot air were demonstrated by the success of Jacques Charles' unmanned hydrogen balloon, soon followed by manned versions. Man was at last free of the earth, and the importance of the new means of 'transportation' immediately brought tumbling forth a multitude of ideas, all wholly impractical, for the use of balloons in warfare. The two most important were for the balloon to be used as a means of landing troops in the enemy's rear (Ben-jamin Franklin wrote how a large body of men 'descending from the clouds might . . . in many places do an infinite deal of mischief before a force could be brought together to repel them', a true understanding of the possibilities inherent in air mobility), and for the balloon to be used as a fighting machine, most visionaries seeing their dreams in the same category as major warships in terms of gun power.

All these notions, to some extent on the right lines, foundered on the total impossibility of using balloons in the ways envisaged. A globular lifting unit with the payload suspended beneath it in a gondola and lacking any means of propulsion, the balloon was and is at the mercy of the winds, thus making it impossible for the balloon's crew to steer their craft in any given direction.

The visionaries, though, tended to ignore the use of the balloon for one of the most important of all military tasks, reconnaissance, perhaps because it appeared so prosaic. This was the balloon's first use in war, however, when the French used a tethered balloon to secure information of the Austrian dispositions in the Battle of Fleurus in 1794.

Gradually, however, the observation balloon began to assume a position of some importance in the world's more modern armies during the last quarter of the 19th century. This was largely the result of improved techniques for the production and storage of hydrogen gas, and the varying success of observation balloons in the American Civil War (1861–1865), the Franco-Prussian War (1870–1871), and various colonial campaigns undertaken by the British in Africa, notably the South African and Sudanese campaigns of 1884 and 1885 respectively. During the Boer War (1899–1902), both the balloon and the newly developed man-lifting kite played important parts in the final success of British arms. By 1900, therefore, most of the world's modern armies had equipped their armies with useful numbers of observation balloons fitted with telephones for the rapid relaying of information to the ground force commanders.

Left: The Avro Triplane helped pave the way for the more efficient and long-lived Avro 504, one of the best aircraft to appear before World War I. Below: Great expectations were entertained for airships as bombers and reconnaissance aircraft, but war dashed these hopes.

The use of lighter-than-air craft as bombers only became a realistic proposition late in the 19th century, thanks primarily to the efforts by French pioneers such as the Lebaudy brothers, in the development of the dirigible airship. Several methods of propulsion were attempted, including steam and electric engines, but it was only with the development of the petrol engine, pioneered in airships by the German Karl Wölfert in 1888, that practical airships became possible.

The man largely responsible for the military adoption of airships was a retired German army officer, *Generalleutnant* Ferdinand, *Graf* von Zeppelin. After a series of disasters, both technical and financial, von Zeppelin finally developed the rigid airship as a viable means of transport, at first for passengers. However, in 1908 the Imperial German Army accepted its first Zeppelin airship, the Z1, and in 1912 the Imperial German Navy followed suit with the L1. Both services at first saw their airships as alternatives to the balloon, but for use in the long-range reconnaissance role. But, as Zeppelin airships were capable of flying reasonably fast (over 40 mph/65 kph), and operating at more than 9,842 ft (3,000 m) with a useful payload, the idea of using the airships for a more offensive role, with bombs, suggested itself to the Germans.

Already, though, the main rival to the airship had appeared. This was the heavier-than-air craft, the aeroplane or aircraft, which finally defeated the airship

Top: *A French lithograph of Louis Bleriot's 1909 crossing of the English Channel exaggerates the 'dash' of the event.* Above: *A typical airship gondola with extensive glazing.*

as a weapon of offensive warfare and ushered in the age of true airpower.

Such prospects were still very far in the future when the Wright brothers made their first flight in a heavier-than-air craft at Kill Devil Hills, Kitty Hawk, North Carolina, on 3 December 1903. The Wrights' Flyer I (a retrospective 'historical' designation) was in all respects a rudimentary experimental aircraft, and it was not until the Wrights took to the air in their Flyer III during 1905 that the world had the opportunity to see its first practical aircraft. The opportunity was ignored, and the brothers thereupon temporarily abandoned actual flying as they sought a buyer for their aircraft. The US War Department turned them down, as

did European nations, thereby throwing away a golden opportunity to steal a march on possible opponents.

But heavier-than-air flight was still in the minds of the military, as indicated by the issuing of the world's first specification for such an aircraft by Brigadier General James Allen of the US Army Signal Corps in 1907. Among the requirements were the ability to lift two men for a flight of one hour, at a maximum speed of 40 mph (64 kph). There were a number of tenders to the specification, but only the Wright brothers, with a modified Flyer Type A, stood any chance of success.

From this time onwards, progress was rapid, and the sceptics were dumbfounded by the success of many aircraft types at the

Orville Wright (above) *pilots one of the 950 successful flights of their glider No. 3 at Kitty Hawk, North Carolina. The Wright brothers based the design entirely on their own research.*

world's first true aviation meeting, *La Grande Semaine d'Aviation*, held at Bétheny outside Reims in August 1909 under the auspices of the champagne industry. Any lingering doubts that heavier-than-air flight had come to stay were finally dispelled. The work started by Louis Blériot when he flew his Type XI monoplane across the English Channel on 25 July 1909 was complete.

So far as the development of aviation for military purposes was concerned, the main stumbling blocks were a reactionary dislike for modern technology on the part of many officers, and the very real obstacle that most military establishments could think of no real purpose to be served

by the aircraft they were so consistently urged by public opinion and their junior officers to adopt. Heavier-than-air craft were still very much in their infancy, and aircraft designers and enthusiasts were satisfied if their aircraft flew. Given the standard of aeronautical design, therefore, the military establishment was in all probability sensible to resist the hasty introduction of aircraft to their inventories, already sorely tried by the adoption of other technical innovations that abounded at the beginning of the 20th century.

Gradually the pressure on the military increased, and it was seen that reconnais-

sance at least could be attempted by aircraft, and so such machines inevitably began to appear in the service of the modern armies. The initial trials soon confirmed that useful reconnaissance could be achieved by aircraft, but also that the serviceability of these early aircraft was low, and that most aircraft had serious defects of one sort or another in their aerodynamics. In this last respect the British were particularly concerned, and soon began to devote considerable public effort to the production of safe, inherently stable aircraft for the reconnaissance role.

From 1910 onwards, the pace of developments in the field of military aviation, or aviation with possible military applications, was relatively rapid, although many of the tentative developments would only see full realization in World War I and later. Firstly, on 30 June 1910, the great American pioneer pilot and constructor Glenn Curtiss undertook the world's first 'bombing' tests, when he flew one of his own biplanes over the outline of a battleship marked out with buoys on Lake Keuka in New York state, and attacked it successfully with dummy bombs.

In August 1910, Jacob Fickel became the first man in the world to fire a rifle from an aircraft, but this was less significant than the first firing of a machine-gun, in this case a Lewis air-cooled light machine-gun, from a Wright biplane by Captain Charles de Forest Chandler in June 1912.

On 14 November 1910, Eugene Ely

The world's first 'military' aircraft was the Wright Flyer Type A bought by the US Signal Corps in 1909 after the completion of a second series of trials, Lt. Selfridge having been killed in the first.

The first crossing of the English Channel was achieved in a Bleriot XI monoplane, and the type was soon adopted for military artillery spotting and reconnaissance. During World War I a cropped-wing version, known as the Penguin, was also used for ground training of pilots.

succeeded in taking off from a platform raised above the bows of the American cruiser *Birmingham*, the aircraft used being a Curtiss biplane. Then on 18 January 1911, Ely achieved the more difficult task of landing on board a ship. The aircraft was again a Curtiss, and the ship the cruiser *Pennsylvania*, some 13 miles (21 km) off San Francisco. Ely then took off again and returned to California. These feats were very much in the nature of stunts but laid the foundations for the development of true aircraft-carriers.

In the field of effective armament for aircraft, a milestone was reached in 1911 when Myron Crissy and Phillip Parmalee became the first men to drop high-explosive bombs from an aircraft, a Wright biplane, at San Francisco during January. Shortly after this, the first bomb-sight was produced by another American, Lieutenant Riley Scott. It is worth noting that the Europeans also managed to undertake some worthwhile armament experiments, a machine-gun being fitted to (but probably not being fired from) a number of aircraft, notably a Nieuport two-seater, and *Capitano* Guidoni of the Italian air service making the world's first drop of an air-launched torpedo.

Another significant event of 1911 was the holding of the world's initial *Concours Militaire* for the selection of military aircraft. This took place near Reims in late October and early November, and set the pattern for a number of similar *concours* held in Germany, Great Britain, Italy and other nations. The selection of standard military types was by means of direct competitive flights by all the contenders. This may give an erroneous impression of the degree of standardization actually achieved in the world's air forces before World War I, and it should be emphasized that although a measure of standardization was achieved, notably by the French and Germans, the concept was more theoretical than practical.

The year 1912 was of crucial importance for military aviation, for it marked the year that large sums began to be spent on the development of air forces. The Royal Flying Corps was formed in April 1912, and a Military Aeroplane Competition to find standard types for the new force was held in August, at Larkhill on Salisbury Plain. The sort of problems besetting air forces may be seen from the fact that the winner of the competition was the Cody Military Trials Biplane, an impressive but wholly impractical machine, of which only two were ordered. By far the best machine present was the Farnborough-designed BE 2, which was not allowed to take part in the competition because it was of government design: it was, nevertheless, built in substantial numbers. Germany also realized during the year that too much attention had been devoted to the intrinsically vulnerable airships with their highly inflammable hydrogen lifting gas, and so started to build up her heavier-than-air service with lavish funds. France, too, realized that aircraft would play an important part in any future war, and made efforts to increase aircraft produc-

Above: *A Deperdussin monoplane returns to its landing field with the results of a reconnaissance flight during French Army manoeuvres before World War I.* Left: *Roland Garros (in a suit) poses with his Morane-Saulnier Type I in which he crossed the Mediterranean to Bizerta in 1913, in one of the classic long-range flights before World War I.* Right: *The first accident on an aircraft carrier. Squadron Commander E. H. Dunning's Sopwith Pup goes over the side of HMS* Furious *despite attempts to hold her on the flight deck, 4th August 1917.*

The Bristol Boxkite was one of the first British aircraft to enter 'series' production. An example of the type is seen here flying over British Army manoeuvres on Salisbury Plain before World War I. The type was derived from the Farman type, and was obsolete by 1914.

tion capabilities, as well as experimenting with the use of aircraft in military manoeuvres. The efforts begun in 1912 began to bear fruit in the last two years of peace, 1913 and 1914, when further technical developments foreshadowed the way aircraft were going to progress during World War I.

By 1912, therefore, the basic elements of the technology of air warfare had already been tested, mostly by the Americans, though the French and Germans had gone a step further with initial research into the problems of fitting a forward-firing machine-gun onto the fuselage of tractor aircraft, using a propeller-geared mechanism to interrupt the action of the gun when a propeller blade was in line with the muzzle of the gun. The only other major technical development during this period was the steady progress made towards the provision of aerial wireless systems, which would allow aircraft to spot efficiently for the artillery. The first wireless set to go aloft did so in the Zeppelin LZ6 during 1909, but this was a cumbersome and weighty apparatus unsuitable for aircraft use. In 1910, though, the Americans had the world's first successes with the transmission of messages from an aircraft to a

ground station by means of radio waves, and by 1914 most countries had experimented with air-to-ground and even air-to-air radio equipment. At the same time, the future of aircraft as reconnaissance machines was made brighter by developments in the field of aerial photography.

It is frequently supposed that it was only in 1914, with the beginning of World War I, that aircraft went to war. There were four other wars, though, in which aircraft had already been used: the Italo-Turkish War in Libya (1911–1912), the 1st Balkan War (1912–1913), the 2nd Balkan War (1913) and the US expedition against Mexico in April 1914. In all these wars air operations were extremely limited and provided no real practical background for future operations, though there were a number of aviation 'firsts', especially in the Libyan and Mexican operations. The Italians deployed a very mixed bag of aircraft to Libya, including Bleriot monoplanes, Etrich monoplanes, various *Taube* monoplanes of German construction, and some Farman and Nieuport biplanes of French design. Among the 'firsts' of this campaign were aerial reconnaissance, bombing, artillery spotting and the first casualty in the air.

The Mexican operation was notable for the use of Curtiss AB flying-boats in a search for mines in front of the US naval squadron heading for Vera Cruz, the first time a naval operation had received air support, though the Germans had experimented widely with the use of airships for this task.

World War I, precipitated by the assassination of the Archduke Franz Ferdinand, heir to the throne of the Austro-Hungarian Empire, on 28 June 1914, finally broke out between 28 July and 3 August of that year. On the side of the Central Powers were Austria-Hungary and Germany, while ranged against them were the Allies: Belgium, France, Great Britain, Russia and Serbia, Belgium having been drawn into the Allied camp by the German invasion of the country as part of the Schlieffen Plan's advance into France.

The air forces deployed by the main combatants were small, and backed by minimal reserves of aircraft and crews, while the tactical doctrine for their constructive use was markedly lacking, and the industrial base on which to build up larger forces, should this prove desirable, was almost non-existent.

The Experimental Stage

The warring powers entered World War I with little or no idea of what the conflict would soon become, and their equipment for the most part reflected this failure to realize that a 'conventional' war of movement would soon be replaced by static trench warfare. However, as the Germans put into effect their long-developed Schlieffen Plan on the Western Front, it appeared that a fast war of manoeuvre was imminent. And here at least, the high commands appreciated that the aircraft they possessed could be of some use for reconnaissance purposes. The trouble lay in the fact that the cavalry was the traditional reconnaissance arm, and many senior officers gravely distrusted the reports of airmen, whom they believed to be eccentrics carried away, perhaps, by the chance to use their 'toys' in war.

It should be noted that the inventories of the combatants' air arms were varied in the extreme. Notable among this diversity of aircraft was the existence of a wide variety of design philosophies with both tractor and pusher types well represented

(a tractor aircraft has its engine in the nose of the fuselage, driving a tractor or 'pulling' propeller, while a pusher aircraft has its engine located at the rear of the central nacelle, driving a propeller that pushes the aircraft forward); monoplanes and biplanes (with the former gradually becoming rarer in the Allied camp as a result of fears for the type's inherent structural integrity) and aircraft with conventional fuselages and others with their empennages (tail surfaces) located at the rear ends of twin booms, so as to give a pusher propeller aircraft room to rotate. Another noticeable feature was the virtual absence of any armament save *flechettes* (darts), and personal weapons such as pistols, rifles and shotguns. Although considerations of weight made it all but impossible with the low-powered aircraft of the time, many of the more farsighted aircrews attempted to take up machine-guns of the air-cooled types, such as the Lewis and Hotchkiss guns, in a valiant effort to shoot down the other side's aircraft and crew.

The proof was not slow in coming, for

on 5 October 1914 *Caporal* Quénault, using a Hotchkiss 8 mm machine-gun for the forward cockpit of a Voisin pusher flown by *Sergeant* Joseph Frantz, shot down an Aviatik two-seater. Although tractor types generally offered superior performance, there was a grave difficulty in fitting such types with a machine-gun in the short term: because the observer, who would have to use the gun, was sometimes not carried, he was located in front of the pilot on the aircraft's centre of gravity, where his absence would not affect the aircraft's balance; in this position he was surrounded by a spider's web of bracing wires in most biplanes, with the wings above and below him, and the whirling propeller directly in front. Indeed, it was facetiously suggested that the best way to check that all the bracing wires were intact was to place a small bird in the observer's cockpit: if it escaped, then a wire was broken. So far as armament was concerned, the location of the gun in this position was next to useless, for the fields of fire possible for the observer/

Aircrew manhandle a Farman M.F.7 Longhorn biplane into position. The later M.F.11 Shorthorn had no forward elevator.

gunner were almost wholly non-existant.

The growing significance of aerial armament was a direct response to the early successes of aircraft in World War I, when the value of aerial reconnaissance reports prevailed over the scepticism of staff officers. At first it was the German airships that seemed to hold the key to air reconnaissance, the Schütte-Lanz airship SL2 flying a mission some 300 miles (480 km) into Russian territory on 22 August 1914 to spot Tsarist forces massing for an attack on the key Austro-Hungarian fortress of Przemysl. Other long-range reconnaissance sorties were flown with some success, but in their other intended role of bomber, the airships proved an abject failure in tactical operations. On 5 August, for example, the Zeppelin ZVI attempted to bomb the Belgian fortress at Liège with modified heavy artillery shells, but was so damaged by small-arms fire at low altitude that she crash-landed on her return journey. On 21 August the Zeppelins ZVII and ZVIII were both lost to 'friendly' small-arms fire after a futile attempt to bomb French positions in the Vosges mountains, and on 28 August the Zeppelin ZV was shot down by Russian small-arms fire while trying to bomb the rail junction at Mlawa in Poland. These early losses for no appreciable advantage swiftly persuaded the Germans that the vulnerable hydrogen-filled airships were of no real value for tactical operations. They decided that maritime deployment would make the best use of the airships' undoubted range, pending the development of attacks against London which, they believed, would force the British out of the war by demoralizing the civilian population and government.

The use of airships in the bombing role was gradually supplemented by that of aircraft. First in the field, again, were the Germans, who established the *Fliegerkorps des Obersten Heeresleitung* (Army High Command Flying Corps), with 36 Aviatik B.Is, in November 1914 for the bombing of London. The unit's commander was Major Wilhelm Siegert, but after a few abortive raids on England and objectives in northern France, the unit was provided with its own rail transport and posted to Galicia, as the world's first mobile 'fire brigade' air formation.

The French had also determined to raise a similar unit, the *1ᵉ Groupe de Bombardement* (1st Bombing Group), which was formed with Voisin bombers on 13 November 1914 under *Commandant* de Göys. The unit first went into action on 4 December, but this and further operations in the immediate future met with little or no success, despite the determination and farsightedness of the French. As with the German force, the adequacy of the concept was wholly unmatched by the aircraft available.

The British also realized that bombing was the up-and-coming thing in air warfare, or at least the Royal Naval Air Service did. No counterpart to the *Fliegerkorps des Obersten Heeresleitung* or *1ᵉ Groupe de Bombardement* was formed, but instead the RNAS decided to tackle the German airships, thought to be the main threat to the Royal Navy and to England, with strikes from forward bases against the Zeppelins' stations. The first raid was made on 22 September from Antwerp against the sheds at Düsseldorf, but failed, largely as a result of poor weather. However, on 8 October another raid was made on the same target, and this time the Zeppelin ZIX was destroyed. Another

raid, this time against the Zeppelin manufacturing works at Friedrichshafen from the French base at Belfort on 21 November, also failed, but persuaded the Germans that the British threat to their airships was a serious one.

At the beginning of 1915, the Germans decided to allow Zeppelin attacks on Allied military targets of strategic importance (that is, targets not directly linked with the conduct of front-line operations), a policy soon extended to allow attacks on Allied cities by night. Certain classes of target (royal residences and the like) remained prohibited, but it is hard to see how airship commanders could hope to avoid such targets at night with inaccurate navigation and the unwieldiness of their craft. The first attack of the campaign was made on 19 January 1915, and thereafter the raids became ever more severe, though not without losses to the Germans. Targets in France were raided (Paris for the first time on 21 March 1915), but it was London (first raided on 31 May 1915) and towns in East Anglia and Kent that were the primary objectives. The airship raids grew in intensity during 1915 and early 1916, though there were some significant losses: on 6 June 1915 Flight Sub-Lieutenant R. Warneford downed LZ37 by dropping bombs on her, the first time an airship had been destroyed by another aircraft; on 10 August 1915 L12 fell into the sea near Ostend after being hit by AA gunfire over Dover, and on 2/3 September 1915 the first airship to be brought down over England fell to 2nd Lieutenant W. Leefe Robinson, flying a BE 2c. This was SL11, one of 14 airships taking part in the largest raid of the war. By the end of 1915, another five airships had been lost to the British defences, and

A replica of the Morane-Saulnier Type N, one of the early fighter types fitted with a machine-gun and deflector plates on the propeller.

although the campaign continued into 1916, the real threat of the airships was over. Sporadic raids continued in 1917 and 1918, the last taking place on 5 August 1918.

Over the Western Front, meanwhile, the importance of aircraft had been fully accepted by the end of 1914, much helped by the accuracy and promptness of reports such as that by an RFC aircraft at the beginning of September 1914 that the right wing of the Germans' great south-westward wheel towards Paris, which should have passed to the west of the French capital to envelop it, would in fact pass to the east of the city. This made possible the counterstroke by the fortress garrison which turned the 1st Battle of the Marne against the Germans.

By the end of 1914, therefore, army commanders were calling for as many aircraft as possible for aerial reconnaissance, both visual and photographic, and for artillery spotting, the importance of the latter having increased significantly with the establishment of fixed defence lines, which commanders considered to be breakable only after prolonged artillery bombardments. The trouble lay in the fact that manufacture of aircraft was a skilled job, and so great had been the pace of technical development before the war that aircraft had been individually made. Now production lines were needed, and current manufacturers lacked the capital to build them quickly. Inevitably the governments of the fighting powers stepped in with financial aid, but it was some time before this had any real practical results.

So important had aerial reconnaissance and artillery spotting now become that special tactics were devised for their integration into the land battle. These tactics were first used by the RFC in the Battle of Neuve Chapelle, which started on 10 March 1915. In the planning stage for the battle, accurate maps of the German defence positions were made possible by the British adoption of French photogrammetric techniques and the arrival of new aerial cameras. This also helped in the control of British artillery fire, for the position of German batteries and strongpoints could be fixed accurately and the fire of British batteries then brought down more precisely with the aid of the new 'clock system' of spotting the fall of shot, relative to the German target, at the centre of a celluloid disc with sectors and ranges marked on it. Improvements in the radio equipment carried in the artillery

The Zeppelin LZ37 plummets down over Belgium after being hit by six 20-lb (9-kg) bombs dropped by Flight Sub-Lieutenant R. Warneford from his Morane-Saulnier monoplane.

spotting aircraft then made it possible for the observer to report to the British artillery with speed and accuracy. At the same time British fighters patrolled the approaches to the German line, ready to report the movement of significant reinforcements into any particular sector. The movement of such reserves was made more difficult by the British bombing plan, which concentrated on rail junctions the Germans would have to use for major reinforcement. However, the impact of the bombing plan was small, for the weight of bombs that could be delivered was minimal. Finally, the high command tried to keep itself informed of the positions of its leading troops by means of 'contact patrols', two of which were flown during

the battle. The idea was for fighters to fly low over the battlefield and spot the locations of the most forward British troops, so that the high command could assess the progress being made, and call down artillery fire to support units held up by German strongpoints.

The RFC played an important part in the initial breakthrough at Neuve Chapelle, but this success could not be exploited for lack of sufficient reserves capable of pouring through the breach quickly enough to keep the Germans off balance, and the usual stalemate resumed. For the air forces, though, Neuve Chapelle was of some importance, for this was the first time that the aviation element had been fully integrated with the land battle to the

A replica of the Vickers F.B.5 Gunbus fighting biplane, which began to arrive in France in February 1915. Note the conventional pusher disposition of the engine and propeller, the boomed tail surfaces and the location of the Lewis machine-gun in the nose of the central nacelle.

tactical advantage of the latter. Particularly useful, though limited, had been the rudimentary contact patrols. The concept was taken a stage further on 9 May 1915 in the Battle of Aubers Ridge, when the troops were issued with strips of cloth to lay out in front of their forward positions, so that aircraft operating at about 5,000 ft (1,558 m) could radio the information back to headquarters. Although few territorial gains were made in the battle, all concerned felt that the contact patrol system was of great worth and so deserved greater development.

At the beginning of 1915, both the French and German specialist bomber units began to use rudimentary bombsights, and to operate in close formation.

This helped to increase the efficiency of the bombers slightly, and fears that the French might press ahead with the development of still more efficient bomber forces persuaded the Germans to form the world's first interceptor fighter force, the *Brieftaubenabteilungen Metz* (Metz Carrier Pigeon Units), in April 1915. But the B type biplanes operated by the force were wholly insufficient for the task, even though the more enterprising crews fitted their aircraft with machine-guns.

The first homogeneous fighter squadron, with effective aircraft, was not formed until July 1915, when the RFC grouped together a number of Vickers F.B.5 pusher biplanes, each armed with a single Lewis machine-gun in the nose of

the crew nacelle. The type had been operational in France since February 1915 after development from the E.F.B.4 and E.F.B.5 of 1914, but had been allocated in 'penny packets' as escorts to general-purpose squadrons.

By the spring of 1915, the value of aircraft in war had reached proportions so great, especially in the reconnaissance and artillery spotting roles, that it was becoming imperative for both sides to find some means of preventing the other from enjoying the fruits of such work without endangering one's own: what was needed was a true fighting aircraft, with a machine-gun aligned along the fuselage and the pilot's line of sight so that the whole aircraft could be aimed at the target.

In early 1915, Roland Garros, a prewar pilot and now a French military pilot, remembered a deflector device of Raymond Saulnier's and persuaded the designer to allow him to use the system in combat, without any attempt at gun synchronization or interruption. As Garros reasoned, only very few bullets would be likely to strike the propeller, and these would be warded off by the deflectors of the Morane-Saulnier Type L which he used.

The crucial date was 1 April 1915, when Garros 'opened the era of true fighter aircraft' by shooting down a German Albatros two-seater, which he had approached head-on, previously a clear indication of safety for the aircraft being approached. During the next three weeks Garros shot down another four German aircraft, occasioning feelings akin to panic among the higher command of the German air service. But the Germans captured Garros and improved on the armament.

The new equipment was fitted to a number of Fokker M.5k monoplanes, which thereupon became Fokker E.I fighter monoplanes. The new type was rushed into production and service, and it

'DH 2s on dawn Patrol', an evocative painting of 1916 by Kenneth McDonough.

seems that the first E.I 'kill' went to *Leutnant* Kurt Wintgens on 15 July, though this was unconfirmed. On 1 August, however, an aircraft of the RFC fell to *Leutnant* Max Immelmann, destined to be one of the very great exponents of the Fokker E types. This date may be taken as the beginning of the 'Fokker Scourge' as it became known in RFC circles. The German fighter, of indifferent performance as an aircraft, gradually came to dominate the skies over the Western Front, despite its small numbers, as a result of being the only real fighter with a forward-firing machine-gun. The British and French tried to respond, notably with Morane-Saulnier Type N monoplanes fitted with deflector plates, but the unreliability of the system merely played into the Germans' hands.

The two key figures in the German air service during this period were *Hauptmann* Oswald Boelcke and *Leutnant* Max Immelmann, both of whom were lionized by the German propaganda machine and became heroes of the German people. However, it was Boelcke whom history recognizes as by far the greater of the two: Immelmann was a good pilot, and fortunate to be amongst the first to receive one of the Fokker E types, but remained only an adequate exponent of the E type, scoring 15 victories before his death on 28 June 1916. Boelcke, on the other hand, was a superior pilot (as proved by the fact that he had amassed the prodigious total of 40 victories by the time of his death on 28 October 1916 in an air accident) and also a first-class organizer and tactical thinker. By September 1915, just as the first improved Fokker E.II monoplanes were being delivered, Boelcke had come to the conclusion that the *ad hoc* allocation of

a few E types to ordinary squadrons was not the most efficient way to make use of Germany's advantage, which he realized could only be temporary. Boelcke therefore reasoned that E types should be grouped together into homogeneous squadrons that could then cut a wide swathe through Allied squadrons. Boelcke convinced Major Hermann von der Lieth-Thomsen, Chief of the Air Force in the Field, of the validity of his ideas, and the two men then decided on the formation of specialized *Jagdstaffeln* (fighter squadrons). Boelcke was at first denied the chance to fulfil his creation by an imperial decree banning him from flying, so *Jagdstaffel Nr 1* was formed on 23 August 1916 under *Hauptmann* Zander. Boelcke formed *Jagdstaffel Nr 2* on 27 August 1916, but was killed shortly afterwards.

The Allies, meanwhile, had been struggling desperately to find a counter to the threat posed by the Fokker, and later the Pfalz E types during the late summer and autumn of 1915. Perhaps the most successful counter was the Vee formation introduced in August by *Capitaine* Felix Happe: when four or six two-seaters operated in a close Vee the weight of the defensive fire that could be thrown up by the French gunners made it too risky an attack for the lightly built E types. Another innovation of the period was the French introduction of *escadrilles de chasse*, homogeneous squadrons of fighters. These later on became worthy opponents to the Germans with the introduction of the Nieuport 11 *Bébé* fighter early in 1916, and of the Nieuport 17 in March 1916.

It thus became clear that although new tactics and organization could ameliorate the situation for the Allies, the only real solution to the 'Fokker Scourge' lay in the

The definitive production variant of the Fokker Eindekker *series was the E.III, fitted with a Parabellum or 'Spandau' machine-gun.*

widespread introduction of new aircraft at least equal to the Fokker E types in fire-power, and superior to the Germans fighters in performance. By February 1916 the Allies had introduced two such fighters, the French Nieuport 11 sesquiplane (a biplane with two wings, usually the lower, of less than half the area of the other two), with an unsynchronized Lewis gun on the top wing firing over the propeller disc, and the British Airco (de Havilland) 2, a trim single-seat pusher biplane, with a Lewis gun in the nose of the nacelle.

At the beginning of 1916, neither side had adequate aircraft manufacturing capability, so the deciding factor in the air war was still very much that of quality. By February, for example, the Germans had produced only 86 Fokker E.IIIs, the French 210 Nieuport 11s, and the British had in France only about 12 DH 2s, sufficient to equip only one fighter squadron. From this time on, the Allies were able to master the 'Fokker Scourge', as demonstrated in the air war over the Battle of Verdun, the great German set-piece onslaught designed to 'bleed France white'. Realizing that they had now to operate in a situation of numerical and qualitative inferiority, the Germans decided that the best option open to them was to patrol over the front, making little effort to penetrate French air space, but denying the French the opportunity to probe into German air space. Germany committed some 150 two-seater types, which thus had to be used for patrol work, a task in which they did not excel, and some 20 Fokker fighters, which bore the brunt of trying to stem the major French effort to operate over the German rear areas. Inevitably, the first major air battles of the war developed over Verdun, and the French were able to secure an advantage and take the war to the Germans.

The importance of the Nieuport 11 is attested by the fact that the Germans secured an initial air superiority against the miscellany of obsolescent types deployed in the sector by the French at the beginning of the battle. But the arrival of *Commandant* du Peuty and the first of the 36 Nieuport 11s to operate in the area immediately tipped the balance the other way, allowing the French to take the air war to the Germans in a decisive fashion.

Amongst the keenest analysts of the French air effort at Verdun was Brigadier General Hugh Trenchard, commander of

The Sopwith Pup appeared in France in 1916. It was a classic fighter of World War I, and one of the most tractable aircraft.

the RFC in France. An avid enthusiast of the offensive, no matter what the cost might be, Trenchard was confirmed in his opinions by the French successes at Verdun. The British commander well appreciated that such tactics could, and at times would, cost the RFC very heavy casualties in men and aircraft, for it was clear that the Germans would respond to the Allies' present technical superiority with a new generation of fighting aircraft. Nevertheless, Trenchard was firmly convinced that his primary responsibility was to the ground forces his air units supported.

Trenchard's decision early in 1916 led to the RFC's concentration on battlefield and deep-penetration missions, two-seaters supplying the ground forces with aid over the battlefield, and with fighter escorts making raids and reconnaissance flights deep into German-held territory. The strengthening bomber forces attacked the German lines of communication, supply dumps and other rear-area targets, and the fighters patrolled deep into German air space to intercept any German aircraft before they could reach the battlefield, and operated over the battlefield itself to support the ground forces with light bombs and machine-gun fire. The one real tactical innovation was the decision that aircraft on contact patrols should operate at low rather than at medium altitude, for the infantry were naturally chary of setting off the flares with which they were supposed to indicate their forward positions: the 'poor bloody infantry' as they have aptly been described were fully aware that the lighting of a flare would immediately bring down round them a hail of German artillery fire.

These developed tactical concepts were put to the test in the 1st Battle of the Somme, which began on 1 July 1916 with the greatest single-day losses ever sustained by the British Army: some 20,000 dead and 60,000 wounded. Despite the losses, the great Allied offensive did manage to make progress as the battle raged on into November 1916. At the beginning of the battle, the Germans were still fully engaged at Verdun, and so could muster only 130 aircraft, including only 30 fighters of the now obsolescent Fokker E and Halberstadt D types; the Allies, whose increased manufacturing capacity was now beginning to bear fruit, could deploy some 385 aircraft, including nearly 140 fighters. Inevitably, the weeks preceding the battle saw a steady increase in the scale of air activity as the Allies strove

Above: *The D.V was the definitive model of the sharklike Albatros biplane fighters, appearing in 1917, but being outclassed by Allied fighters later in the war.* Right: *The end of an Albatros fighter over Arras, at the hands of a Sopwith Pup in a high-altitude dogfight.*

to build up a comprehensive map of the German positions, and prepare for the battle by bombing German dumps and lines of communication, while whittling away the German air strength with fighter activities. The mainstays of the Allied air units were as before, with the addition of the Sopwith $1\frac{1}{2}$ Strutter, a two-seater of respectable performance and agility, and the first British combat aircraft to be fitted with a synchronized forward-firing machine-gun. There were also increasing numbers of the Royal Aircraft Factory FE 2b pusher two-seater, a cumbersome but nonetheless effective fighting aircraft. During the 1st Battle of the Somme these types were joined by the Allies' first truly effective fighters, the Sopwith Pup and Spad S.7, both armed with a single synchronized Vickers machine-gun. Whereas the Pup relied on the tactical advantage of extreme agility and moderate performance, the Spad called on excellent performance and stability as a gun platform, allied with very great structural strength.

Inevitably, therefore, the German aircraft suffered heavily in the opening phases of the battle: the only reason Allied air superiority failed to score more heavily being lack of targets and the German decision to stay on their own side of the lines. Their loss of air superiority was instrumental in a German reassessment of their basic air policy during August 1917: the Verdun offensive was called off, freeing aircraft for the Somme front, and it

was decided to expand the air service very greatly. The service's first commander of general rank was appointed on 8 October, in the form of General Ernst von Hoeppner, with *Oberst* von der Lieth-Thomsen as his chief-of-staff. Von Hoepnner concurred with von der Lieth-Thomsen in the latter's earlier decision that fighter aircraft should have priority so that they could protect the basically more important two-seaters from enemy interference. Fighters were thus formed into specialist *Jagdstaffeln* of 14 aircraft each, and specifications for new fighters were drawn up, with the emphasis on speed, climb and manoeuvrability. The first of a new generation of fighters was just entering service: the Albatros D.I and D.II were markedly superior to Allied fighters in terms of performance, and the D.II had the additional advantage of two machine-guns synchronized to fire through the propeller disc.

It is clear, therefore, that the Germans had once again regained air superiority by the closing months of 1916, and this fact was confirmed during the first months of 1917 by the arrival of the Albatros D.III. This definitive version of the sleek fighter family had two guns, better streamlining and aerodynamics, and superior performance thanks to an uprated engine. Only in speed figures was the D.III slightly inferior to the D.II, though it was still faster than most Allied fighters.

The fighter arm was now all that the Germans could wish, but the air service

still had grave difficulties: early experiments with contact patrols had been a failure; artillery spotting was not as good as the Allies', largely as a result of the general inferiority of German radio equipment. Ground support tactics and liaison were deficient, and airships had proved inadequate for attacks on enemy 'strategic' targets. At the end of 1916 and the beginning of 1917, therefore, the German air service made strenuous efforts to improve its performance in these four main categories. Greater emphasis came to be placed upon the first three during April 1917, when the United States of America entered the war on the Allied side, and the German high command was quick to realize that only victory within the coming year would suffice to bring hostilities to a successful conclusion before the advent of massive American forces in France.

The Germans still placed great store on the strategic campaign against England, and the gradual phasing out of the airship attacks coincided with the increase in the reliance placed on bombers, the first important type being the Gotha G.II and G.III, which entered service in the second half of 1916. The mainstay of the strategic bomber force, however, was the Gotha G.IV, which assumed the brunt of the attacks on England from June 1917, carrying up to 1,102 lb (500 kg) of bombs over short ranges, and having a defensive armament of three machine-guns. The Gothas were supplemented later by a few examples of the Zeppelin (Staaken) R.VI giant bomber, with four engines, a maximum bombload of 3,968 lb (1,800 kg) and a defensive armament of four machine-guns. Germany saw a great future for giant bombers, and a considerable number of experimental and limited-production types were produced for flight and operational testing, to the detriment of the more relevant aspects of the German air effort. The importance of the campaign against England was signalled by the formation during the autumn of 1916 of the so-called *Englandgeschwader*, whose formal title was *Bombengeschwader Nr 3*. This unit was to have an operational strength of 30 Gotha twin-engined bombers, and carry out a campaign against London with the intention of causing the civilian population of the capital such casualties that the government would be forced to come to terms. In fact the concept was far in advance of Germany's means of carrying it out.

This campaign against London was linked in German policy with the start of a campaign of unrestricted U-boat attacks on Allied shipping and shipping plying to Allied ports, which had the unwanted side-effect of bringing the USA into the war on 6 April 1917. As part of the U-boat campaign, the Germans increased that part of their effort designed to protect U-boats in Allied coastal waters from the attentions of flying-boats and escort airships. There thus developed, in parallel with the air war over the Western Front, an air war in the English Channel, the North Sea and other coastal areas. The Allies made extensive use of large flying-boat bombers, of the Felixstowe, F.B.A. and Curtiss types, while the Germans

Rittmeister *Manfred,* Freiherr *von Richthofen was the ace World War I pilot.*

responded with a number of floatplane fighters such as those built by Albatros, Friedrichshafen and Hansa-Brandenburg. The British also concentrated on German U-boat construction yards, and this led the RNAS into the field of heavy bombing of a strategic nature, with the excellent Handley Page O/100 entering service towards the end of 1916. This could carry up to 2,000 lb (907 kg) of bombs over a short range, and had a defensive armament of up to five machine-guns. The O/100 was supplemented in 1918 by the basically similar but more powerful O/400, and would have been joined in 1919 by substantial numbers of the Handley Page V/1500, which was a four-engined bomber capable of lifting up to 7,500 lb (3,402 kg) of bombs, including a specially developed 3,300 lb (1,497 kg) weapon, and of carrying a useful load as far as Berlin. As with the German effort, though, this concept remained a threat rather than a reality.

The winter of 1916–1917 was a hard one, with little air activity possible. The Allies were preparing a double offensive for the following spring, and therefore concentrated their efforts on the build-up of fighting squadrons, which was hampered by the shortage of adequate aircrew to man the ever increasing flow of new aircraft reaching the front from improved production facilities. The Germans, realizing what the Allies planned, were preparing the so-called Hindenburg Line, to which they intended to make a strategic withdrawal as soon as possible. This line, with carefully prepared defences, would allow the German armies to hold out against the numerically stronger Allies until their own preparations for the decisive 1918 offensives were ready. Before the Allies could launch their own drives, the Germans fell back to the Hindenburg Line between 23 February and 5 April. Thereupon, the Allies launched their own offensives. Soon after large-scale mutinies broke out in the French army, making the Allied position precarious in the extreme should the Germans be able to capitalize on the fact. The result in strategic terms was that for the rest of the year the British had to draw the weight of the Germans onto themselves to give France time to rebuild her army.

The British offensive at Arras between 9 and 15 April 1917 coincided with the return of reasonable weather, and the battle was marked by intensive air operations, starting just before the ground offensive and ending after it. Justifiably, the month became known to the RFC as 'Bloody April', as British aircraft fought their way with dire losses over the lines to photograph and bomb German positions. Though the battle pitted 385 British fighters against only 115 German aircraft, British losses for the month were 151 aircraft to the Germans' 70. Determined to give the ground forces all the support he could, however, Trenchard insisted on the maintenance of offensive air operations despite the terrible losses. Especially heavy were the losses to the British two-seaters: the BE 2 family was by now totally obsolete, the Royal Aircraft Factory RE 8 proved quite vulnerable to German fighters when not well flown, and the Bristol F 2A was new to service, and had not had suitable tactics devised for its use.

The Early Peak

The terrible losses of 'Bloody April' were largely attributable to the tactical employment of the mass of Allied aircraft, and the relative inexperience of the crews facing the elite of the German fighter force, but also to the recent introduction of new aircraft, which meant that crews were not yet fully competent, and adequate tactics for each type had not been evolved. For this was the period in which the latest generation of Allied aircraft, designed to counter the superiority of the German Albatros fighters, were beginning to enter service. Prime examples were the magnificently agile and fast-climbing Sopwith Triplane, which entered service in November 1916; the potentially first-class Bristol F 2A, a two-seater fighter with a forward-firing machine-gun for the pilot, and a flexible machine-gun for the rearward-facing gunner, which entered service in March 1917; and the great Royal Aircraft Factory SE 5 single-seat fighter, which entered service in April 1917, and had the unusual armament of one fixed machine-gun on the forward fuselage, fitted with a synchronization gear, and one quadrant-mounted machine-gun above the upper wing to fire over the propellor disc. In their fully developed forms as the F 2B and SE 5a, two of these aircraft were amongst the best fighters of the war, being joined by the Sopwith Camel and the Spad S.13 in June and September 1917 respectively. The Camel and S.13 were both twin-gun fighters, the one supremely manoeuvrable and the other a high-performance aircraft of great strength and an excellent gun platform.

To pit against these four main Allied fighters, which were appearing in steadily increasing numbers during the summer of 1916, and being used to greater advantage by more skilled aircrew, the Germans could muster only the Albatros D.III, the slightly improved Albatros D.V and D.Va, the incredibly agile Fokker Dr.I triplane, introduced in August 1917, the L.F.G. (Roland) D.II and D.III, and the Pfalz D.III, which entered service in September 1917. For further improvements in performance, the Germans would have to wait for the next generation of fighters, which appeared in early 1918, allowing only one of them, the Fokker D.VII, arguably the war's best fighter, to enter widespread service.

Inevitably, therefore, the Germans found themselves pushed onto the defensive, with even their fighters forced into the escort role to safeguard the two-seaters going about their unglamourous but essential work of artillery spotting and photographic reconnaissance.

The importance of air fighting to the land battle was now clear for all to see, and considerable efforts were made to improve the direct impact of the air forces on the conduct of surface operations. The best means seemed to be by a closer co-ordination of the air effort with the plans of the infantry. On 11 May 1917, for example, FE 2b two-seaters, escorted by fighters, made a co-ordinated attack on German positions just beyond the British barrage before an infantry attack, and then went in to eliminate pockets of German resistance as the barrage lifted and the infantry moved forward.

Such experiments were watched closely by the Germans, who had also realized that air forces could be of great value in the land battle, the more so because they could help to speed up the otherwise laggardly pace of most land advances, a factor that featured prominently in Germany's plans for her decisive offensives to knock France and Great Britain out of the war in spring 1918 before the Americans could make their presence felt. The Germans made their first attempt with such tactics on 10 July 1917, when a whole *Staffel* of aircraft was used with such success that the high command immediately ordered the formation of a number of *Schlachtstaffeln* (battle squadrons) for ground-attack work. Thus while the

The Bristol F 2B was undoubtedly the best two-seat fighter of World War I.

German two-seaters (C types), used for reconnaissance, artillery spotting and light bombing, continued to enjoy a high production priority, they now had to vie with the new CL types for the *Schlachtstaffeln*. The C types had been derived from the earlier unarmed B types, and had evolved by 1917 into useful fighting aircraft with a standard armament of one forward-firing synchronized gun for the pilot, and one flexible gun for the observer/gunner. The CL type, of which the best known are the Halberstadt CL.II and CL.IV, and the Hannover CL.II and CL.IIIa, appeared in 1917, and were superficially similar to the C types except

that they were lighter, smaller, and were intended for low altitude work with de-rated engines and structures designed to absorb a fair amount of small-arms fire from the ground. Perhaps the most prophetic of such machines was the Junkers J.I, an all-metal, low-level reconnaissance and close-support aircraft with armour protection and cantilever wings, and an armament of two fixed and one flexible gun. These CL types, designed to co-operate with the 'stormtroopers' of the new fast-moving German tactics, were to be a key element in the Germans' plans for 1918.

The importance of the new ground-

attack tactics was demonstrated on 7 June 1917 in the opening phase of the Battle of Messines – by the British rather than the Germans. On this date the German line was split open by the detonation of a huge mine located directly under the front, a breach quickly seized by the infantry with carefully planned air support by fighters and two-seaters operating at low level in direct support.

So great were the now commonplace air battles that the Germans decided to increase the size of the basic unit that could be controlled by one man: on 26 June 1917 the establishment of *Jagdgeschwader Nr* I, comprising *Jastas* 4, 6, 10 and 11 and

The Fokker Dr I triplane was produced in response to the highly manoeuvrable Sopwith Triplane, and was a classic dogfighting aircraft.

under the command of the redoubtable von Richthofen, was promulgated. The object of this change was to establish under proven leaders formations of fighter aircraft, complete with their own transport, spares and the like, that could be shuttled between threatened points in the German line, and so make up for lack of German numbers by quality and mobility. This was all the more important because the Allies were increasing use of their light bomber forces to supplement the offensive work of the 'corps' two-seaters, whose primary responsibility was artillery spotting and reconnaissance.

The first full use of the developed German ground-attack tactics took place on 30 November 1917, when the Germans counter-attacked to retake the salient seized by the British, with the first mass use of tanks, on 20 November in the Battle of Cambrai. To a great extent the German success was attributable to the use of all *Schlachtstaffeln* that could be rushed to the area, with cover provided by the fighters of *Jagdgeschwader Nr* I.

Despite this tactical reverse, the Allies felt that their position at the beginning of 1918 was a good one: the French had largely recovered from the effects of the April/May 1917 mutinies, and the full implications of the 3rd Battle of Ypres, culminating in the Battle of Passchendaele, had not yet been brought home to the British. So far as the air forces were concerned, production was adequate, and at last the quality of replacements reaching the front was sufficient, if not all that could be desired. The relative importance of the various types of aircraft at this time may be gauged from the fact that in January 1918 the RFC had in France four fighter-reconnaissance, 17 bomber, 18 army co-operation and 27 fighter squadrons, a balance reflected in other air arms.

On 21 March 1918, however, the Germans launched the first of the five offensives in which they hoped to defeat the British and French before the Americans, now beginning to arrive in France in great numbers, could play a decisive part in concluding hostilities against a Germany rapidly approaching exhaustion. The German situation at the beginning of their offensive was a good one, for the final end of major hostilities with Russia after the Russian revolutions of 1917 and the Treaty of Brest-Litovsk of 3 March 1918 had freed considerable forces for service on the Western Front.

For these offensives, the Germans had evolved new tactics, whose principal

Airco (de Havilland) 9 bombers of No 108 Squadron, Royal Air Force, start an attack on Ostend on 3 September 1918. The DH9 was the successor to the magnificent DH4.

architect had been General Oscar von Hutier. Without a long artillery bombardment, lightly equipped stormtroopers were to advance with all speed behind a creeping barrage, their task being to break through the Allied front, bypassing all centres of resistance, to reach the rear areas to knock out the Allied guns and disrupt the lines of communication and command. Following up in the wake of the stormtroopers were the conventional infantry, who would mop up the bypassed centres of resistance and consolidate. The *Schlachtstaffeln* had a vital part to play in these tactics, acting as flying artillery for the *Sturmtruppen* and otherwise doing the work of contact patrols.

The five German offensives took place

between 21 March and 19 July 1918, and at first swept the Allies before them in total disarray, not least because of the new combined *Schlacht* and *Sturm* tactics. In a desperate effort to halt the rout of their armies, the British and French committed all their forces, as well as a number of American units, together with all available air units. By day and night air fighting continued, with losses sometimes reaching 33% in ground-attack missions. Gradually, though, the Allies got the measure of the Germans, and could take comfort in the fact that they could replace their losses, in *matériel* if not wholly in men, whereas the Germans could not. Moreover, the German air effort was beginning to feel the fuel shortage occasioned by the

29

Allied blockade of German supply lines.

The scale of the air fighting may be gauged by the fact that during May 1918, the Germans lost 180 aircraft, and the Allies over 400 machines, their highest monthly loss during the war so far. Most of these losses, it should be emphasized, were the result of ground fire with rifles and machine-guns, as aircraft strafed and bombed forward troop positions.

These five offensives were the last efforts of the exhausted German forces, which now prepared themselves for the inevitable Allied counteroffensives, made the more formidable by the injection of powerful American forces. The Allies had also realized the signal importance of concentrated air support for ground actions, the French leading the way with the formation of the *Division Aérienne* on 18 April 1918: this consisted of two *groupements*, one made up of 12 *escadrilles* of Spad S.13 fighters and nine *escadrilles* of Breguet 14 bombers, and the other of 12 Spad *escadrilles* and six Breguet *escadrilles*. A single air commander could thus call on the services of some 600 aircraft. Intended as a mobile force to secure local air superiority over critical sectors of the front, the *Division Aérienne* immediately began to prove its worth as a defensive formation in the third German offensive (on the Aisne between 27 May and 17 June 1918), the fourth German offensive (between Noyon and Montdidier between 9 and 13 June 1918) and the fifth German offensive (in Champagne and on the Marne between 15 and 19 July).

The British too had formed a special air force, with the establishment under Major General Sir Hugh Trenchard, lately Chief of the Air Staff at the Air Ministry (headquarters of the new Royal Air Force), of the Independent Air Force on 6 June

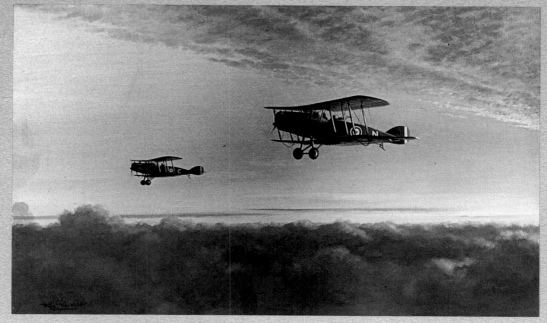

Above: *A pair of Bristol F 2B Fighters patrol just above the clouds during the late afternoon. With a sting in nose and tail, the F 2B was greatly feared by German aircrew.*
Below: *The SE 5A was fast, rugged, and a first-class gun platform.*

1918. This was the first air formation specifically established for the large-scale conduct of strategic bombing operations against the enemy's heartland. Moves in this direction had already been made, for in July 1917 the RNAS had formed a special bomber wing to operate with the French from a base near Luxeuil in a campaign against Germany. The French too thought the air war against southern Germany a worthwhile one, and by February 1918 had six *groupes de bombardement* with 27 *escadrilles*. The efforts of the RNAS No 3 Wing had been shortlived, as the bombers were soon removed to aid in the 3rd Battle of Ypres in Flanders. In response to the German bombing of London in the night campaign that started in September 1917, the 41st Wing was formed in October 1917 for the bombing of Germany, and this was eventually raised to the strength of a brigade when adequate aircraft became available. However, the force was able to inflict little damage in the 57 raids flown between October 1917 and June 1918.

The object of the Independent Air Force was a decisive campaign against the German armaments industry, and to allow the force to operate without hindrance from local army commanders, it was made wholly independent of the normal chain of command. For the rest of the war the bombers of this formation undertook a series of raids that caused little real damage, because of the limited tonnage of bombs that could be delivered, but caused the Germans sufficient concern to divert numbers of fighters from the front to form *Kampfeinsitzerstaffeln* for home defence, the pilots being second-line men. For the first time, though, it had been realized that decisive results could be achieved by a force of heavy bombers operating under a single command against a carefully selected list of strategic objectives.

Despite the German spring offensives, the Allies had continued with the planning for their own final offensives, the first of which was unleashed on 18 July in the form of the Aisne-Marne offensive by French and American forces. Major Allied air forces were committed, and losses for July topped the 500 mark. Yet the Germans could not counter the weight of the Allied thrust, and by the offensive's end on 5 August 1918, the Marne salient had been retaken. Again, the tactical use of airpower had played a decisive part in keeping the Germans off balance.

By this time, the Allied fighter force was able to operate in great concentrations,

the Germans seldom meeting formations of less than 12 aircraft. At the same time, the various capabilities of Allied fighters meant that corps two-seaters operating at low level could be given close escort by Sopwith Camels, medium-altitude cover by SE 5as, and high-altitude cover by Bristol F 2B Fighters, this system giving the German fighters little chance of getting to the two-seaters. Nevertheless, losses could be great, as shown on 8 August 1918, the start of the great Allied offensive with the British push in the Battle of Amiens. For the loss of 49 of their own aircraft, the Germans could claim 83 Allied aircraft, the highest single-day losses of the war. Given the very numbers of Allied aircraft operating, however, it was not surprising that the German fighters and ground forces could dispatch so high a number.

Losses during September 1918 reached 773 Allied aircraft, the highest monthly total for the war, but this was largely attributable to the use of even the 'independent' forces for tactical operations, under the command of Colonel William Mitchell, field commander of the American Expeditionary Force's air units in France. For the rest of the war, however, the Allied air units continued to dominate the skies over the Western Front and provide the Allied armies with considerable support with bombing and strafing.

In general, air operations over other fronts followed the pattern set over the Western Front, though on a smaller scale. However, the Eastern Front and Italian Front saw the widespread use of 'heavy'

bombers before the Western Front. On the Eastern Front, the Imperial Russian air service had adopted before the outbreak of war the world's first four-engined bomber, the Sikorsky *Ilya Muromets*, and although few of the type were built, fairly extensive operations were conducted. Results were small, but so well defended were the Russian bombers that the Germans were unable to shoot any down. Over the Italian Front, moreover, the Caproni bombers used by the Italian air service conducted numerous raids against Austro-Hungarian targets, mainly the naval facilities in the Adriatic, and various armament factories in Austria-Hungary proper. The Adriatic was also the scene for a widespread war of naval aircraft, mostly floatplane and flying-boat fighter operations.

Air operations also played a small, but nevertheless important, part in the British campaigns in Palestine and Mesopotamia. In the former campaign, Australian squadrons particularly distinguished themselves by their daring and expertise. Of some portent was the virtual destruction of the Turkish 7th Army by aircraft of the RAF on 21 September 1918. Attempting to pull back to the north from Nablus in Palestine, the 7th Army was eliminated as a fighting force by continuous RAF raids on the head of the column as it wended its way through a number of ravines: two aircraft attacked every three minutes, with six or more aircraft attacking every 30 minutes. By the end of the day the army had broken up, handfuls of men surrendering or trying to pull back to the north of their own.

Colonel 'Billy' Mitchell was one of the architects of American airpower.

Air-to-Air Armament
World War I

Manfred von Richthofen prepares to open fire with the twin machine-guns of his Albatros D-III fighter on an FE 2b, whose gunner prepares precariously to return fire with the single flexible Lewis gun available to him for rearward fire.

Air-to-air armament is used in an offensive manner, but is basically defensive in character. The object of such armament is to protect one's own aircraft, and by destroying aircraft of the other side to allow the aircraft of one's own side to go about their business unmolested by armed opponents.

The first aircraft to be armed on an official basis was a Wright biplane of the US Army's Signal Corps, which was fitted with a Lewis light machine-gun in April 1912, and air-tested in June of the same year by Captain Charles de Forest Chandler. The installation was primitive, the forward end of the air-cooled gun's jacket resting on the rudder bar. Nevertheless, Chandler scored a good number of hits on a white sheet spread out on the ground in College Park, Maryland, though the performance of the gun failed to persuade the US authorities to adopt the weapon, the 'invention' of Colonel Isaac Newton Lewis, an American. It is from these trials, though, that the development of airborne armament may best be traced.

Disgruntled by the US armed services' failure to adopt his gun in place of the Benet-Mercié (Hotch-kiss), the world's other main air-cooled machine-gun of the pre-war period, Lewis left for Europe, where in January 1913 he established the Armes Auto-matiques Lewis in Liège, Belgium, to manufacture his gun. European efforts towards the development of armed aircraft had hitherto been beset by the problem of weight: most water-cooled machine-guns weighed at least 40 lb (18.14 kg) without their un-wieldy, and additionally heavy ammunition belts, whereas the Lewis gun turned the scales at 27 lb (12.25 kg), and the Hotchkiss at $27\frac{1}{4}$ lb (12.36 kg). Amongst other factors, it was the weight of the weapons available that had defeated the pioneer efforts of men such as the German Franz Euler, who patented the idea of a fixed forward-firing machine-gun on 23 July 1910, and the British Major Robert Brooke-Popham in 1910 and 1911. Even when the gun could be taken up in an aircraft, the extra weight so affected the performance of most types that they became impractical fighting machines.

Practical development of the Lewis gun as a basic weapon for aircraft continued in the period before World War I, notably in Belgium and Great Britain, in which countries trial firings were per-formed by Lieutenant Stellingwerf of the Belgian Army in September 1912 and November 1913 respectively. The Lewis gun was finally ordered for RFC and RNAS service in July 1914, by which time France had adopted the 8 mm Hotchkiss (the Lewis was made in 0.303 in calibre) as a standard aircraft gun, together with 37 mm and 47 mm cannon. The prime users of these weapons were the large numbers of Voisin pushers: these were massive enough to absorb the recoil of the cannon, and their pusher configurations made the location of a 'flexible' gun in the nose of the nacelle a practical military proposi-tion. The British had also experimented with cannon, using the Coventry Ordnance Works' 1 pounder (0.45 kg) weapon. Inevitably, recoil was the worst problem encountered with the aerial use of weapons of this calibre, and several ingenious palliatives were tried. At the moment of firing, lead shot to the weight of the cannon's round was discharged from the rear of the weapon to counteract the recoil, or a high-velocity stream of gas was released to the rear by another charge. Thus the recoil was kept within manageable proportions, but only at the expense of greatly reduced flexibility for the gun, which could not be fired in any position in which the counter-weight or gases would hit the parent aircraft, its rigging, its engine or its propeller.

The problem with machine-guns other than the Lewis and the Hotchkiss was their weight, size and unwieldiness. For whereas the Lewis and Hotchkiss were compact and had easily manageable ammuni-tion supplies (a 47-round drum on the Lewis, and 9-, 14- or 30-round metal strips on the Hotchkiss), weapons such as the British Vickers and Maxim, German MG08, and Austro-Hungarian Schwarz-lose M07/12 used canvas belts for their ammunition. Though this conferred far greater ammunition capacity without the need for reloading, the canvas belts themselves were all but unmanageable in flight, making the task of the gunner exceptionally difficult. This factor became all too clear in trials with the Vickers 'Destroyer' in 1913: though the lighter Vickers (Maxim) gun was substituted for the initial Maxim gun, problems with the belt feed made the whole concept unworkable.

For pusher types, which predominated in the period up to 1914, provision of a machine-gun on a simple ball and socket mounting at the front of the nacelle provided perfectly adequate armament, especially if a drum- or strip-fed machine-gun were used, or if some means of containing the belts of heavier weapons could be devised. However, there was clearly a considerable tactical advantage in fitting machine-guns to the best aircraft available, and by 1913 these were almost invariably of the tractor type, with the engine and propeller mounted at the front of the fuselage and pulling the aircraft through the air, rather than driving it as in the pusher types. Clearly a machine-gun could be fitted to such a type, but only to fire over the rear vertical hemi-sphere of the gunner's field of vision. The problem facing designers in this type of aircraft was thus a twofold one: the aircraft could be provided with a defensive armament easily enough, though to pro-vide the gunner with an adequate field of fire his position would have to be changed with that of the pilot (pilots generally occupying the rear seat in two-seaters so that when no passenger was carried, the removal of weight would be near the centre of gravity having little effect upon the balance of the aircraft), but the aircraft could be provided with offensive armament only if some means could be devised of allowing the machine-gun to be fitted on the forward fuselage to fire along the pilot's line of sight but miss the whirling blades of the propeller. This last might be turning at 40 revolutions a second, and the gun firing 10 rounds per second, making it

An early Allied solution to the problem of forward-firing armament was the location of the weapon on the upper wing, to fire over the propeller disc, as on this Nieuport scout.

inevitable that a blade would be hit even in a short burst of a few rounds. Yet every designer who turned his mind to the subject came to the conclusion that only a machine-gun aligned along the pilot's line of vision and the aircraft's line of flight would produce an effective weapon: the alignment of the gun in any other direction produced problems of deflection shooting beyond the abilities of all but a tiny minority of superlative shots.

Yet for a variety of reasons the location of the machine-gun in the forward fuselage had a number of advantages: a belt-fed type, which was inherently more reliable, could be used; its greater weight did not matter as the weapon was located closer to the aircraft's centre of gravity; the location of the gun near the centre of gravity did not have so detrimental an effect on the manoeuvrability of the aircraft as a weapon mounted at the front of a pusher's nacelle, together with a gunner to use it; and a fixed gun could be fed by a long belt housed in an ammunition tank and brought up to the gun by means of chutes, thus obviating the problems of exposed canvas belts becoming tangled as they had in experiments with such guns on flexible mountings.

Thus the advantages were many, but there remained the problem that a two-bladed propeller revolving 1,200 times per minute had a blade in front of the muzzle 20 times per second, in which time some 10 rounds would be fired towards it. There were two basic methods of getting round the problem: firstly, to arrange the machine-gun so that it fired down a hollow propeller shaft; and secondly, to

devise a mechanism that would interrupt the action of the gun when a blade was in front of the muzzle, or better, to synchronize the action of the gun so that it fired only when there was no blade in front of the muzzle. The first method was feasible with rotary engines, or with inline engines with geared drives moving the axis of the propeller to a position in line with the inside of the V between the cylinder banks; but it also raised problems with ammunition feed and the position of the gun breech where the pilot would find it difficult to clear a blockage or jam. In fact the only really successful use of this method during World War I occurred in 1917 and 1918 when a few French aces such as Georges Guynemer and René Fonck used a Spad fighter fitted with a *moteur-canon* in the V of the Hispano-Suiza inline engine. Guynemer closed in to very close range, where a single shot from the explosive cannon shell was sufficient to cause the destruction of an enemy aircraft, and Fonck relied on his phenomenal shooting to down a few aircraft with single cannon rounds. Even so, both men found the difficulties of loading single rounds into the awkwardly placed breech hardly worth the effort. The system, it should be noted, had been devised in 1912 by Franz Schneider, a designer for the German firm *Luft-Verkehrs Gesellschaft* (LVG). Schneider, a Swiss national, had experimented with the system in the period immediately before the outbreak of World War I, but had given up after perpetual oiling-up problems with the spark plugs of the Daimler engine which he had to invert for the system.

Schneider, who had been a designer for the French Nieuport firm before joining LVG, was not deterred by the impracticality of his first attempt to provide an aircraft with a fixed forward-firing armament. On 15 July 1913, Schneider patented for LVG a relatively simple mechanism to relate the firing of a machine-gun to the position of the propeller. Early in 1914, Schneider asked the German military authorities for a machine-gun so that he could conduct experiments with his creation, but was refused the loan of such a weapon. Examination of the patent reveals that in some respects Schneider had erred, but there seems little doubt that early failure would have served merely to put this talented engineer on the right lines, once he got down to the practical task of making his gear work. Extraordinarily, the German magazine *Flugsport* published details of Schneider's mechanism some two months after the beginning of World War I, though this seems to have provided the Allied nations with no stimulus towards their own development of a gun synchronizing gear.

By 1914, however, designers in several countries had come to appreciate the advantages of a fixed forward-firing armament for tractor aircraft, and

devised methods for (or at least had patented principles of) achieving these ends. In Russia, for example, a Lieutenant Poplavko received some governmental support for his efforts in this direction, though in England the Edwards brothers' attempts met with total indifference.

On 22 January 1914, a patent was granted to Armand Deperdussin for the concept of a fixed machine-gun that could be made to fire through a revolving propeller disc 'by means of electrical control or a similar device'. However, as Deperdussin was in gaol at the time after a conviction for embezzlement, there was little that he could do to turn his concept into a workable device. Indeed, the patent had been applied for by the official receiver of Deperdussin's SPAD firm, which had no real interest in developing a synchronizer as envisaged by the firm's founder.

Shortly after this, on 24 February 1914, the Italian firm of Nieuport Macchi SA applied for a patent of more realistic terms. For whereas Deperdussin's patent had described only the concept of his notion, the Nieuport Macchi application described the device envisaged: from the rear of the engine a

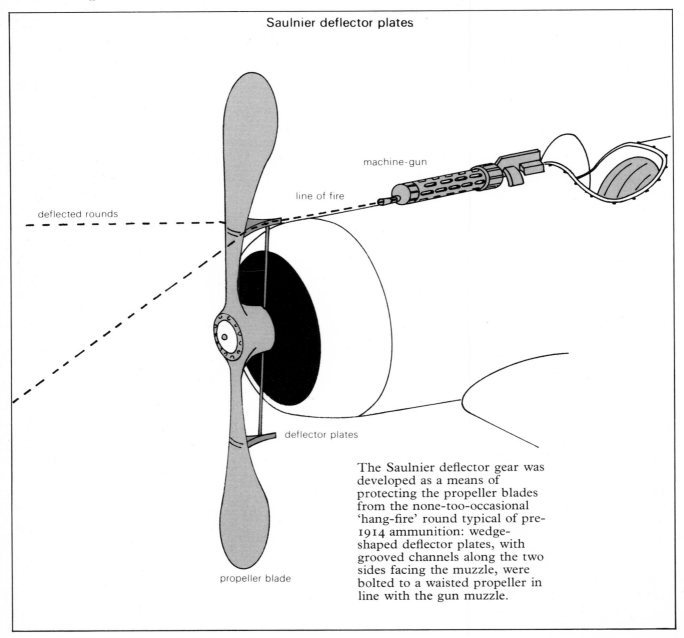

Saulnier deflector plates

machine-gun

line of fire

deflected rounds

deflector plates

propeller blade

The Saulnier deflector gear was developed as a means of protecting the propeller blades from the none-too-occasional 'hang-fire' round typical of pre-1914 ammunition: wedge-shaped deflector plates, with grooved channels along the two sides facing the muzzle, were bolted to a waisted propeller in line with the gun muzzle.

drive shaft would operate, through a series of bevelled joints, a cam to regulate the firing of the machine-gun.

Back in France again, the prolific but somewhat eccentric genius of Robert Esnault-Pelterie led to the application for a remarkably far-sighted patent on 26 March 1914: not content with the design of a potentially workable synchronizing gear, Esnault-Pelterie submitted a design for a two-seat fighting aircraft. Power was to be provided by a horizontally mounted rotary engine: the propeller was driven through a bevelled drive, a rearward extension of which controlled the firing of the pilot's machine-gun, which was provided with a measure of flexibility by its mounting. The second member of the crew was also provided with a machine-gun, this time a fully flexible weapon to protect the rear of the aircraft. The gunner's weapon was to be provided with a frame to prevent its movement into areas in which the aircraft itself would be hit. Esnault-Pelterie also envisaged the location of the crew in an armoured cabin to protect them from hostile fire. Given the power of current engines, the whole scheme was probably impractical, though its individual elements were all workable, and did indeed feature in later aircraft.

Most important, however, was the application by Raymond Saulnier of the Morane-Saulnier concern, in April 1914, for a patent covering a workable machine-gun synchronizing gear. Realizing the implications of his device, Saulnier immediately wrote to the French Inspector General of Aeronautics, General Bernard, on 5 May 1915, but received no reply. Although Saulnier's idea, the detail design of the installation appears to have been that of Louis Peyret, Morane-Saulnier's chief draughtsman. Once completed, the device was tested on the ranges of the Hotchkiss machine-gun company near the Eiffel tower. The trials showed that the synchronizing gear worked perfectly at engine speeds of 1,200 revolutions per minute, but that the device was made impractical for service use by the imperfections of the standard French machine-gun ammunition: occasional rounds detonated slightly later than they should have (or 'hung fire'), with the result that the bullet, instead of passing between the blades of the propeller, struck one and shattered it. Such an occurrence in the air, of course, would be disastrous. Colonel de Boigne, a director of the Hotchkiss firm and the controller of the experiments, could offer little hope of completely standardized ammunition, especially as nitro-cellulose propellants were still relatively new, and peacetime economic measures meant that strict quality control of ammunition manufacture was impossible, and indeed not needed for any other applications of the standard 8 mm round.

To see what could be done to mitigate the effects of bullet strikes on the propeller blades, Saulnier removed the mechanical linkage between the engine and the gun, and fired whole 'strip' magazines of ammunition at a blade armoured with one of three types of wedge-shaped deflector plates specially produced for the purpose. The object of the exercise was to develop the optimum deflector, which could then be used in conjunction with the synchronizing gear to ward off the occasional 'hang-fire' round.

However, with the outbreak of World War I the experiments came to a premature end, Saulnier's permission to use a Hotchkiss machine-gun being revoked. In a way this was fortunate, for the Hotchkiss was totally unsuitable for large-scale development as a synchronized aerial machine-gun on two counts: the firing pin was part of the breechlock, with consequent mechanical problems in arresting the movement of a relatively heavy part of the mechanism; and the limitations of the weapon as a result of the strip-feed ammunition method.

Roland Garros, a test pilot for Morane-Saulnier, had known of the experiments, but had played no part in them. Mobilized at the outbreak of hostilities, Garros finally managed in December 1914 to get semi-official permission to return to the Morane-Saulnier factory and resume work on the synchronizing mechanism. Thus Garros made the first aerial trials of the system, still without the mechanical linkage between engine and gun. The initial deflectors were too clumsy for realistic service use, and it was Garros who devised the idea of 'waisting' the propeller blade in line with the gun muzzle so that considerably smaller deflectors, specially made by Panhard, could be fitted. At the instigation of Jules Hue, Garros' mechanic, the faces of the deflector on each side of the apex were channeled so as to deflect the bullet without breaking it up, the splinters of other bullets having damaged the propeller blades.

After a total disaster with the first trial aircraft, a Morane-Saulnier Type G which broke up on the ground when subjected to intense vibration after centrifugal force threw off one of the deflectors, Garros and Hue were allocated a Morane-Saulnier Type L parasol-wing monoplane for their experiments. This machine proved ideal, especially after Hue had devised and built the machine-gun bearers, a device to improve the ammunition feed arrangements, and a means of disposing of used cartridge cases. Official trials were conducted to the satisfaction of all, and Garros was soon afterwards ordered to Dunkirk for combat evaluation of the deflector plate system against the German bombers raiding the town and port on a regular basis. At the same time, the armed Type L monoplane was ordered into production.

But just at this moment the Germans ended their campaign against Dunkirk, disappointing Garros by the removal of his anticipated prey. He did, however, manage to attack three German aircraft bombing Furnes, though without success. Then a storm brought down the hangar in which Garros' Type L was sheltered, destroying the aircraft utterly. Garros' already lowered spirits were further dampened during a visit to Paris during which he received the news that the 10 armed Type Ls ordered earlier had been cancelled just as they were approaching completion. However, on his return to Dunkirk he found that Hue had fitted up another Type L for his use, though the weather made operational flying all but impossible.

The great day finally came on 1 April 1915: while *en route* to attack a German railway station with two modified 155 mm artillery shells, Garros met and shot down in flames a German two-seater. Another German aircraft fell to the novel head-on form of attack on 15 April, and a third on 18 April. *Escadrille M.S. 23*'s most celebrated pilot had revolutionized air warfare in two and a half weeks.

Late on 19 April, though, Garros accompanied *Capitaine* de Malherbe in a bombing attack on Courtrai station. Diving from 6,562 ft (2,000 m) to 2,297 ft (700 m) to drop his bombs, Garros was forced to crashland near Ingelmunster after the engine of his aircraft had been hit by ground-fire. German troops immediately closed in on the scene of the crash, and although Garros managed to escape capture for some hours, he was only partially successful in destroying his valuable aircraft, which was immediately moved to Iseghem for closer examination once the Germans had appreciated the potential of the inbuilt armament.

The fact that the Germans were still proceeding with the development of aircraft with fixed armament for the pilot is attested by the first flight, at about this time, of the LVG E.VI, designed by Schneider. This featured both a fixed gun for the pilot and a flexible gun for the observer. The latter is of considerable interest, for although the prototype was lost while being flown to the front for operational evaluation, no further examples being built, the ring-mounted Parabellum machine-gun installation became standard on all subsequent German two seaters. The ring mounting round the observer's cockpit allowed the gun to be moved in azimuth through 360°, while the gun mounting on the moving part of the carriage allowed the gun to be elevated and depressed through a considerable angle. The problem of the ammunition belt whipping about in the slipstream was neatly solved by winding the belt on a rotating drum attached to the feed side of the gun's receiver, from which it was pulled by the gun's feed pawl as necessary. The British evolved a similar mounting, the type bearing the name of its inventor, Warrant Officer F. W. Scarff, RN. Scarff, who worked in the Admiralty Air Department, designed his definitive No 2 Ring Mounting in 1916: it consisted of a fixed ring round the gunner's cockpit, on which rotated a movable ring. Mounted on the latter was an elevating bridge consisting of a pair of quadrants, on which the gunner's Lewis machine-gun (sometimes two such guns in later aircraft) was fixed, the weight of the gun or guns being balanced by 'bungee' elastic cords. The mounting could only be moved when a lever had been actuated, release of the lever locking the mounting. The Scarff No 2 Ring Mounting entered British service in July 1916, and became the standard Allied flexible gun mounting for the rest of World War I, remaining in RAF service for many years after the end of the war.

The Parabellum gun had been designed for ground use, but from 1915 onwards was used almost exclusively as an air weapon. In essence, the weapon was a highly refined version of the German version of the Maxim machine-gun, the MG08. In 1911 the designer Karl Heinemann had moved to the *Deutsche Waffen und Munitions Fabriken* (DWM), or German Weapons and Munitions Factory, whose telegraphic address was Parabellum, Berlin, to develop an air-cooled and considerably lightened version of the MG08. Compared with the original weapon, the Parabellum had a locking toggle that moved upwards rather than downwards, a wooden stock, and the water jacket retained, to support the recoiling barrel, but fretted out for lightness. The original MG08 had weighed $58\frac{1}{2}$ lb (26.54 kg), but the Parabellum weighed only 22 lb (10 kg). The weapon's rate of fire was also increased from the MG08's 400 rounds per minute to about 700 rounds per minute. Calibre remained the same, both weapons firing the 0.312 in (7.92 mm) *Patrone* 98 (1898) standard German round. Later in the war, it should be noted, the Parabellum came to be fitted with a close fitting barrel casing in place of the fretted water jacket of earlier models. This reduced drag considerably, and made the weapon easier to handle in the air.

The Allied equivalent to the Parabellum was the Lewis gun, which was adopted by all Allied air forces in the absence of a superior air cooled weapon. Designed for ground use, the Lewis was cooled by a current of air drawn past the cooling fins inside the bulky radiator casing, both of which were soon found to be unnecessary for aerial use and so discarded, leaving the Lewis with an apparently fragile, unsupported barrel. So far as cooling was concerned, moreover, it was found that it was freezing rather than overheating that was the main problem with guns in the air. The rate of stoppages with Lewis guns was therefore high until special lubricants were developed for use at high altitude. Weighing only 27 lb (12.25 kg) in its ground form, and less in its aerial version, the Lewis proved an admirable weapon, its only main disadvantage being the limited capacity of its circular ammunition drum, only 47 rounds, increased in July 1916 by the adoption of the 97-round double drum. Even so, this compares poorly with the 250-round belt of the Parabellum. The rate of fire of the Lewis gun was also inferior to that of the Parabellum, being only 550 rounds per minute, though this was later increased by the fitting of a muzzle attachment.

During the early part of 1915, both the Parabellum and Lewis became increasingly frequent as observers' weapons, the Lewis gun also being found on extemporized mountings designed to give the pilots of single-seaters a modicum of firepower. A few Morane-Saulnier Type Ls were fitted with Lewis guns and deflector plates, as were some Morane-Saulnier Type Ns and other single-seat scouts such as the Sopwith Tabloid and the Bristol Scouts C and D. In other

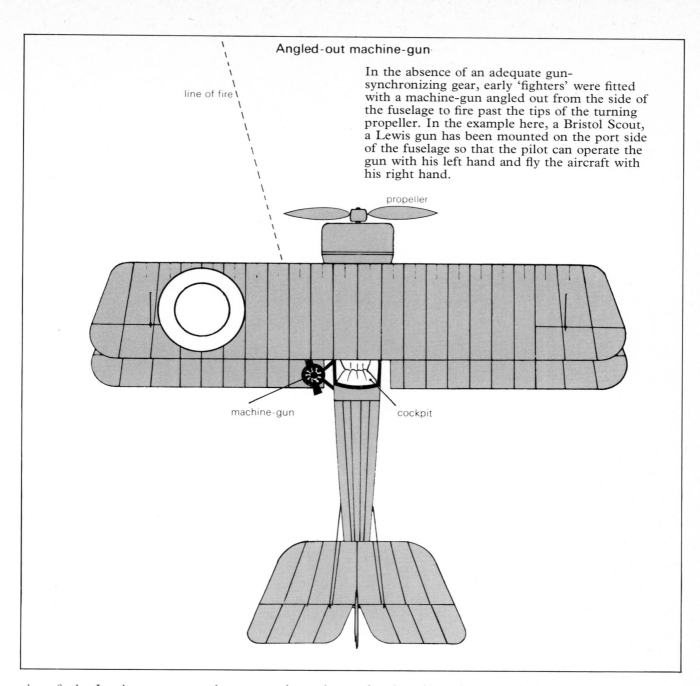

Angled-out machine-gun

line of fire

propeller

In the absence of an adequate gun-synchronizing gear, early 'fighters' were fitted with a machine-gun angled out from the side of the fuselage to fire past the tips of the turning propeller. In the example here, a Bristol Scout, a Lewis gun has been mounted on the port side of the fuselage so that the pilot can operate the gun with his left hand and fly the aircraft with his right hand.

machine-gun   cockpit

aircraft the Lewis was mounted at an angle to the fuselage so that the stream of bullets would clear the tips of the turning propeller. This made sighting all but impossible, and it took an exceptional pilot to calculate a deflection shot perhaps 45° different to his line of flight. Such angled mountings had also been tried with rifles and carbines, but were at best only desperate expedients pending the development of an Allied synchronizing gear. Although some successes were gained with angled guns, they can be considered little better than devices such as bombs dangled on the end of long lines, to be detonated electrically when entangled with the rigging of an enemy aircraft below. There were other, equally eccentric weapons in use: grappling hooks towed on the ends of long lines to break the enemy aircraft's propeller; *fléchettes* (small steel darts) dropped in vast numbers by the French and British alike; and Ranken darts, designed by Engineer Lieutenant Francis Ranken, RN, principally as an anti-Zeppelin weapon. The explosive darts were released in salvoes of three from a 24-dart container above the target, four vanes spreading from the dart in flight to hook

the dart into the target's fabric covering and so allow the warhead to detonate inside the enemy aircraft. And these were only the more realistic of the devices tried, or at least contemplated. The Lewis gun appeared to be the best solution to the immediate need for aircraft armament, in both single- and two-seater aircraft, but there was an acute shortage of the guns, the factory in Liège having fallen into German hands, and production at the Birmingham Small Arms factory being slow to get under way. Demand for the Lewis was great, especially as the type was proving invaluable for trench warfare, and by the middle of 1915 it was possible to issue only a few weapons to each squadron. Mountings had to be improvised, and it was the practice to allocate Lewis guns only to those aircraft dispatched for a sortie beyond the lines, leaving those intended for missions over the lines to look after themselves as before, with *ad hoc* armament systems. The Germans were better off in this respect, for adequate supplies of the Parabellum were available for use on the new C class of armed biplane two-seaters which had begun to appear in the spring of 1915 as replacements for the earlier B class of unarmed two-seaters. Generally fitted with engines of about 150 or 160 hp, aircraft such as the Albatros C.I, Aviatik C.I and Rumpler C.I were generally superior to types such as the Royal Aircraft Factory BE 2b and Caudron G.3. The only real matches for the German C type aircraft were the Vickers F.B.5 and the Nieuport 10. However, with the introduction of the next generation of C types, aircraft such as the Albatros C.V and DFW C.V with 200 or 220 hp engines, the Allies were outclassed in terms of two-seaters.

After the capture of Garros' Morane-Saulnier Type L, the Germans quickly appreciated the value of their prize, and immediately decided to copy the armament system. The first attempt, by Simon Brunnhuber, was a failure; so *Hauptmann* Helmuth Förster, adjutant to Major Hermann von der Lieth-Thomsen, the Chief of Field Aviation, called in the flamboyant Anthony Fokker, a Dutch national working in Germany. Fokker was given the propeller of Garros' aircraft, a Parabellum machine-gun and a supply of ammunition, and ordered to produce a copy of the system for use on German aircraft. Fokker decided to go one better than his order, for he probably knew of Schneider's 1913 patent, though probably not of two current Russian synchronizing mechanisms, those of Poplavko and Smyslov-Dibovsky. Only a week later he was back at Döberitz to inform the authorities that he had invented a viable gun synchronizer, altogether superior to the primitive device used by Garros. And although Fokker, a natural publicist, claimed all the credit for himself, it is certain that he played only a minimal part in the development of the Fokker synchronizer gear. The real credit should therefore go to three of Fokker's designers, Fritz Heber, Leimberger and Heinrich Lübbe. The mechanism was basically simple: when the pilot operated the firing mechanism, the engine itself actuated the trigger mechanism by means of cams and a push-rod except when a propeller blade was in line with the muzzle of the gun. The system was tested on one of Fokker's own aircraft, the M.5k (A.III) unarmed reconnaissance aircraft, itself a copy, by a quirk of fortune, of the French Morane-Saulnier Type G. The gun used was the Parabellum, and the whole system worked perfectly. Early tests revealed the reliability of the system, and also the redundancy of the headrest, positioned behind the cockpit so that the pilot could align his head, and so his vision, exactly along the aircraft's line of flight. It seems that the idea was an 'improvement' upon a headrest in Garros' Type L; on the Frenchman's aircraft, however, the headrest had been located on the front edge of the cockpit, so that the pilot pressed his head forward onto it, close to the sights of the gun. The armed Fokker monoplane henceforward became the M.5k/MG, and the type was ordered into production as the E.I, the E standing for *Eindecker* or monoplane.

The E.I production aircraft were modelled closely on the M.5k/MG with the exception that the Parabellum machine-gun was replaced by an MG08/15, otherwise known as the leMG08, or as the 'Spandau' to the Allies as a result of the fact that many of the weapons were manufactured at the Spandau Arsenal near Berlin, and were so stamped, persuading the Allies that this was the official name of the weapon. The MG08 had been developed into the MG08/15 quite simply because, although the earlier weapon had proved very useful in the field, it was very heavy, turning the scales at $58\frac{1}{2}$ lb (26.54 kg) for the gun alone (with water), the tripod weighing another $70\frac{1}{2}$ lb (31.98 kg), and the alternative sled mount 83 lb (37.65 kg). The MG08/15 dispensed with the water pump and tripod/sled mounting, for a plain water jacket, bipod mount, shoulder stock and a reel-type drum magazine holding a 50-round canvas belt. Both the water-cooling and the belt feed were unusual features in a light gun, but avoided the need for extensive redesign of the basic weapon. Weight of the 7.92 mm MG08/15 was only 39 lb (17.7 kg), but rate of fire remained unchanged at about 400 rounds per minute.

With Parabellum production needed for observer mountings, it seemed natural to try the MG08/15 as the pilot's weapon. The weight of the weapon could be reduced because water-cooling was not necessary in an aircraft whose high speed through the air would provide more than adequate air-cooling, though the water jacket had to be kept (fretted out for lightness) to support the barrel; the bipod and shoulder stock could be eliminated; and the belt-feed mechanism of the weapon was ideally suited for a fixed-gun installation over a high-capacity magazine with a chute leading up to the receiver to keep the slipstream off the canvas belt. (It is interesting to note that in 1918 there appeared the MG08/18, adapted from the aircraft MG08/15 for ground use with the air-cooled barrel, which had no bipod and was very prone to overheating.) The MG08/15 installation was tried on the second M.5k/MG, and proved immediately successful, to the extent that the type became the standard fixed machine-gun for German aircraft during World War I.

The Fokker E.I entered service in June 1915, and immediately proved itself a decisive weapon, despite the generally poor performance and agility of the basic airframe, which had never been intended for air fighting. Nevertheless, the possession of a fixed forward-firing machine-gun made the E.I, and its successors the E.II, E.III main production variant, and E.IV masters of the air during the period between late summer 1915 and early summer 1916, despite the fact that no more than 475 were built. From the armament point of view, the interesting factor about the E.III/IV was that it could be fitted with twin MG08/15 guns, though this reduced performance so drastically that only one gun was normally fitted; and one E.IV was specially modified for the ace Max Immelmann to carry three MG08/15 guns. Despite the extra power of a 160 hp engine, performance was low, and the complexities of the triple synchronizer gear once caused Immelmann to shoot off both blades of his propeller.

It was soon abundantly clear to the Allies that it was the Fokker's synchronizer gear which made the E types such formidable opponents, yet for some still unexplained reason the Allied air authorities made no immediate effort to develop comparable gears of their own design, or even to copy the Fokker gear from German aircraft that fell into Allied hands. Consequently the German fighters had a field day, downing Allied aircraft in great numbers during what became known as the 'Fokker Scourge'.

Given that the Allies were slow to develop synchronizing gears for their own fighters, it becomes clear why the winter of 1915 and spring of 1916 witnessed the arrival of a large number of Allied aircraft types designed to counter the superiority of the Fokkers by a number of odd recourses. In Britain there appeared the Armstrong-Whitworth F.K.12 escort triplane with a pair of gun nacelles mounted on the extended-span central wing outside the disc swept by the conventional tractor propeller; the Blackburn Triplane pusher, with a large nacelle probably intended to mount a Davis recoilless gun; the Robey-Peters Davis Gun Carrier biplane, with a pair of nacelles under the upper wings, each to carry one Davis recoilless gun; the Sage Type 2 tractor biplane with a two-man enclosed cockpit filling the space between the fuselage and the upper wing, through a hole in which the gunner poked his torso

to use the Lewis gun it was intended to carry; the Sopwith LRTTr three-seat anti-Zeppelin triplane with a second gunner in a streamlined nacelle in the upper wing centre section; the Pemberton Billing P.B. 29E and Supermarine P.B. 31E pusher and tractor quadriplanes, each with an upper wing position for armament intended for use against airships; and the Vickers F.B. 7 twin-engined biplane with a 1 pounder (0.45 kg) quickfiring gun in the fuselage nose. The French also produced a number of oddities, including the Breguet *de Chasse* pusher biplane escort with a Davis 2 pounder (0.91 kg) gun in the nacelle nose; the Breguet 12 Ca.2 pusher with a 37 mm Hotchkiss cannon; the Dufaux fighter, with its pusher propeller mounted behind the cockpit in a 'conventional' fuselage, the two halves of which were joined by a tube through the hub of the propeller, and a Lewis gun in the nose of the fuselage; the FBA *Avion Canon* with the engine mounted between the biplane wing cellule, set above the fuselage and driving a pusher propeller, the armament consisting of a 37 mm Hotchkiss cannon in the fuselage nose; and the SPAD A.2 and A.4 'pulpit' fighters, with gun-equipped 'pulpits' carried in front of the tractor propeller on each type.

These are only a few of the many weird and wonderful expedients tried at various times to evade the difficulties imposed by lack of an Allied synchronizer

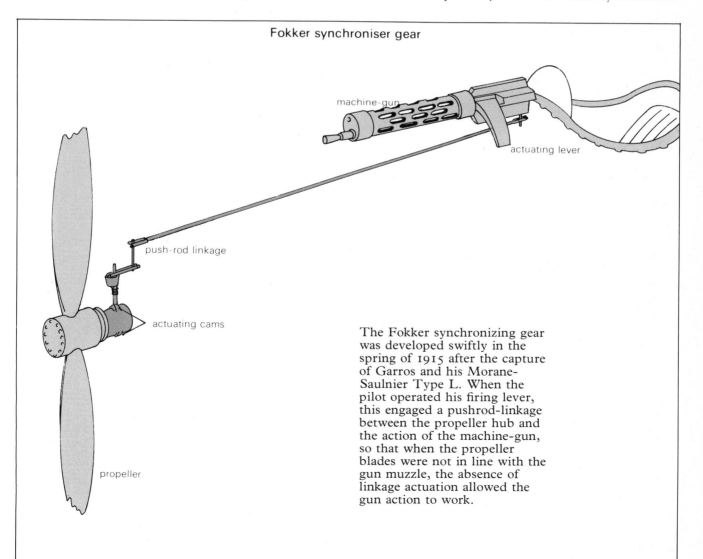

Fokker synchroniser gear

machine-gun

actuating lever

push-rod linkage

actuating cams

propeller

The Fokker synchronizing gear was developed swiftly in the spring of 1915 after the capture of Garros and his Morane-Saulnier Type L. When the pilot operated his firing lever, this engaged a pushrod-linkage between the propeller hub and the action of the machine-gun, so that when the propeller blades were not in line with the gun muzzle, the absence of linkage actuation allowed the gun action to work.

gear, or to use for combat purposes weapons heavier than the Germans were apparently contemplating. Even without a synchronizer gear, though, the final success of the Allies in defeating the Fokker Scourge was inevitable once they had realized that the E types' weakest spot lay in their very performance as aircraft, which at its best was mediocre. During the spring of 1916, therefore, the Allies introduced two aircraft basically superior to the Fokker types: the French Nieuport 11 *Bébé*, armed with a single Lewis gun above the upper wing where it could fire over the disc swept by the propeller, and the Airco (de Havilland) 2 trim pusher biplane, with a forward-firing Lewis gun in the front of the central nacelle. Both these aircraft could outperform the E types, and gradually wrested air superiority back for the Allies.

Yet the success of the Nieuport 11 and DH 2 could not obscure the fact that in their synchronizer gear the Germans had a decided technical advantage, which if combined with an adequate airframe would once again give the Germans a decided qualitative edge. The Allies could no longer 'make do' without an equivalent gear, therefore, and soon the first of such gears began to appear. The most notable were the French Alkan, designed by Sergeant-Mechanic Alkan for use with a Lewis gun; and the British Arsiad (designed by Major A. V. Bettington and named for his Aeroplane Repair Section, No 1 Aircraft Depot), the Ross, the Scarff-Dibovsky (developed into a practical gear by Warrant Officer Scarff from the basic design of the Russian Lieutenant-Commander V. V. Dibovsky), the Sopwith-Kauper and the Vickers-Challenger. All the British gears were designed for use with the Vickers machine-gun, which rapidly became the standard aircraft fixed machine-gun in British, French and Italian service. The gears were all mechanical, and basically similar to the Fokker type. Unfortunately for the Allies, having previously suffered from an absence of such gears, they now had too many – the three main types being the Arsiad, fitted to only a few aircraft; the Scarff-Dibovsky, fitted to aircraft of the Royal Naval Air Service; and the Vickers-Challenger, used in most Royal Flying Corps and French air service aircraft. The first aircraft with a synchronizer gear to reach France was a Bristol Scout, on 25 March 1916; on 24 May of the same year the first batch of new aircraft to use the gear arrived, in the form of a flight of Sopwith 1½-Strutter fighter/reconnaissance aircraft. At much the same time the Nieuport 17, also fitted with a synchronized gun, made its appearance in French service.

Some efforts were made to provide a synchronizer for the Lewis gun, which some authorities felt to be a better aircraft gun because of its light weight and earlier problems with the Vickers gun. But it was soon realized that the Vickers, in an air-cooled version, would be ideal for aircraft use: it was more reliable, having been designed for the sustained-fire role, was belt- rather than drum-fed and so had far greater ammunition capacity, and its extra weight, compared with the Lewis, was hardly significant when the gun was located in a fixed mounting on or near the aircraft's centre of gravity. Adopted for service with the British Army in 1912, the Vickers machine-gun was a progressive development of the 0.45 in (11.43 mm) Maxim and 0.303 in (7.7 mm) Vickers-Maxim machine-guns, retaining the calibre of the latter, but being made considerably lighter and more efficient by the use of improved metals. Whereas the Vickers-Maxim weighed 60 lb (27.21 kg), the Vickers weighed 33 lb (14.97 kg), and was lightened still further for aircraft use by the fretting out of the water jacket and the elimination of the sights, spade grips and other ground-use items. Though the Vickers gradually became the Allies' standard fixed machine-gun for aircraft use, normally in association with the Vickers-Challenger synchronizer gear produced by the same company, the machine-gun was not without problems in its initial versions. The use of a mechanical synchronizer gear meant that the rate of fire was very low when the engine was throttled back (the same trouble had beset both the Saulnier and Fokker gears), and there was an alarming tendency for the expended end of the canvas ammunition belt to pass under the gun and re-enter the breech, the resulting double feed being difficult for the pilot to clear.

It was mechanical problems such as these, and jams caused by the lack of uniformity in the ammunition available at the time, which were largely responsible for the standard installation of fixed guns with their breeches accessible to the pilot. Only thus could he try in flight to clear the many feed and jamming problems that were endemic to World War I machine-guns. But even the best laid-out armament installations were relatively difficult to get at, and the need to clear stoppages often resulted in aircraft undertaking the most unlikely and unintended manoeuvres as the pilot tried to hold the control column between his knees and operate on the guns with his hands. It should be noted, though, that another reason for the standard location of guns in the forward fuselage just in front of the pilot was an aerodynamic one: the guns and their associated ammunition tanks were amongst the heaviest items in the aircraft, especially when the full load of ammunition was carried, and their location on or near the aircraft's centre of gravity meant that manoeuvrability was not adversely affected to an unwelcome extent. Indeed, the Sopwith Camel, the war's most successful fighter, owed much of its success to its phenomenal agility in the air: this was largely the result of the designer's genius in locating all the major heavy 'components' of the aircraft (engine, fuel, guns/ammunition and pilot) in the forward 6 ft (1.83 m) of the fuselage. This factor also played a great part in the agility of the Fokker Dr I triplane fighter, which concentrated the main masses into the front 6½ ft (1.98 m) of the fuselage.

By the end of 1916, most Allied fighters (the best being the French Nieuport 17 and Spad S.7, and the British Sopwith Pup) had mechanically synchronized single fixed machine-guns, while most two-seaters

Typical of the armament carried by two-seaters in World War I is that of this RE 8 reconnaissance/artillery spotting aircraft: a fixed Vickers gun for the pilot (on the port side of the fuselage) and a Lewis gun on a Scarff mounting for the gunner.

were now fitted with the Scarff No 2 Ring Mounting for their flexible Lewis guns (the Hotchkiss of the French and the Revelli of the Italians having been almost entirely superseded) in place of the earlier pillar-and-socket, or Nieuport ring mountings. For use on single-seat aircraft there appeared the Foster mounting, designed by Sergeant Foster of No 11 Squadron, RFC. This sliding-rail mounting with a quadrant coming down from the upper wing towards the fuselage in front of the cockpit replaced earlier overwing mountings for Lewis guns: the ability to pull the gun back and down, so that the breech and ammunition drum were just in front of the pilot, being a great blessing. On earlier mountings, the pilot had frequently been compelled to stand up in the cockpit, holding the control column between his knees, to change the ammunition drum or clear a stoppage. In one celebrated incident, a British pilot trying to remove a stuck ammunition drum had lost the control column from between his knees, the aircraft promptly rolling onto its back and the pilot falling out of the cockpit. Suspended from the leather handle of the recalcitrant drum, which he now prayed would not come off, the pilot finally managed to get his feet and lower legs back into the cockpit and so pull himself back into his still inverted aircraft. Only then could he let go of the ammunition drum and right his aircraft. With the new Foster mounting such incidents became unlikely. The usual

method of firing a gun mounted on the top wing to clear the disc swept by the propeller was a Bowden cable running up from the cockpit to the trigger mechanism of the Lewis.

Although basically simple, and able to control the firing of two MG08/15 machine-guns, the Fokker synchronizer gear depended for reliable operation on frequent inspection and adjustment of the pushrod mechanism. During 1916, therefore, the Germans set about improving the basic nature of the gear with a view to improving its capabilities and reliability. While the Allies realized the inadequacy of their synchronizer gears, none of which could control the fire of more than one machine-gun, the Germans were introducing new fighters (Albatros D.II/III and LFG (Roland) D.I) armed with twin machine-guns. During the late autumn and early winter of 1916, therefore, twin-gun fighters of these types superseded the single-gun interim biplane fighters (Albatros D.I, Fokker D types and Halberstadt D.I, D.Ia, D.II, D.III and D.IV) that had taken over the main burden of fighter operations from the Fokker and Pfalz E types during the late spring of 1916. Soon joined by more advanced twin-gun fighters, these German fighters marked a great step forward in fighter design, with double the armament of earlier types, and far superior performance and structural strength. The culmination of this German move was the infamous 'Bloody April' of 1917, when the Royal Flying Corps in particular suffered disastrous losses while trying to take the air war to the the Germans over the major Allied ground offensives of the period.

It was only during May 1917 that the Allies found the solution to the Germans' latest bout of air superiority, by introducing large numbers of new aircraft types on the Western Front. Marked by higher performance and considerably greater structural integrity than earlier Allied aircraft and current German types, it was aircraft of the new generation (Bristol F.2A Fighter, Royal Aircraft Factory SE 5, the Sopwith Triplane and the Spad S.13) that finally turned the tide in favour of the Allies for the rest of the air war with a few local exceptions. With the exception of the Spad S.13, these aircraft had only a single fixed machine-gun in the fuselage, though the Bristol Fighter and SE 5 had a Lewis gun (flexible in the two-seat Fighter and wing-mounted in the SE 5) each. More importantly, perhaps, these were only the precursors of the latest generation of Allied fighters, the classic examples of which (such as the Sopwith Camel) were armed with twin Vickers machine-guns. This had been made possible during 1916 by the development of the CC synchronizer gear, so named after its two inventors, Georgiu Constantinescu, an expatriate Romanian mining engineer, and Major G. C. Colley. The new C.C. gear worked on hydraulic rather than mechanical principles, the firing impulse being transmitted from the engine to the trigger mechanism by means of oil pressure on a plunger. The new gear was far simpler than the old mechanical system, and could be applied with little modification, other than a lengthening or shortening of the oil pipe, to any aircraft. Just as importantly, the C.C. gear was capable of controlling the fire of two fixed guns. The first aircraft fitted with the C.C. synchronizer gear, Airco (de Havilland) 4 light bombers, arrived in France in March 1917, and the gear was soon in widespread service on fighters, two-seaters and light bombers.

At about the same time the Germans introduced their own new synchronizer: the long and relatively unreliable push-rod linkage from the engine was abandoned, and the guns were now controlled from the engine cam-shaft, the pilot's trigger operating a clutch mechanism in the device.

Twin fixed machine-guns, usually of the Vickers or MG08/15 type, remained the standard fighter armament for the rest of the war, controlled by C.C. or redesigned Fokker synchronizer gears. Late in the war, the Allies in particular tried to improve on the weight of fire currently standard by the addition of extra guns, but such efforts were bedevilled by the need to keep the guns' breeches within reach of the pilot, and the inherent limitations of the C.C. gear. Aircraft such as the Sopwith 5F1 Dolphin, for example, had twin synchronized Vickers guns, and also one or two Lewis guns mounted on the centre-section frame of the low upper wing. The Lewis guns were angled to fire forwards and upwards, and so clear the tips of the propeller blades without the need

for a synchronizer gear. In any sort of crash landing, however, the pilot was fortunate to emerge without his face badly damaged by striking the rear of the Lewis guns. Other such expedients were tried, but production single-seat fighters with an armament of more than two machine-guns were rare.

The Vickers, Lewis, MG08/15 and Parabellum were the four most widely used air-to-air weapons of World War I, but these were by no means the only weapons employed. Many other machine-guns were tried and used in limited numbers (the 8 mm French Hotchkiss machine-gun being the most common example), and a number of cannon and rocket installations received some considerable experimental attention and limited service use.

Amongst service weapons, the most notable were the Austro-Hungarian Schwarzlose MG05/12, a slow-firing and not very reliable 0.315 in (8 mm) weapon whose most unusual feature was that it was blowback-operated, an unusual feature in a machine-gun designed for the sustained-fire role. To make the system work, the Schwarzlose's designer, the German Andreas Schwarzlose, had to use a breechlock of considerable mass, which inevitably reduced the rate of fire, which was only 400 rounds per minute. The gun itself was quite heavy, at 44 lb (20 kg). The most common mountings from 1917 onwards were two double installations using the revised Fokker synchronizer: either well forward in the nose, on each side of the standard inline engine's cylinder block, where the guns were kept warm (essential in the Schwarzlose to facilitate used round extraction) but were out of reach of the pilot; or farther back towards the cockpit, where the pilot could reach the breeches, but in a position where long tubes stretching forward from the muzzles were essential to prevent the hot propellant gas igniting petrol fumes in the engine compartment. The Fokker types of synchronizer gear could not be used with the Schwarzlose at low engine revolutions, so early aircraft had a gun above the upper wing.

The main Italian-designed machine-gun used in aircraft was the Fiat (Revelli) Model 1914 0.256 in (6.5 mm) weapon, designed by *Maggiore* Abiel Botel Revelli. Like the heavier-calibre Schwarzlose used by Italy's main opponent, the Model 1914 was a retarded-blowback weapon, and used a small oil pump (worked automatically by the action of the weapon) to lubricate each round and so facilitate spent-round extraction. The Model 1914 also had an feed arrangement consisting of a 'mousetrap' type magazine with 10 compartments each holding five rounds. For aerial use the Model 1914 was lightened by the removal of the water jacket, which was replaced by longitudinal fins along the barrel, serving to help cool and strengthen the barrel. Fire was 500 rounds per minute.

Another weapon used by the Italians was the 0.35 in (9 mm) Villar Perosa. Extraordinarily, this was the world's first true sub-machine gun, and was designed by Revelli. The standard weapon consisted of two barrels, side-by-side, fed from a pair of 25-round

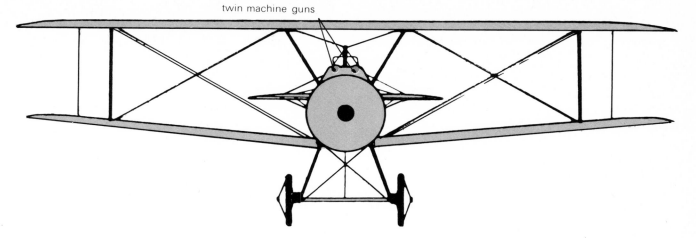

twin machine guns

1918 3-second weight of fire: on average, pilots could keep opponents in their sights for about three seconds at a time, and in this period the twin 0.303-in (7.7-mm) Vickers guns of the Sopwith Camel could deliver a weight of fire of 1.24 lb (0.56 kg), the equivalent weight for the Fokker D VII's twin MG08/15 machine-guns being 1.41 lb (0.64 kg).

vertical box magazines. Action was again retarded blowback, rate of fire 2,400 rounds per minute, and weight 14.3 lb (6.2 kg). The usual mounting was on the rear of the upper wing centre-section so that the pilot could fire obliquely upwards, operating the thumb trigger with his free hand. The weapon was not particularly effective, but a number of captured examples were pressed into service by the Germans and Austro-Hungarians in late 1917.

Although most American aircraft (largely of British and French origins) used the Vickers machine-gun as primary fixed armament, the Americans also developed the 0.3 in (7.62 mm) Marlin gun for aerial use. Basically an adaptation of the Model 1914 Colt-Browning after the designs of A. W. Swebilius of the Marlin-Rockwell Corporation, the Marlin was unusual amongst World War I machine-guns in being gas-operated, and was the first weapon of such operation to be synchronized effectively, with both mechanical and hydraulic gears. Only aircraft built in the USA, mostly DH 4 bombers, were fitted with the Model 1918 Marlin gun, which weighed 22½ lb (10.2 kg) and had a rate of fire of 630 rounds per minute. A relatively useful weapon, the Marlin was hampered by poor ammunition feed characteristics, especially when the canvas belt was wet.

A number of other machine-gun installations were tried, but did not see widespread service use for a number of reasons. In France, large numbers of the Darne 0.295 in (7.5 mm) machine-gun were ordered for service in 1919, and most were cancelled at the end of the war. The Darne was potentially an excellent weapon, for its design was first class, but the workmanship of most examples was shoddy for some unexplained reason. Designed by Regis and Pierre Darne of St Etienne, the Darne gun was gas operated, and because of its very short bolt stroke had the extremely high rate of fire of 1,700 rounds per minute. The weapon was of clever design in general, and made extensive use of stampings in its construction, there being few machined parts and only one forging,

this helping to make the Darne possibly the cheapest machine-gun ever designed. Work on the weapon continued in the 1920s and 1930s, and it finally became an effective aircraft weapon. Another potentially useful weapon was the machine-gun designed by Lieutenant (later General) André Berthier: this was gas operated, fed from a 30-round magazine, and had a rate of fire of about 450 rounds per minute. Few wartime orders were forthcoming for this machine-gun, but the principle of the weapon later found effective expression in the Vickers GO gun of the 1930s.

Italy produced the useful 0.256 in (6.5 mm) S.I.A. machine-gun designed by Giovanni Agnelli and manufactured by the *Società Italiana Ansaldo*. The gun was slightly too late to see service in World War I, however.

Germany was especially prolific in the testing of special and new weapons on aircraft. In 1916, for example, the Bergmann MG10 was tried as an observer's weapon. The weapon, designed in 1910 by Theodor Bergmann, was in many respects superior to the MG08 adopted as the standard German Army weapon, and was a short-recoil operated weapon with excellent feed characteristics using an aluminium-link belt and a mechanism that could handle badly positioned rounds that would have jammed other weapons. Despite its impressive performance, however, the Bergmann was not widely adopted. Another experimental German machine-gun was the Gast twin-barrel gun, developed by Karl Gast of Barmen. Spring-fed drum magazines were positioned on each side of the weapon, one to each barrel. Operation was on the locked-breech recoil principle, with the recoil of one barrel reloading, firing, extracting and ejecting the rounds of the other barrel. Rate of fire was excellent at 1,600 rounds per minute. In service the weapon proved very useful, especially as it came with a telescopic sight and was highly accurate, but the end of the war came before many such weapons could be delivered.

The Germans also had high hopes for the 'motor gun', in which a number of barrels would be rotated around a common axis by the engine, in the fashion of the 19th-century Gatling gun, to secure a high rate of fire. Major Wilhelm Siegert, the Inspector of Aviation Troops, called for such a weapon in August 1916: prototypes were produced by Autogen, Fokker, Gebauer (in Austria-Hungary), Gotha, Siemens and Szakatz-Gotha, and the theory seemed to be sound. Fortunately for the Allies, none of the weapons reached fully operational status, though at least one Allied aircraft was apparently shot down with the Siemens gun. Rate of fire was, in one case, 7,200 rounds per minute.

As noted earlier, high hopes were entertained for cannon-armed aircraft, but in general the cannon (firing an explosive shell) proved ineffective during World War I. The main types tried were the British Armstrong-Whitworth 1 pounder (0.45 kg), the Coventry Ordnance Works 1 pounder (0.45 kg), the Vickers 1½ pounder (0.68 kg), the American Davis recoilless 1½ pounder (0.68 kg), the French 1.46 and 1.85 in (37 and 47 mm) Hotchkiss guns, and the 1.46 in (37 mm) Puteaux gun specially modified for *moteur-canon* installation in the Spad S.12 and S.14 for Guynemer and Fonck. The Germans had the 20 mm Hispano cannon used by the Allies in World War II.

Marc Birkigt, the Hispano-Suiza engineer who had modified the 37 mm Puteaux gun for aircraft use, also devised another engine-mounted weapon: a cannon whose round consisted of 32 ball bearings which spread out like pellets from a shotgun after firing. The weapon was too late to see service, but would probably have been most effective at close range.

Such then were the weapons and synchronizer gears of air-to-air fighting in World War I. Also worthy of short examination are the sights used to aim the aircraft guns of the period, and also the ammunition employed with the guns.

In general sights were primitive: at first they were nonexistent, pilots merely aiming their aircraft at their opponent, or using the iron sights usually fitted to the machine-gun when produced for ground service. Later, however, the ring-and-bead sight appeared: this featured a metal pillar surmounted by a bead, mounted as far forward along the fuselage nose as possible, and an iron ring, containing an elementary graticule, on a pillar in front of the pilot. To aim, the pilot lined up the centre of the ring sight, the bead and the target before firing, making allowance for deflection within the scope provided by the ring sight's graticule. Naturally enough, the system lacked sophistication, but was generally adequate for the short ranges and slow speeds of World War I. The best sight of the war was the British Aldis sight, which was a telescopic, gas-filled sight aligned with the gun. From autumn 1917 this gave pilots a great advantage in air-to-air engagements, but proved a distinct liability in ground-attack missions, many pilots failing to pull out in time when using the Aldis

sight. For use against airships and bombers operating at night, the British developed special illuminated sights to complement the paired Foster-mounted Lewis guns that proved superior to twin Vickers guns, the latters' muzzle flash blinding the pilot temporarily.

In general, ball ammunition proved adequate for air-to-air fighting against other aircraft. But for operations against balloons and airships, which were filled with highly inflammable hydrogen, incendiaries were essential, especially as a few dozen bullet holes would do little to bring down gas-filled aerostats. Perhaps the most celebrated incendiary bullet was the Buckingham, named after its British inventor, J. F. Buckingham of Coventry: the round combined incendiary properties with a noticeable smoke trace, and was adopted early in World War I by the RNAS. It resembled the standard 0.303 in (7.7 mm) bullet, but had a hollow nose containing 8 grains (0.52 grams) of phosphorous. As the bullet rotated in flight, the phosphorous was slowly ejected through a hole in the side by centrifugal force. Similar in concept, but improved in performance, were the Brock and Pomeroy rounds, adopted slightly later. Other rounds available were the armour-piercing, explosive and explosive-incendiary. Although the use of ball and tracer was officially encouraged in air-to-air fighting, the use of the other rounds was generally discouraged. Notwithstanding, by 1918 most ammunition belts for general use were made up of a mixture of ammunition types, such as a repetition of three ball, one tracer, one armour-piercing and one incendiary. During 1918, the French developed a special 0.433 in (11 mm) Vickers gun for use against balloons.

The original anti-balloon weapon had been the exciting, but not very effective Le Prieur rocket, designed by Lieutenant Y. P. G. Le Prieur of the French naval air service. The rocket entered service in 1916, and was usually mounted in a vertical row of four rockets on the two interplane struts of types such as Nieuport single-seaters. All eight rockets were fired in a single salvo when the pilot threw a switch in the cockpit. The development of effective incendiary ammunition rendered the type obsolete, and it disappeared during 1917.

Finally, in World War I, mention must be made of the Prideaux disintegrating-link belt, which came into British service during 1917 and was soon adopted by the other Allies as the most effective means of ridding themselves of the expended end of an ammunition belt. The Prideaux belt, designed by a dentist of that name with the help of a patient, Major Lanoe G. Hawker, VC, consisted of a series of interlocking metal links which fell away as each round was fired, usually being ejected safely into the slipstream down a chute. Hawker, it should be noted, had been a prolific inventor before his death at the hands of Manfred von Richthofen: he had developed gun sights, hangars, and assisted a designer named French in the development of the 97-round drum for the Lewis gun.

Air-to-Surface Armament
World War I

In the early stages of World War I both bombs and bomb-aiming were rudimentary, as this illustration of a Royal Naval Air Service bombardier in action reveals.

The utility of the air-launched torpedo was proved in the second half of World War I. The Sopwith Cuckoo was the first aircraft designed for such operation from aircraft-carriers.

Air-to-surface weapons fall into two main categories: those which are unguided and those which are guided. Within these two main categories there are a number of sub-categories: unguided weapons which fall freely under the influence of aerodynamics and of gravity (free-fall bombs), and unguided weapons which are powered (unguided missiles, often referred to simply as rockets); guided weapons without motive power (glide-bombs), and guided weapons with motive power (air-to-surface missiles).

The simplest, and oldest, of these weapons is the free-fall bomb. The first such weapon was probably the type used by *Oberleutnant* Franz Uchatius of the Austrian army: Uchatius designed and received permission to use in the siege of Venice in March 1849 a number of paper balloons carrying $29\frac{3}{4}$-lb (13.5-kg) bombs, released over the city (it was hoped) by time fuse. No casualties were caused.

The Italians used primitive bombs, basically artillery shells converted for the purpose by the addition of sheet metal fins, in their conquest of Libya from the Turks in 1911–1912. Little damage was caused by the weapons, though the effect on the totally unprepared Turks was at times useful. Inevitably, their first use was accompanied by Turkish claims that the bombs had hit a hospital.

The first bombs of World War I were usually small weapons specially made for the purpose, or heavy artillery shells converted by the addition of fins. The main French weapon was the 6.1-in (155-mm) shell, and the Germans even managed to drop some of their monstrous 16.54-in (420-mm) shells from airships. Gradually, though, properly designed bombs were developed by all the major powers, in ever increasing weight as the bomb-carrying capacity of aircraft increased.

Typical of World War I bombs were the German Carbonit and P.u.W. ranges. The Carbonit type of bomb was made by Sprengstoff AG 'Carbonit' at Schlebusch. Characteristic of the type was a plumb-bob shaped body, with a steel nose for extra penetrative qualities. The body was made of cast iron, and a cylindrical fin assembly was mounted behind the body. The normal filling of the bombs was TNT, and four sizes were produced: 9.92-lb (4.5-kg), 22.05-lb (10-kg), 44.09-lb (20-kg), and 110.2-lb (50-kg).

There was also a Carbonit incendiary bomb. This was of the same basic design, but had a cylindrical body of sheet steel rather than the teardrop body of cast iron. The filling of the bomb, which weighed 22.05-lb (10-kg) in all, was one part benzol, five parts kerosene and a little liquid tar, to a weight of 7.7 lb (3.5 kg) for the incendiary mixture. Also used for incendiary purposes was the Goldschmidt bomb: this had an inner cylinder filled with thermite, and an outer cylinder filled with benzol, and the whole was wrapped in tarred rope. The Goldschmidt bomb burned at the extremely high temperature of 3,000°C, and weighed about 22.05 lb (10 kg). Both the Carbonit and the Goldschmidt types of bomb were used between 1914 and 1916, having replaced the A.P.K. type developed by the *Artillerie-Prüfungs-Kommission* (Artillery Test Commission) in 1912 and 1913, and being replaced in turn by the P.u.W. type developed by the *Prüfanstalt und Werft der Flieger-truppe* (Air Force Test Establishment and Workshop), in conjunction with Görz-Friedenau, makers of optical instruments, including bomb sights.

The A. P. K., Carbonit and Goldschmidt bombs had all been useful in their time, but were of limited use as aircraft performance rose and the bombers had to operate at higher altitude. All the earlier models of bomb were woefully deficient in their aerodynamic qualities, and were thus increasingly inaccurate as bombing height increased. P.u.W. and Görz-Friedenau thus developed the true ancestor of the modern type of bomb, with clean lines and

German World War I bombs

Typical of the bombs of World War I are the German *Prüfanstalt und Werft der Fliegertruppe* (PuW) weapons illustrated here. There was also a 12.5-kg (27.6-lb) PuW bomb.

The dropping of bombs exclusively by eye was never particularly accurate, even from low-flying aircraft.

fins designed to rotate the weapon in flight for greater stability and accuracy. And instead of cast iron, the new streamlined bombs were made of good quality steel so that the bombs had greater penetrative capabilities, a factor increased by the thickening of the metal in the bombs' nose sections. The P.u.W. bombs were made in five different sizes, for a total of six bombs. The smallest type was the 27.56-lb (12.5-kg) weapon, which was made in HE and incendiary versions. The HE version was 3.54 in (90 mm) in diameter and 29.53 in (750 mm) in length, and the explosive comprised 12% of the total weight; the incendiary version was 5.51 in (140 mm) in diameter, 33.47 in (850 mm) in length, and filled with about the same percentage weight of inflammable materials. Next up in size was the 110.25-lb (50-kg) bomb, 7.09 in (180 mm) in diameter, 66.93 in (1,700 mm) in length, and with explosive comprising 46% of the total weight. The 220.5-lb (100-kg) bomb was 9.84 in (250 mm) in diameter, 74.8 in (1,900 mm) in length, with explosive comprising 60% of the weight. There was then a considerable increase in size, the next bomb weighing 661.5-lb (300-kg), with a diameter of 14.37 in (365 mm), a length of 108.27 in (2,750 mm) and explosive taking up 60% of the weight. Largest of the family was the 2,205-lb (1,000-kg) weapon, with a diameter of 21.65 in (550 mm), a length of 157.68 in (4,005 mm), and an explosive content of 68% of the total weight.

The last major bomb to be perfected by Germany in World War I was the 'Elektron' incendiary, designed for the attacks on London but completed just too late to see active service. The bomb was highly efficient, but weighed only 2.2 lb (1 kg), so

that Germany's giant bombers could have carried a very considerable number of these deadly little devices.

Allied bomb design was not as advanced as that of the Germans in World War I, the British, French and Italian bombs being less well streamlined, and fitted with fins producing considerably more drag but not guiding the bomb as accurately. To Britain, though, goes the distinction of having produced the largest free-fall bomb of World War I, the monstrous 3,300-lb (1,497-kg) weapon intended for carriage by the Handley Page V/1500 four-engined bomber over short ranges. Generally, however, the Allies were content with bombs in the order of 250-lb (113.4-kg), designed for maximum blast rather than penetration. Also notable were the 20- and 25-lb (9.07- and 11.34-kg) Cooper bombs intended for anti-personnel attacks by fighters fitted with about four of the weapons on external racks.

Bomb aiming was a primitive affair at the beginning of World War I, the bomb aimer/dropper generally leaning out of his cockpit to aim without the benefit of any optical instrument, and then drop his bomb manually at what seemed the best moment. Needless to say, accuracy was minimal unless the pilot brought the aircraft down over the target, and this frequently yielded good results where absence of AA gunfire made it possible. By 1915, however, the first rudimentary sights began to appear: these generally worked on the principle of telling the bomb-aimer his speed over the ground, and giving him a reasonable estimate of drift across the ground as a result of side winds. The most common of the sights were the British CFS sight, designed at the Central Flying School by 2nd Lieutenant R. B. Bourdillon and 2nd Lieutenant G. M. B. Dobson; the French Dorand and Lafay sights; the German Görz-Friedenau; and the best of all, the American Sperry gyroscopically stabilized sight. Although the Sperry sight was the best of the lot, and pointed the way forward, it was some time before it would be ready for operational use. The CFS sight, typical of its kind, worked thus: a timing scale on the sight allowed the aimer to sight on an object at two times measured exactly by stop-watch, and so calculate his speed over the ground, and also to get a good estimate of drift; the aimer then set the movable foresight to the time interval recorded in the speed calculation, and released the bombs when the sight was centred on the target.

During the 1920s and 1930s considerable effort was devoted to the development of better bombs, with a more effective aerodynamic shape, improved safety before the bombs were dropped, reliable fusing after the weapon had been dropped, and the right impact angle and detonation effect on the ground. The type generally evolved was a cast-iron casing filled with the relevant explosive, fitted with four fins, fused aerodynamically by nose and tail fuses, and designed largely for blast effect and a slight degree of penetration, called the general-purpose bomb.

Air-to-Air Armament
Between the wars and World War II

Typical of the manually-
operated flexible defensive gun
armament of interwar bombers
are these twin Vickers 'K' guns.

In the period of financial retrenchment soon after World War I ended on 11 November 1918, it was inevitable that the vast armed forces of the Allied nations should be trimmed right back, and that little or no new allocations would be made towards the development of the weapons being prepared for service in 1919 and 1920. This applied most strongly to the air forces of the war, which found themselves reduced to absolute minima by the early 1920s and forced to operate with aircraft left over from the war, or with very small numbers of aircraft that had appeared in the closing stages of hostilities.

Only towards the middle of the 1920s did governments give favourable attention to the need for re-equipment programmes for their air forces, to ensure that the quality of fighting aircraft kept up with the technological advances of the day. The air forces themselves, eager to get whatever they could at a time when armies and navies were trying to exert as much authority as they could over the autonomous and semi-autonomous air forces, were forced into a double policy: acquiring for service use limited numbers of aircraft which used the latest developments brought up to production level; and funding very small numbers of experimental aircraft to push forward the boundaries of aerodynamics so that the results could then be incorporated in the next generation of service aircraft.

For a variety of reasons, therefore, progress in military aircraft between 1920 and the early 1930s was seen basically in terms of aerodynamics and structures, and little attention was devoted to developing the armament of aircraft. Improvements in air-to-air armament were made, but these were concerned basically with increasing the reliability of World War I service weapons, and bringing towards acceptance a number of weapons under development at the end of World War I. What remained basically unaltered was the widespread belief that the armament standards of World War I were still basically sufficient: for single-seat fighters two rifle-calibre machine-guns; for two-seaters (now generally becoming general-purpose aircraft capable of fulfilling the light bomber, reconnaissance, liaison, and army co-operation roles) a single rifle-calibre machine-gun for the pilot, plus one or two flexible weapons of the same calibre for the gunner/observer; and for bombers a variable number of rifle-calibre machine-guns located in open mountings to protect the aircraft's most vulnerable points. Despite the fact that prolonged service use had removed most of the mechanical problems with belt-fed machine-guns, and that growing experience with nitro-cellulose propellants had led to far greater ammunition reliability, it was still the practice in most countries to locate the breeches of the machine-guns where they could be reached by the pilot. This inevitably meant that the design of the forward fuselage was circumscribed quite severely by the need to accommodate the guns, ammunition tanks, feed mechanisms and synchronizer gear as well as the pilot, engine and fuel/lubricant tanks.

In the second half of the 1920s, though, metal structures for the basic airframe of military aircraft were standard, and many continental European designers began to give serious thought to the adoption of cannon (firing explosive rounds) as a more certain way of ensuring the destruction of the target aircraft. Among the principal designers of cannon during the decade were Hotchkiss in France, Madsen in Denmark, and Oerlikon and Solothurn in Switzerland. For a variety of reasons, the calibre used for cannon at the time was 0.79 in (20 mm): it was the smallest practical calibre for an explosive shell with adequate destructive properties; the firing of a shell of this type at a high muzzle velocity produced recoil forces that could be handled acceptably by current airframes; reasonably high rates of fire were possible; and the cannon itself could be made quite compact, to fit relatively easily into the more stream-lined aerodynamic shapes becoming imperative for high performance.

The most successful of the early cannon was the Oerlikon, which was recommended for mounting in the V of geared inline engines so that the mass of the engine could be used to absorb the recoil forces, and the hub of the propeller, offset from the line of the engine's crankshaft by the reduction gearing, could be used as the muzzle port, so obviating the need for a synchronizer gear. However, the design of such an installation, undertaken by the French Hispano-Suiza engine company using the celebrated HS 12X engine, was not a success when it emerged in 1933. So early cannon-armed fighters, such as the French Dewoitine D.37, featured a pair of 20 mm weapons mounted in the wings outboard of the propeller disc. Seeing the difficulties they had encountered with the design of an engine mounting for the Oerlikon cannon, the Hispano-Suiza designers determined to try their hands at the design of a new 20 mm cannon specifically tailored to the concept of an engine mounting in the HS 12 series of engines. Design of the weapon, based on the German Becker of World War I, began in 1933, and eventually led to the celebrated 20 mm Hispano cannon used to such good effect by the British in World War II. One of the first service aircraft to use the new weapon was the Dewoitine D.510 low-wing monoplane fighter of 1934. So impressive was the performance of the new Hispano gun that the governments of Belgium, Japan, Sweden, the UK, the USA and the USSR all purchased examples of the weapon for evaluation with a view to possible use and even manufacture. Thus the Hispano 20 mm Type 404 *moteur-canon* can justly be regarded with the 20 mm Oerlikon weapon as the first effective aircraft cannon.

The military world was at this time fairly evenly divided into two camps so far as aircraft armament was concerned. Both camps believed firmly that the most important target for the fighters of the middle and late 1930s would be the bomber, the great 'scare' weapon of the time, but were divided on the best means of shooting down large numbers of the latest examples, which could confidently be expected to

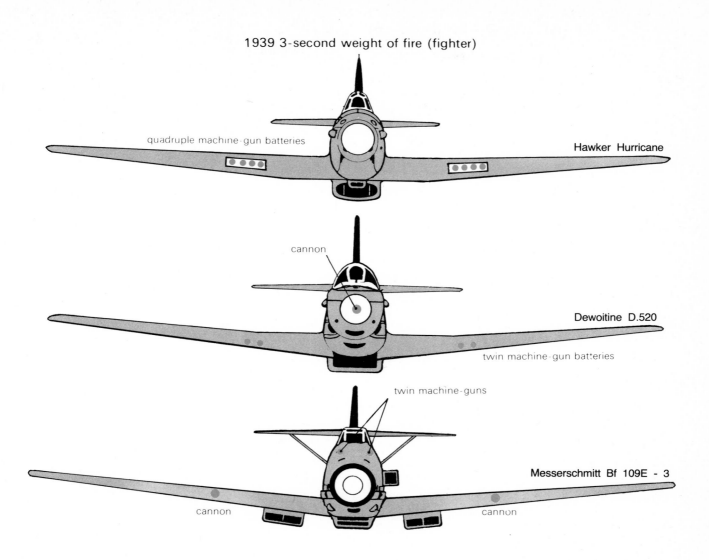

1939 3-second weight of fire (fighter)

quadruple machine-gun batteries

Hawker Hurricane

cannon

Dewoitine D.520

twin machine-gun batteries

twin machine-guns

Messerschmitt Bf 109E - 3

cannon   cannon

1939 3-second weight of fire: on average, pilots could keep opponents in their sights for about three seconds at a time, and in this period the eight 0.303-in (7.7-mm) Browning machine-guns of the Hawker Hurricane could deliver a weight of fire of 10.94 lb (4.96 kg), the equivalent weight for the Dewoitine D.520's one 20-mm Hispano-Suiza 404 cannon and four 7.5-mm (0.295-in) MAC machine-guns being 12.57 lb (5.7 kg) and for the Messerschmitt Bf 109E-3's two 20-mm MG FF cannon and two 7.92-mm (0.312-in) MG17 machine-guns 19.29 lb (8.75 kg).

advance rapidly in capabilities already shown to be formidable by the first bombers to make extensive use of the technological advances of the 1920s: machines such as the American Boeing B-9 and Martin B-10, already in service, and designs such as the Russian Tupolev SB-2, the German Dornier Do 17 and Heinkel He 111, and the Italian Savoia-Marchetti SM.79 twin-engined metal cantilever medium bombers destined for service in the mid-1930s. So though air armament experts were convinced that a radical reform of aircraft armament was both inevitable and necessary in view of the threat posed by the bomber, they were sharply divided as to the best means of countering the threat. One camp (the Americans, British, Italians and Japanese among the major world powers) finally came to the conclusion that although cannon offered a good chance of causing serious damage with a few hits, the chance of scoring the necessary hits with the one or two cannon that could be carried aloft by fighters in the immediate

future was too small, and that multiple batteries of machine-guns would give the fighters a significantly improved chance of downing the bomber by scoring a very large number of individually less effective strikes, whose cumulative effect would surpass that of a few cannon shell strikes. The other camp (France, Germany, gradually Japan as she began to shift from the other group, and the USSR) maintained that cannon batteries, supplemented by machine-guns, offered the optimum chance of inflicting mortal damage. By 1937 Britain too began to shift into the camp of the cannon-advocates, but by this time her latest generation of fighters was in service, fitted with multiple machine-guns. The Japanese and Italians also began to drift towards the cannon camp, leaving only the Americans firmly committed to machine-gun primary armament. The machine-gun camp had also been divided internally, the British deciding that a battery of eight rifle-calibre machine-guns, mounted in the wings of aircraft such as the Hawker

In the late 1960s, the world's major aerospace powers began to appreciate the limitations of their current air-to-air missiles, which stood little chance of scoring a hit on close-range manoeuvring targets. Seen here under the wing of a Hawker Hunter fighter is an AATV (Air-to Air Test Vehicle) for the proposed British SRAAM (Short-Range Air-to-Air Missile) dogfighting weapon.

Hurricane and Supermarine Spitfire, was the best way to employ machine-guns. The Americans opted initially for a mixture of rifle- and heavy-calibre machine-guns, then for a battery of six or eight wing-mounted heavy machine-guns; Italy and Japan believed in a mixed battery.

By 1939, therefore, the major powers had generally adopted as their main fighters single-engined, single-seat, low-winged monoplane aircraft fitted with retractable undercarriages (many of them also having refinements such as variable-pitch or constant-speed propellers, flaps, enclosed cockpits, self-sealing fuel tanks, armoured windscreens and a measure of armour protection for the pilot), with a wide mixture of armament installations. On what was to be the Allied side the following are representative: the American Curtiss P-36C with one 0.5 in (12.7 mm) and three 0.3 in (7.62 mm) machine-guns; the British Supermarine Spitfire with eight 0.303 in (7.7 mm) machine-guns; the French Morane-Saulnier M.S. 406 with one 20 mm cannon and two 0.295 in (7.5 mm) machine-guns; the Polish PZL P-11c with four 0.303 in (7.7 mm) machine-guns; and the Russian Polikarpov I-16 with two 20 mm and two 0.3 in (7.62 mm) machine-guns. On what was to be the Axis side, Germany deployed the Messerschmitt Bf 109E, armed with two 20 mm cannon and two 0.312 in (7.92 mm) machine-guns, and the Messerschmitt Bf 110C twin engined fighter, armed with two 20 mm cannon and four 0.312 in (7.92 mm) machine-guns; Italy used the Macchi C.200, armed with two 0.15 in (12.7 mm) machine-guns; and Japan's army air arm the Nakajima Ki-27, armed with two 0.303 in (7.7 mm) machine-guns, while the navy's air arm used the Mitsubishi A6M1, armed with two 20 mm cannon and two 0.303 in (7.7 mm) machine-guns.

In 1939, therefore, the world's fighters were armed with a catholic selection of weapons — medium machine-guns, heavy machine-guns and 20 mm cannon. And though the trend later in the war was towards cannon, it is worth remembering that for all their destructive potential, the cannon used in the early stages of the war, with the exception of the French and Russian weapons, were recoil-operated weapons of relatively low muzzle velocity and rate of fire, firing thin-walled shells of limited explosive capabilities. There was much to be said, accordingly, for the British design philosophy, which placed great emphasis on hitting the target as many times as possible in the average two seconds it would be in the pilot's sights. The pilot of a Bf 109E, for example, could get off only 34.66 20 mm and 73.33 7.92 mm rounds in two seconds, whereas the pilot of the Spitfire I or Hurricane I could fire 320 0.303 in rounds in the same time, giving him a far greater chance of hitting his target, though not perhaps so damagingly as a 20 mm strike. Nevertheless, as armour plating, bullet-proof windscreens and self-sealing fuel tanks were only just becoming standard, multiple medium machine-gun strikes often proved more effective than a single 20 mm strike.

As the war progressed, better cannon with higher muzzle velocities (and hence flatter, more accurate trajectories at medium and long ranges) and more effective ammunition became the norm, together with heavy machine-guns to counter the better protection of later aircraft, whose protection was usually equal to the potential harm that could be caused even by multiple medium machine-gun fire.

The most common weapons in service at the beginning of World War II were the medium machine-guns, firing standard rifle-calibre ammunition. The standard British weapon of the type was the 0.303 in (7.7 mm) Browning machine-gun. A recoil-operated weapon, the Browning was evolved from an experimental 0.3 in (7.62 mm) weapon designed towards the end of World War I and manufactured by Colt-Browning. Although the Air Ministry tried the weapon in 1918, no orders were forthcoming. Then, after the war, Armstrong Whitworth bought the manufacturing rights from Colt-Browning, though the buyers knew that the Air Ministry was more interested in the purchase of a new 0.5 in (12.7 mm) machine-gun than in the replacement of the well-proved Vickers with a weapon of similar calibre. In 1926, though, the Air Ministry ordered six examples of the Colt-Browning, made by Armstrong Whitworth in 0.303 in (7.7 mm) calibre. The guns were not delivered for trials until 1929, by which time Armstrong Whitworth had amalgamated with Vickers to become Vickers-Armstrong, and the Air Ministry had decided that the combination of several factors precluded the replacement of the 0.303 in (7.7 mm) Vickers gun with a 0.5 in (12.7 mm) weapon. The Vickers-Armstrong versions of the Colt-Browning were once more in the running, therefore, though trials did not take place until 1931.

Tested in an Armstrong Whitworth Siskin fighter, two guns were enough to convince the Air Ministry: one fired 14,400 rounds with only three stoppages (only one of them the fault of the gun), and the other 5,200 rounds with no stoppages. In 1930, however, Colt-Browning had redesigned the gun in two forms, as a pilot's gun with a short barrel, and as a gunner's weapon with a long barrel and a muzzle attachment intended to increase the rate of fire to 300 rpm more than the pilot's model. Vickers-Armstrong again manufactured 0.303 in (7.7 mm) versions, which were tested in 1932. Although the long-barrel version of the Model 1930 Browning failed to find favour as an observer's weapon because of its belt feed, it was otherwise preferred for its high rate of fire and great accuracy. Accordingly, in 1934 the long-barrel Browning was tested with a view to replacing the Vickers Mark III, its main competitors being the Vickers Central Action Gun and the Darne, other weapons such as the Gebauer, Hotchkiss, Lahti and Madsen having been eliminated earlier. Decision was reached in June 1934 that the Browning was superior to the Mark III Vickers on a number of counts: rate of fire was higher (1,100 rpm to 800 rpm), reliability was considerably greater, weight was 5 lb (2.27 kg) less, the gun was less prone to

This Supermarine Spitfire I had high firepower but careful streamlining, and so the four Browning machine-guns in each wing of the Spitfire are hardly evident.

breakages, and the pitch of the ammunition belt was less. As Vickers-Armstrong had dropped their manufacturing licence for the weapon, the Air Ministry bought the rights, controlled the final development of the Browning for British service, and then contracted manufacture of the weapon to Vickers and Birmingham Small Arms, the only two manufacturers capable of making the weapon at the time. The only major modification to the basic American gun was to the action of the gun: in the basic weapon the breech chambered a round and halted in the forward position, with the firing-pin cocked, at the end of a burst. But alone of the major powers, the British still used as small arms propellant a nitro-glycerine based substance (cordite) rather than nitro-cellulose. The trouble lay in the fact that the heat of a prolonged burst so warmed the chamber that the round left in the breech 'cooked off' and destroyed the gun; rather than burning, the propellant exploded. Redesign cured the problem by making the action such that at the end of a burst the breechlock was retained at the rear of its movement. Despite this failing, and also its tendency to wear out barrels quickly by its high heat and high fouling characteristics, cordite had two main recommendations for the army, the main users of small-arms ammunition: its long 'shelf life', and its great stability in hot and humid conditions as found in many parts of the British empire. Thus it was only after World War II that Britain finally discarded the use of cordite in favour of nitro-cellulose propellants. By 1939, however, the 0.303 in (7.7 mm) Browning machine-gun was the

standard British fixed aircraft gun, proving itself hard-hitting, reliable and effective when firing a mixture of ball, tracer and De Wilde incendiary ammunition. The gun was $44\frac{1}{2}$ in (113.03 cm) long, weighed 24 lb (10.87 kg), had a rate of fire between 1,100 and 1,200 rounds per minute, and fired a 0.344 ounce (9.74 gram) projectile with a muzzle velocity of 2,660 ft (811 m) per second.

The 0.3 in (7.62 mm) Browning used by the American air services was in all respects similar to the British version, the latter having been derived from the American weapon. The major differences were the end-of-burst closed breech position of the American Browning M2 gun, made possible by the use of nitro-cellulose propellant, the original 0.3 in (7.62 mm) calibre, and internal arrangements to use rimless 0.3 in (7.62 mm) ammunition, whereas the British Brownings used 0.303 in (7.7 mm) rimmed ammunition. The American 0.30-06 ammunition had a complete round length of 3.33 in (84.58 mm) compared with the British round's 2.21 in (56.13 mm), and the bullet weighed 0.43 oz (9.72 gms).

Other similar rifle-calibre machine-guns in service at the beginning of World War II were the 0.295 in (7.5 mm) FN-Browning, used by Belgium and France, the French *Manufacture d' Armes de Chatellerault* (MAC) 1934-M39 0.295 in (7.5 mm), the Italian Breda-SAFAT Model 1935 0.303 in (7.7 mm), the Japanese Type 89 Model 2 0.303 in (7.7 mm), derived from the British Vickers, and the Type 97 0.303 in (7.7 mm), the Polish KM Wzor 33 0.303 in (7.7 mm), the German Rheinmetall-

Borsig MG17 0.312 in (7.92 mm) and the Russian ShKAS 0.3 in (7.62 mm).

Of these, the best were the German MG17 and the Russian ShKAS. The MG17 was designed in 1934, was 42.44 in (1,078 mm) long, weighed 22.49 lb (10.2 kg), and fired a 0.453 ounce (12.8 gram) bullet at a muzzle velocity of 2,970 ft (905 m) per second at the rate of 1,180 rounds per minute. Most impressive of all, though, was the ShKAS (Shpitalny *Komaritsky Aviatsionny Skorostrelny* or Shpitalny rapid-fire aircraft gun). It weighed only 22.05 lb (10 kg), and fired a 0.34 ounce (9.575 gram) bullet with muzzle velocity of over 2,707 ft (825 m) per second at the prodigious rates of 1,800 rounds per minute (unsynchronized) and 1,600 rounds per minute (synchronized). The effective range of all these rifle-calibre weapons was about 656 yards (600 m).

Heavy machine-guns, with a calibre of about 0.5 in (12.7 mm) gradually came to replace rifle-calibre machines almost entirely during the war, but there were only three such weapons in service in 1939: the American Browning M2, the Italian Breda-SAFAT and the Russian UBS (*Universalny Berezina Skorostrelny* or Beresin all-purpose rapid-fire gun). The Italian gun was in no way distinguished, and was in essence a scaled-down version of the 0.303 in (7.7 mm) Breda-SAFAT also used by the Italian air arm. The American and Russian heavy machine-guns were highly effective weapons, classics of their kind. Weighing only slightly more than 47 lb (21.3 kg), the UBS fired a 1.8 ounce (50.97 gram) bullet with a muzzle velocity of more than 2,805 ft

(855 m) per second at the rate of 900 rounds per minute. The American Browning M2 was an almost comparable weapon, derived from the ground-service heavy machine-gun of the same calibre. This weapon received definitive modification towards the end of World War II to produce the superb AN-M3 heavy machine-gun. A recoil-operated weapon capable only of automatic fire, the AN-M3 weighed $68\frac{3}{4}$ lb (31.18 kg) with its recoil adaptor, and was $57\frac{1}{4}$ in (1,454.15 mm) long overall, the barrel being 36 in (914.4 mm) in length. The ammunition used was of the M2 series, the ball round being 5.45 in (138.43 mm) long overall and weighing 4.11 ounces (116.43 grams). The bullet weight was 1.62 ounces (45.86 grams), which the 0.55 ounces (15.52 grams) of propellant fired with a muzzle velocity of 2,840 ft (865.6 m) per second at the cyclic rate of fire of 1,150–1,250 rounds per minute. The original M2 aircraft gun was basically similar to its successor, but had a lower rate of fire.

Such, then, were the machine-guns in general service at the beginning of World War II. As the machine-gun was quickly supplemented and then largely supplanted by the shell-firing cannon, only a few new types of machine-gun entered service during the war, most of them in German or Japanese service. The best of these weapons was the German MG131, developed by Rheinmetall-Borsig in 1938 as an aircraft heavy machine-gun, with a calibre of 0.512 in (13 mm). The weapon was 45.98 in (1,168 in) long and weighed 45.19 lb (20.5 kg). A complex weapon, the MG131 featured mechanical or electric/pneu-

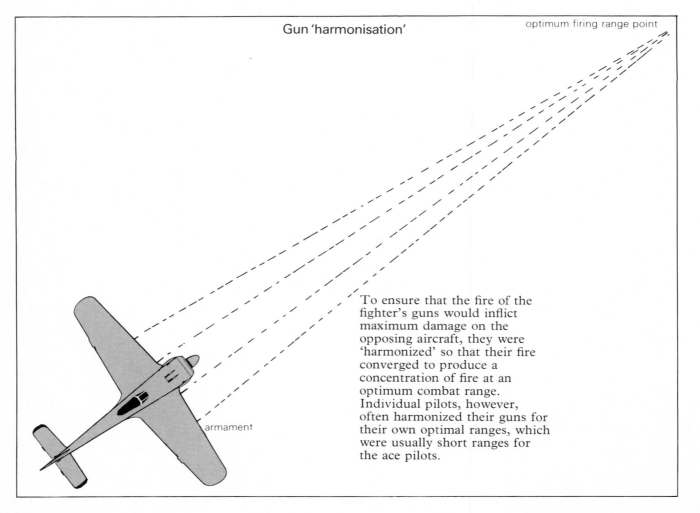

Gun 'harmonisation'

optimum firing range point

armament

To ensure that the fire of the fighter's guns would inflict maximum damage on the opposing aircraft, they were 'harmonized' so that their fire converged to produce a concentration of fire at an optimum combat range. Individual pilots, however, often harmonized their guns for their own optimal ranges, which were usually short ranges for the ace pilots.

matic loading and firing, with electric ignition of the round. The complete round weighed 2.54 ounces (72 grams), the bullet itself weighing 1.2 ounces (34 grams). Muzzle velocity was 2,461 ft (750 m) per second, and rate of fire 930 rounds per minute, the latter being slightly higher than the rate attainable with the M2 Browning. The Japanese introduced their Type 1 (Ho-103) heavy machine-gun during the war. This was modelled closely on the M2 Browning, with a number of improvements. Weight was 48 lb (21.77 kg), length overall 49 in (1,244.6 mm), muzzle velocity 2,560 ft (780 m) per second, and rate of fire 900 rounds per minute. The 0.5 in (12.7 mm) Type 1 was used on aircraft of the Imperial Army air force, while the equivalent weapon for the Imperial Navy's fighters was the the 0.52 in (13.2 mm) Type 3 heavy machine-gun. This weighed 66 lb (29.94 kg) and was 61 in (1,549.4 mm) long overall. The complete round for this weapon weighed 4.2 ounces (118.76 grams), the bullet itself weighing 1.84 ounces (52.07 grams); the 0.53 ounce (15 grams) of propellant fired the bullet with a muzzle velocity of 2,592 ft (790 m) per second. Rate of fire was 800 rounds per minute. The effective range of all these heavy-calibre machine-guns was between 820 and 984 yards (750 and 900 m) depending on bullet shape and weight, and the muzzle velocity of the weapon.

As the war progressed, it became standard to equip fighters with cannon of 20 mm calibre or more, the Germans being the leaders in the development of new weapons, and the Russians generally fitting their aircraft with cannon of a calibre slightly larger than other nations. Towards the end of the war, moreover, the Germans and Japanese made great efforts to develop special heavy cannon that would give their fighters a better chance than hitherto of downing Allied bombers with short bursts from long range.

The cannon in service in 1939 were the Hispano-Suiza HS 404 *moteur-canon* already discussed, the Swiss-designed Oerlikon and its derivatives, the Russian ShVAK (Shpitalny-Vladimirov *Aviatsonnaya Krupno Kalibernaya* or Shpitalny-Vladimirov large-calibre aircraft gun), and two Japanese weapons, the Type 97 (1937) (otherwise known as the Ho-1 and Ho-3) used by the army, and the Type 99 (1939) used by the navy. By far the best of these weapons was the ShVAK: it weighed 92 lb (41.75 kg), and fired its 3.5 ounce (100 gram) 20 mm round at a muzzle velocity of 2,821 ft (860 m) per second and at the rate of 800 rounds per minute. The HS 404, on the other hand, weighed 109 lb (49.45 kg), and fired its 4.42 ounce (125 gram) round at a muzzle velocity of 2,821 ft (860 m) per second and at the rate of 700 rounds per minute. Both these weapons were gas-operated, and although the French weapon was very heavy it fired a better round than the Russian weapon at a slightly lower rate of fire. The German MG FF was a licence built Oerlikon-Bekker weapon. It was 52.68 in (1,338 mm) long and weighed only 57.98 lb (26.3 kg), and fired a 4.73 ounce (134 gram) shell from its 7.14

ounce (202 gram) round. However, as the MG FF was recoil-operated its muzzle velocity and rate of fire were low, at 2,297 ft (700 m) per second and 540 rounds per minute respectively. (In service use these figures were often lower, typically 1,952 ft/595 m per second and 350 rounds per minute.) In general, therefore, the MG FF and its motor-mounted model, the MG FF/M, were inferior to both the HS 404 and and ShVAK despite firing heavier rounds. The main trouble with the latter was that it was a thin-walled projectile with low penetrating capabilities. The ShVAK was belt-fed, and therefore had better ammunition supply than the HS 404, which was fed from a 60-round drum, and the MG FF, which was fed from a 30- or 60-round magazine or drum.

The Japanese army's Type 97 20 mm cannon was evolved from a 20 mm anti-tank cannon of the same designation, and was a recoil-operated weapon. There were two versions, the Ho-1 and Ho-3, the former for flexible use with a 15-round magazine and the latter for fixed use with a 50-round magazine. The Ho-3 weighed 95 lb (43 kg), and was 69½ in (1,765 mm) long. Muzzle velocity was 2,690 ft (820 m) per second, rate of fire 400 rounds per minute and effective range (as with other cannon of the same calibre, except the MG FF) about 985 yards (900 m). The Imperial Navy's Type 99 was also a 20 mm weapon, and was used in ever-improving models throughout the war. The early Type 99 Model 1 weighed 51 lb (23.13 kg) and was 52½ in (1,333.5 mm) long, and had a rate of fire of about 450 rounds per minute and a muzzle velocity of 1,970 ft (600 m) per second. The late Type 99 Model 2 Marks 4 and 5 weighed 82.6 lb (37.47 kg) and were 74.4 in (1,890 mm) long, with muzzle velocities of 2,493 ft (760 m) and rates of fire of 750 rounds per minute. Range increased from 875 yards (800 m) to 1,094 yards (1,000 m). The Type 99, it should be noted, was basically a development of the Oerlikon-Bekker cannon.

Realizing that the cannon offered the only real hope of inflicting mortal damage on large and/or protected aircraft, which were appearing in the last years of the 1930s, the RAF decided in 1937 that cannon armament was essential. The weapon selected for adoption, after considerable improvement, was the HS 404, which had high penetrating power (double that of the Oerlikon/MG FF and half as much again as the ShVAK) thanks to its large shell and high muzzle velocity. The weapon was introduced as the Hispano Mark I in 1940, in the closing stages of the Battle of Britain, and did not at first prove successful. The main trouble lay in the fact that the British had decided that two wing-mounted guns were essential, and the wings of aircraft such as the Spitfire were not rigid enough for cannon designed for fully-rigid mounting on an engine. Thus feed and other problems plagued the Mark I and Mark II Hispano cannon, the former built from French drawings and the latter from British drawings, but otherwise similar. By 1942 most of the problems had been overcome, and the gun redesigned

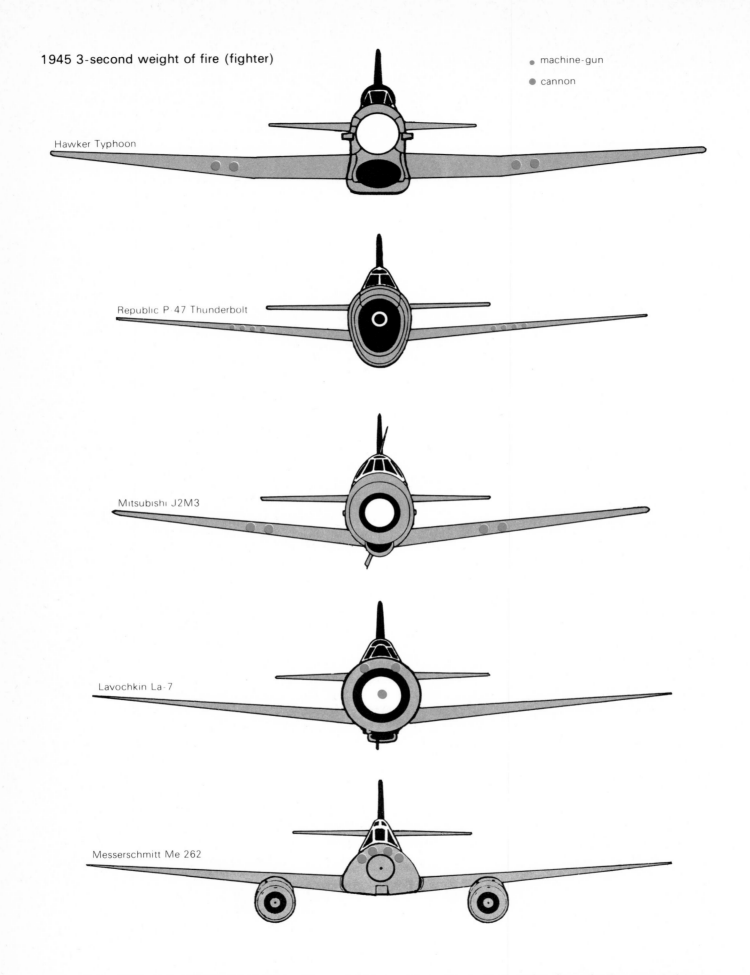

1945 3-second weight of fire (fighter)

● machine-gun

● cannon

Hawker Typhoon

Republic P-47 Thunderbolt

Mitsubishi J2M3

Lavochkin La-7

Messerschmitt Me 262

1945 3-second weight of fire: on average, pilots could keep opponents in their sights for only three seconds at a time, and in this period the four 20-mm Hispano cannon of the Hawker Typhoon could deliver a weight of fire of 39.7 lb (18 kg). The equivalent weight for the Republic P-47D Thunderbolt's eight 0.5-in (12.7-mm) Colt-Browning machine-guns was 30.93 lb (14.03 kg), for the Mitsubishi J2M3's two 20-mm Type 99-I and two 20-mm Type 99-II cannon 39.7 lb (18 kg), for the Lavochkin La-7's three 20-mm ShVAK cannon 41.66 lb (18.9 kg), and for the Messerschmitt Me 262's four 30-mm MK 108 cannon 96 lb (43.56 kg).

to use a belt rather than drum feed. This latter meant that far more ammunition could be carried, and that large bulges in the wings of Hispano-armed aircraft were unnecessary. The Hispano Mark I/II in its developed form weighed 109 lb (49.45 kg) and had a rate of fire of 650 rounds per minute. The Hispano remained the standard British fixed gun (often supplemented by 0.5 in/12.7 mm Brownings) for the rest of the war, the last version being the Hispano Mark 5, with a longer barrel, greater ease of manufacture and a cost considerably lower than that of the Mark II. The Mark 5 weighed 84 lb (38.1 kg) and had a rate of fire of 750 rounds per minute, though the prototype had weighed only 79 lb (35.83 kg) and had a rate of fire of 820 rounds per minute. Muzzle velocity was 2,790 ft (850 m) per second with a projectile weighing 4.88 ounces (138 grams).

By the end of the war, most British fighters (such as the de Havilland Mosquito N.F.30, the Gloster Meteor III, the Hawker Typhoon IB, the Hawker Tempest V and the Supermarine Spitfire 21) were armed with four 20 mm cannon, usually with 150 rounds per gun.

The USA dabbled with cannon armament, such as the 25 mm hub-mounted weapon of early Bell P-39 Airacobra prototypes and the 37 mm Oldsmobile T9 or M4, with 30 rounds used in early production models, but finally decided that although heavy cannon offered good chances of inflicting heavy damage if a strike were scored, such strikes would be too infrequent, and so fitted their fighter aircraft with a standard armament of 0.5 in (12.7 mm) Colt-Browning M2, MG53-2 or AN-M3 heavy machine-guns. The Lockheed P-38 had four such guns, the North American P-51 four or six 0.5 in (12.7 mm) guns, and the Republic P-47 six or eight heavy machine-guns. Ammunition stowage was a minimum of 267 and a maximum of 500 rounds per gun. US Navy fighters such as the Grumman F6F and the Vought F4U had six guns with 400 rounds per gun. The increase in firepower between the early fighters (one 0.3 in/7.62 mm and one 0.5 in/12.7 mm gun, mounted in the upper forward fuselage) and the late fighters (up to eight 0.5 in/12.7 mm guns with 425 rounds per gun in the wings) may readily be imagined. Most of the late fighters could also carry useful loads of bombs and rocket projectiles, unlike the early machines.

Although the standard armament of the US fighters was the 0.5 in (12.7 mm) Browning, some aircraft apart from the P-39 and its P-63 Kingcobra derivative also had cannon as part of their armament. The Americans manufactured a version of the Hispano Mark II as the Hispano M1 cannon. Four such weapons were carried in a belly pack on the Douglas P-70 night-fighter; one as a supplement to the four 0.5 in (12.7 mm) machine-guns in the nose of the Lockheed P-38F/G long-range fighter and fighter-bomber; one M2(C) 20 mm cannon as well as four 0.5 in (12.7 mm) guns in the P-38H to P-38M; four wing-mounted 20 mm cannon in the P-51 ground-attack aircraft; four nose-mounted 20

mm cannon in the Northrop P-61 night-fighter; and four wing-mounted cannon in the F4U-1C fighter-bomber. As can be seen from the types of aircraft fitted with cannon, it was for special purposes such as ground-attack that the American authorities thought cannon useful. They rightly thought that no German or Japanese aircraft was heavily enough armoured to withstand the pounding of a multiple 0.5 in (12.7 mm) heavy machine-gun battery firing ball, tracer and armour-piercing/incendiary rounds.

The Russians remained content with their 1939 weapons throughout World War II, though the performance of the ShVAK was improved, and the ShKAS was largely phased out as part of the fixed armament of fighters in favour of the UBS. However, triple ShVAK mountings became quite common, and the Yakovlev Yak-9T had a 37 mm Nudelman-Suranov NS cannon, though this was intended primarily for use against German armoured vehicles and fixed fortifications.

Aware of the limitations of the MG FF cannon, the Germans had started the development of harder-hitting weapons even before the outbreak of war, Mauser designing the not very effective 0.59 in (15 mm) MG151 in 1935, and the scaled-up 20 mm MG151/20 in 1937. The MG151/20 became the standard small-calibre cannon in *Luftwaffe* service during the war. The MG151, in the unusual 15 mm calibre, was 77.17 in (1,960 mm) long and weighed $94\frac{1}{4}$ lb (42.75 kg). The complete round for the gun weighed 6.7 ounces (190 grams), and the projectile 2.54 ounces (72 grams). Rate of fire was 700 rounds per minute, and muzzle velocity very high, at 3,412 ft (1,040 m) per second. For its hitting power the gun was heavy, however, and was more used as a flexible weapon than as part of fighters' fixed armament.

The MG151/20 was an altogether superior weapon, and appeared in two forms (with and without synchronization capability). Both versions were 67.32 in (1,710 mm) long and weighed 93.7 lb (42.5 kg), and used the same 20 mm round. This weighed 7.77 ounces (220 grams), of which the shell amounted to 4.06 ounces (115 grams). Rate of fire for the unsynchronized version was 780–800 rounds per minute, and for the synchronized version 550–750 rounds per minute. Muzzle velocity was 2,591 ft (790 m) per second. In terms of performance the MG151/20 was comparable with the ShVAK, and inferior to the Hispano in hitting power.

Cocked and loaded electro-pneumatically, the main advantage of the MG151/20 was that the ammunition was detonated electrically. This meant that whereas the MG17 (sometimes retained as a sighting weapon) and the MG131 had to be synchronized mechanically, effective electrical synchronization was possible for the MG151/20: when a propeller blade was in line with a muzzle, an engine-driven cam merely broke the electrical firing-circuit until the blade was out of the way.

Excellent though the MG151/20 was, the Germans realized early in 1942 that the increasing scale of heavy bomber attacks (soon to be supplemented by

Fighter armament layout (1914-1945)

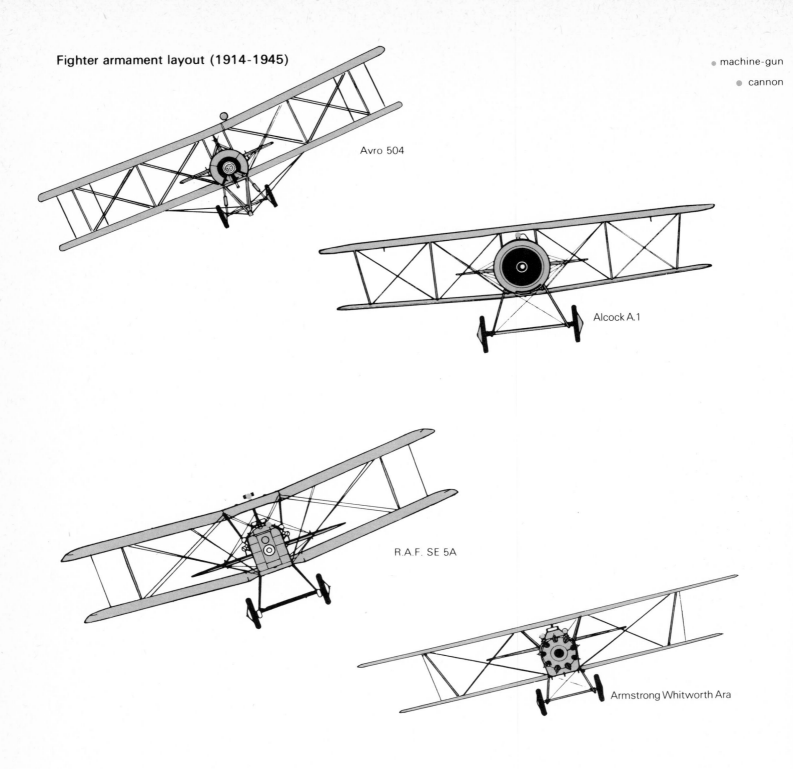

Avro 504

Alcock A.1

R.A.F. SE 5A

Armstrong Whitworth Ara

Armament layout, 1914-1945 (top to bottom): a single 0.303-in (7.7-mm) on the top wing to fire over the propeller blades; a single 0.303-in (7.7-mm) on the top of the forward fuselage to fire through the propeller disc with the aid of a synchronizing gear; two 0.303-in (7.7-mm) machine-guns, one on the upper wing to fire over the propeller disc, and the other on the top of the forward fuselage to fire through the propeller disc with the aid of a synchronizing gear; two 0.303-in (7.7-mm) machine-guns on the top of the forward fuselage to fire through the propeller disc with the aid of a synchronizing gear; two 7.62-mm (0.3-in) machine-guns in the forward fuselage to fire through the propeller disc with the aid of a synchronizing gear, and two 20-mm cannon in the wings to clear the propeller disc; eight 0.303-in (7.7-mm) machine-guns in the wings to clear the propeller disc; four 20-mm cannon in the wings to clear the propeller disc; and four 30-mm cannon in the nose (jet aircraft).

the inevitable American effort) could not be countered by conventional, or at least current, weapons. Operational analysis revealed that against heavy bombers machine-guns were of little or no use, and that to knock down a four-engined Allied bomber needed on average 20 strikes by 20 mm cannon shells. Yet the average pilot managed to get perhaps only 2% of his aimed fire onto the target, meaning that to hit a target 20 times he would need to fire about 1,000 rounds (more than was carried in any fighter), which would take a four-cannon fighter some 25 seconds (most fighters could keep a bomber in their sights for a maximum of three seconds). Clearly, therefore, the *Luftwaffe* had to adopt quicker firing or considerably heavier cannon, preferably a type that combined both factors.

The Germans were lucky that Rheinmetall-Borsig were already developing two such weapons, both in 1.18 in (30 mm) calibre: the MK103 and the

MK108. (The abbreviation MG, it should be noted, stands for *Maschinengewehr* or machine-gun, MK for *Maschinenkanone* or cannon, and BK for *Bordkanone* or cannon carried on an external mounting.) Of these two weapons, whose design had been started in 1941 and 1942 respectively, the Germans selected the MK108 as the new anti-bomber cannon. Some 41.6 in (1,057 mm) long and 127.87 lb (58 kg) in weight, the MK108 fired a round weighing 16.96 ounces (480 grams), including the 11.66 ounce (330 gram) shell, with a muzzle velocity of 2,165 ft (660 m) per second and at a rate of 520 rounds per minute (later raised to 850 rounds per minute). The gun was loaded and cocked electro-pneumatically, and the rounds were fired electrically. The MK108 entered service in 1943 on the Messerschmitt Bf 109G-6 (one gun mounted to fire through the propeller hub), the Focke Wulf Fw 190A-8 (two guns in gondolas under the wings outboard of the under-

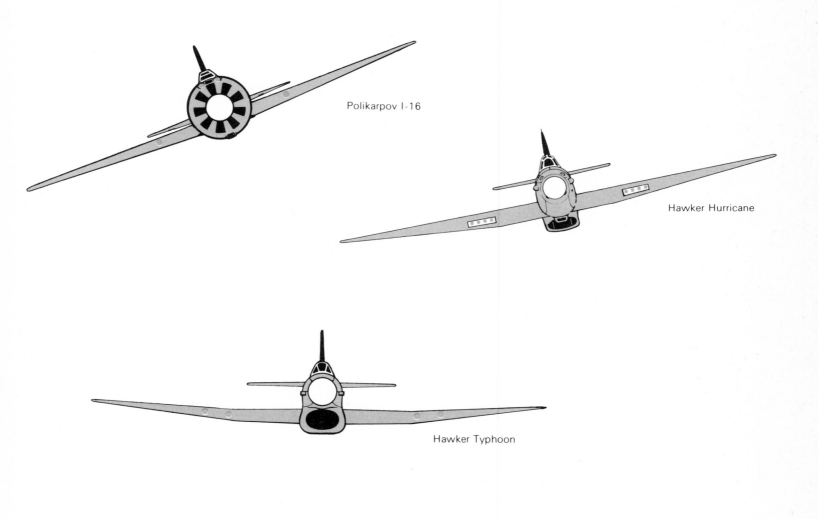

Polikarpov I-16

Hawker Hurricane

Hawker Typhoon

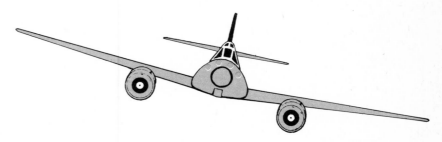

Messerschmitt Me 262

carriage legs), and the Messerschmitt Bf 110G-2 (two guns in the nose). The result of the widespread introduction of the MK108 was an immediate increase in the *Luftwaffe's* success rate. The MK108 was not a total solution to the *Luftwaffe's* problem, however, for the gun's rate of fire was slow and the muzzle velocity too low for fighters to be able to fire from a safe distance. So although the effect of the 30 mm shell was devastating, the German fighters often suffered very heavy losses from the bombers' defensive fire as they closed in to the effective range of under 547 yards (500 m). The measure of the MK108's effectiveness may be gauged from the fact that three or four rounds were usually enough to down a heavy bomber – only one-fifth the number of 20 mm shell hits needed. And one 30 mm hit was normally sufficient to destroy a fighter or twin-engined bomber. The most effective MK108 installation was in the Messerschmitt Me 262 jet-engined fighter, which was armed with four MK108 cannon in the nose, the upper pair having 100 rounds per gun and the lower pair 80 rounds per gun. The Me 262 was the most heavily armed 'conventional' fighter of World War II, being able to fire 123.68 lb (56.1 kg) of shells in a three-second burst at 850 rounds per minute.

To cause this crippling damage, though, fighters armed with MK108 batteries had to close in to potentially suicidal ranges, and the Germans quickly extemporized other measures. The MK103 was substituted for the MK108: although the MK103's rate of fire was slower (only 440 rounds per minute) and its weight far higher (321.87 lb/146 kg), the MK103 was far longer (91.26 in/2,318 mm), especially in the barrel, and had a muzzle velocity of 2,821 ft (860 m) per second with a more massive round. This weighed 34.63 ounces (980 grams), the shell weighing 18.73 ounces (530 grams). The MK103 was a bomber-destroyer of magnificent performance, but was very bulky and heavy, with a consequent adverse effect on performance. Other expedients tried were the BK3,7 and the BK5. The BK3,7, fitted to the Messerschmitt Bf 110G-2/R1, consisted of a 37 mm Flak 18 gun fitted under the belly of the aircraft in a wood fairing covered with canvas. Some 142.52 in (3,620 mm) long and weighing 936.96 lb (425 kg), the BK3,7 fired a shell weighing 14.3 ounces (405 grams) at the rate of 160 rounds per minute with a muzzle velocity of 3,839 ft (1,170 m) per second. Magazine capacity was 72 rounds, located in the rear cockpit. The muzzle velocity of the weapon made possible long-range fire, but the bulk and weight of the weapon seriously hampered performance. More effective, however, was the installation of the BK5 on the Messerschmitt Me 410A-2/U4 and B-2/U4. Derived from the 50 mm KWK39 tank gun by Rheinmetall, who had also produced the Flak 18, the BK5 fired a shell weighing 56 ounces (1,585 grams) at the rate of 140 rounds per minute with a muzzle velocity of 2,821 ft (860 m) per second. The weapon was 170.94 in (4,342 mm) long, and had to be carried semi-recessed in the lower fuselage. The trajectory of the shell was quite flat, but again the weight and bulk of the weapon so hampered performance that the Me 410 was relatively easy prey for the North American P-51B escort fighter which was encountered in increasing numbers at the beginning of 1944.

The weapon that might possibly have provided the Germans with the answer to their aerial problems appeared just too late to see active service. This was the MG213/20, designed by Mauser during 1944 and 1945. Mauser realized that the basic limitation in the performance of other weapons was the speed at which the reciprocating breechlock could move, extracting and ejecting the empty case as it moved back, and chambering a fresh round from the magazine as it moved forward to the locked position once again. Such a breechblock was necessarily of some mass, and gun design could not make this mass move any faster than it already was in the confined space available. The Mauser designers came up with an ingenious and basically simple solution: the feed mechanism and breechblock of earlier weapons were replaced by a cylinder rotating parallel to the bore sight of the gun; this cylinder contained five 'breeches', allowing five separate elements of the loading and ejection cycle to be carried out at the same time. The action of the gun was electro-pneumatically powered, and rounds fed in from the left of the receiver in their disintegrating metal-link belt. Arriving in the 7pm (looking at the cylinder from the rear) position, the round is positioned behind the empty chamber; the cylinder rotates anti-clockwise, and at the 5 pm position the round is rammed partially into its chamber; moving on to the 2 pm position, the round is completely chambered, the individual link of the belt having been discarded to the right; at 12 am the round is fired; and at 10 am the empty case is thrown out of the case ejector chute just as a fresh round, five rounds along the belt from the original round, is positioned for chambering. The success of the Mauser designers' efforts can be seen from the performance figures of the weapon: the MG213/20 was 75.98 in (1,930 mm) long and weighed 165.35 lb (75 kg), but fired at the prodigious rate of 1,300 rounds per minute with a muzzle velocity of no less than 3,494 ft (1,065 m) per second. Each round was electrically fired, and the shell was about double the usual weight of 20 mm shells at 7.4 ounces (210 grams). The basic design was also to have been used in a 30 mm equivalent, designated MG213/30. This latter weapon was to have weighed the same, but been only 64.17 in (1,630 mm) long. Muzzle velocity would have been low, at 1,772 ft (540 m) per second, but rate of fire extraordinarily high for a 30 mm weapon, at 1,180 rounds per minute. Also under design in 1945, were two fixed weapons derived from the MK108, the 55 mm (2,165 mm) MK112 and MK114. The former was to have weighed 597.45 lb (271 kg) and been 79.2 in (2,102 mm) long, firing a 52.3 lb (1,480 gram) shell to a range of 995 yards (910 m) at a muzzle velocity of 1,968 ft (600 m) per second and a rate of 300 rounds per minute. The

MK114 was to have weighed 1,560.86 lb (708 kg) and fired a shell to the effective range of 1,985 yards (1,815 m) with a muzzle velocity of 3,445 ft (1,050 m) per second at the rate of 150 rounds per minute. These last two, though, smack more than a little of desperation measures.

Japan also suffered terribly at the hands of heavy bombers, and developed a number of heavy cannon to try to crush the American offensive. The Imperial Japanese army air service quite quickly supplanted its initial 20 mm Type 97 cannon first with a small number of imported MG151/20 weapons, and then one of the war's best 20 mm weapons, the Type 1 (Ho-5) of 1941. This was based on the design of the 0.5 in (12.7 mm) Type 1 (Ho-103) heavy machine-gun, and was a lightweight weapon weighing only 58 lb (26.3 kg); it was 58 in (1,475 mm) long, and fired at the rate of 850 rounds per minute with a muzzle velocity of 2,461 ft (750 m) per second, giving it an effective range of 947 yards (900 m). Designed specifically as a bomber destroying weapon, the 30 mm Ho-105 cannon was used in limited numbers at the end of the war in aircraft such as the Nakajima Ki-84-Ic: it was 79½ in (2,020 mm) long and weighed 97 lb (44 kg), firing 450 rounds per minute at a

muzzle velocity of 2,346 ft (715 m) per second up to a range of 947 yards (900 m). Next up in calibre amongst army weapons was the 37 mm Type 98 (1938) cannon, basically a copy of a French infantry cannon of the same calibre, and used in the ventral armament tunnel of the Kawasaki Ki-45: the gun was only 54 in (1,372 mm) long, but weighed 269 lb (122 kg), and had to be hand fed at the rate of 15 rounds per minute with ammunition that had an effective range of 1,094 yards (1,000 m) at a muzzle velocity of 2,000 ft (610 m) per second. Next up in size was the most unusual weapon used by the army, the 40 mm Ho-301, used in limited numbers only by the Nakajima Ki-44-11c fighter: the gun was only 58½ in (1,485 mm) long and weighed 291 lb (132 kg), and fired very odd ammunition without a cartridge. Instead, the propellant charge was contained in the base of the shell and, after ignition, exhausted through 12 ports in the base to drive the shell forward up the short barrel. Though this had a number of advantages that helped to make the rate of fire 450 rounds per minute, it also had disadvantages such as a low muzzle velocity of only 760 ft (232 m) per second, and an effective range of a mere 164 yards (150 m). Under development at the end of the war

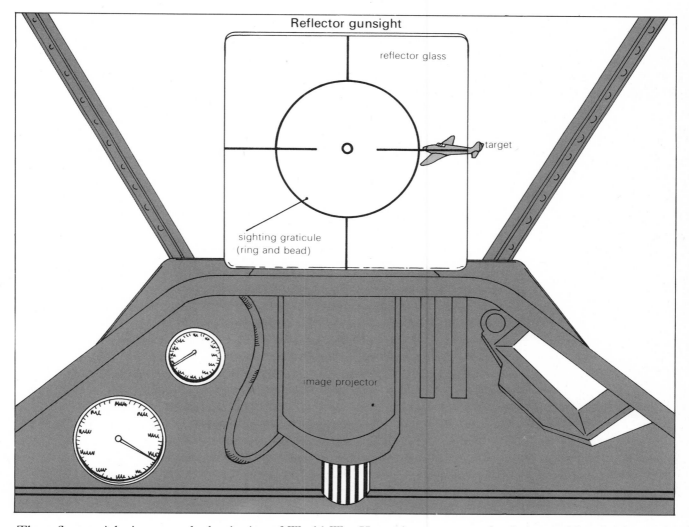

The reflector sight in use at the beginning of World War II was in essence a refined ring-and-bead sight, with the image of the ring and bead projected onto a special glass in front of the pilot's eyes in such a way that they were visible only if the pilot were looking along the aircraft's longitudinal axis. The image was also focussed at infinity to relieve the pilot of the impossible task of trying to focus his sight on two different distances at the same sight. The outer ring provided a measure of deflection calculation capability.

was the 57 mm Ho-401, used on types such as the Kawasaki Ki-102b: it weighed 353 lb (160 kg), and fired its shells at a muzzle velocity of 1,700 ft (518 m) per second at the rate of 90 rounds per minute. The Imperial Japanese army air arm also has the distinction of having produced the largest-calibre air-to-air gun of the war, the 75 mm Type 88 carried in the Mitsubishi Ki-109. The weapon was essentially the Type 88 (1928) 75 mm AA gun adapted for carriage in an aircraft. Some 15 rounds of ammunition were carried and hand-loaded individually, and muzzle velocity was 2,362 ft (720 m) per second.

The Imperial Japanese navy air arm did not have so great a responsibility as the army for the air defence of the Japanese home islands, and so did not need to develop heavy cannon specifically to knock down the American strategic bombers raiding Japan. Only two new weapons were added to the fixed-weapon inventory of the Imperial Navy air arm: the Type 3 (1943) 13.2 mm machine-gun and the 30 mm Type 5 (1945) cannon. Otherwise, the standard weapons remained the 0.303 in (7.7 mm) Type 97 machine-gun and the 20 mm Type 99 cannon. The Type 3 machine-gun was widely used, especially on the Mitsubishi A6M fighter's later models: it was 66 lb (30 kg) in weight and 61 in (1,550 mm) long, and had a range of 947 yards (896 m) at 800 rounds per minute with a muzzle velocity of 2,592 ft (790 m) per second. The Type 5 cannon was in essence an enlargement of the Type 99: the magazine held 42 rounds, weight was 154 lb (70 kg), length $82\frac{1}{2}$ in (2,095 mm), muzzle velocity 2,416 ft (750 m) per second, rate of fire 400 rounds per minute, and range 947 yards (900 m).

Such, then, were the main types of gun used for air-to-air fixed mountings in World War II. Some of them were effective weapons throughout the war, others were rendered obsolete as the technical pace of the conflict speeded up, and yet other examples were only approaching fruition towards the end of the war. But no matter how effective the weapon, it was next to useless unless the pilot could aim accurately. And here great advances were made over the standards of World War I and the inter-war years, the period in which simple ring-and-bead sights or the Aldis sight had sufficed because of the short ranges at which most air battles had taken place (or were anticipated to occur), and the relatively low performance of biplane aircraft.

Increasing performance and air-to-air combat ranges meant that the simple sights were no longer sufficient, especially where there was a call for deflection shooting (all shooting in which the relative speeds and flight courses of the two aircraft involved differed, thus necessitating calculation of the amount of 'lead' necessary to ensure a hit). Although the outer ring of the ring sight's graticule allowed a certain amount of calculation to be achieved, there were problems of the sights obscuring the target, the difficulty of seeing the foresight in poor conditions of weather or light, and the impossibility of focussing on the rear sight (close to the eye) and the target (at optical infinity) at the same time. During the 1930s, therefore, the reflector sight became standard: this obviated the need for a ring-and-bead sight, replacing it with a piece of reflector glass on which the pilot could see, when his head was in the right position to see along the aircraft's line of flight, the image of a ring sight produced by a light projector below the inclined glass panel. The image was focussed at infinity, and the brightness of the image could be adjusted to suit the conditions. With the aid of the ring sight the pilot could try to assess the factors necessary for him to calculate the amount of deflection involved and make the right allowances for relative course and speed. By 1939 most major air forces were using such reflector sights: the American ST 1A, the British GM 2, the French Baille-Lemaire or OPL *Modèle* 1931, the German Revi 12c, the Italian San Giorgio, and the Russian PBP-1.

But although the reflector sight made the pilot's task easier so far as the physical problems of aiming were concerned, there still remained the difficult problem of deflection, for which the reflector sight was intrinsically no superior to the ring-and-bead sight. It was only in 1939 that designers at the Royal Aircraft Establishment at Farnborough in Hampshire started work on a new type of sight working on totally different principles: that if the pilot of the attacking aircraft holds his sights on his opponent in a turn, the attacking fighter's rate of turn is proportional to the angle of deflection necessary to hit the opponent. The designers at the RAE thus produced a sight based on the reflector sight, but coupled with a gyroscope that measured the rate of turn and 'instructed' the light projector to move the sighting graticule on the reflector glass to the right position by the angle of deflection required. Naturally enough, the angle value so arrived at was true for only one range, and so the infant gyro gunsight was provided with a device which allowed the pilot to set the diameter of the ring graticule to a position corresponding to the wing span of known enemy aircraft. Using a device on his control column, the pilot was then able to keep the graticule diameter at the same apparent size as the span of the aircraft he was engaging. This allowed the sight to compute the range of the target and so allow for this factor in deciding the deflection angle required.

The development of the new sight was a complex business, and it was the end of 1943 before the Gyro Gunsight Mark IID was ready for mass production for the RAF, the USAAF (as the K-14) and the US Navy (as the Mark 18). Although the new sight was first greeted with scepticism, the more so because its use involved the pilot in a fair degree of extra manual dexterity before and during combat, the results of air combat soon revealed that the gyro gunsight improved the 'kill' rate by almost 100%, particularly at long range (500 yards/457 m or more) and at large deflection angles (45° or more). The Germans also developed a gyro gunsight, the Askania EZ 42, but this had reached only the trials stage by the end of the war.

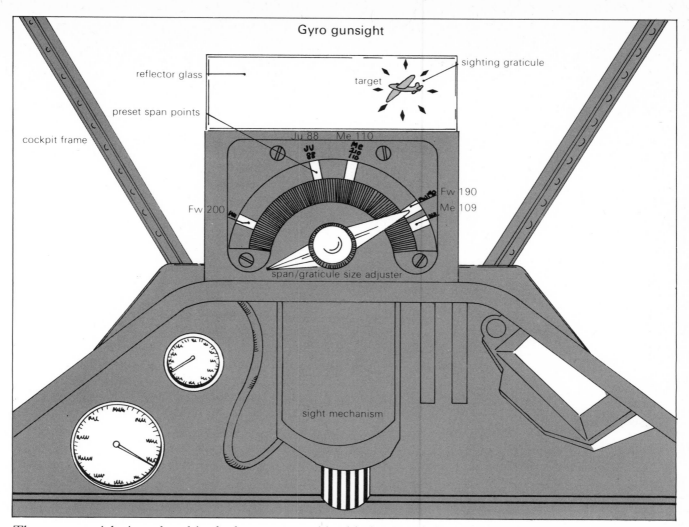

Gyro gunsight

reflector glass

preset span points

cockpit frame

sighting graticule

target

Ju 88   Me 110

Fw 200

Fw 190

Me 109

span/graticule size adjuster

sight mechanism

The gyro gunsight introduced in the late 1943 considerably improved the standard of aerial marksmanship attainable by the average pilot by easing his problems in association with deflection shooting. All the pilot had to do was set the control on his sight's panel to the span of the opposing aircraft's wings, and then follow the other aircraft into a turn. The attacking pilot then adjusted the size of the graticule to match his opponent's apparent diameter, and the gyro mechanism in the sight produced the right deflection for the range and rate of turn, so that when a pilot had his enemy in the right-sized graticule, his fire would strike the aircraft.

The gun was by far the most important and successful air-to-air weapon of World War II, but was supplemented by several other weapons of varying capabilities, some of which might have been developed into useful types had the war continued longer.

The earliest of these to see service was an unguided air-to-air rocket, the 3.23 in (82 mm) RS-82, designed by I. Kleymyenov and G. Langyemak in late 1936 and early 1937, and built by the Gas Dynamics Laboratory in Moscow. The type was first tested on a Polikarpov I-16 Type 10 monoplane fighter in July 1937, three rockets being mounted under each wing. The type entered service in December 1936, and scored some successes in Spain and in the Siberian and Mongolian border clashes with Japan in 1938 and 1939. Considerable thought had been given in the 1930s to the feasibility of unguided rockets as bomber-destroying weapons: it was anticipated that a salvo of such weapons, fired at high velocity, would have a flat trajectory, low dispersion and therefore an excellent chance of scoring a direct hit on an enemy bomber. The RS-82 was rather 'fat' for its length of 24.6 in (325 mm), and although its impact-fused 1.1 lb (0.5 kg) warhead would no doubt cause considerable damage with a

direct hit, the motor gave the 15 lb (6.8 kg) missile a maximum velocity of only 1,148 ft (350 m) per second. This suggests that the salvo of six missiles would not have had a flat trajectory, and that dispersion would have been great. The Russians also produced a 5.17 in (132 mm) version, the RS-132, but this seems to have been even less successful than the RS-82.

The other main protagonists of unguided missiles were the Germans, looking for yet another possible method of destroying heavy bombers operating by day. As soon as the need for unguided missiles became clear, the *Luftwaffe* instituted a crash programme to develop such weapons, but had to turn to modified army weapons for use in the period before the specialized weapons were ready for service use. During 1943, therefore, the *Luftwaffe* adapted the army's Rheinmetall-Borsig 8.27 in (21 cm) *Nebelwerfer* 42 round for airborne use. (The *Nebelwerfer* 42 was the German Army's five-barrel rocket-launcher, mounted on a highly mobile light chassis.) Emerging as the Wfr.Gr.21 (8.27 in *Werfergranate* or 21 cm rocket projectile), the missile was carried in the launch tubes mounted on struts beneath the wings of fighters such as the Messerschmitt Bf 110G series. At launch the Wfr.Gr.21 weighed 248 lb (112.5 kg):

of this the propellant comprised $40\frac{1}{4}$ lb (18.27 kg), the whole warhead 90.39 lb (41 kg), and the high explosive filling of the warhead 22.42 lb (10.17 kg). The rocket was spin-stabilized, and provided with a time fuse to detonate the warhead after the missile had travelled a preset distance between 601 yards (550 m) and 1,203 yards (1,100 m). The propellant vented through 22 venturi, angled to impart spin to the missile, but maximum velocity was only 1,017 ft (310 m) per second, far too low too give the missile a relatively flat trajectory, necessary if the warhead were to explode not more than 33 yards (30 m) from the target.

As a result of its crash programme to develop a specialized air-to-air missile, the *Luftwaffe* was able to use the Rheinmetall-Borsig R4M unguided missile in the closing stages of the war. This highly successful missile was 31.89 in (810 mm) long and 2.17 in (55 mm) in diameter, weighing 7.72 lb (3.5 kg) complete, of which the high-explosive warhead comprized 1.1 lb (0.5 kg). Although still not very high, the missile's velocity of 1,722 ft (525 m) per second was just high enough for accurate aiming. Combined with its light weight, this meant that fighters could carry large numbers (24 on the Messerschmitt Me 262) on low drag wood racks under the wings, for ripple-salvo firing at individual bombers. From a range of 601 yards (550 m), the missiles spread out into a roughly circular pattern about 98.4 ft (30 m) in diameter, and one strike from an impact-fused R4M was usually sufficient to knock down an American bomber.

The main failing of the R4M was that its effective range was limited, with the result that the fighters carrying the type had to close in to within the bomber boxes' useful defensive fire zone. Rheinmetall-Borsig therefore developed the R 100/BS: this was a large unguided rocket some $72\frac{1}{2}$ in (1,841.5 mm) in length and a diameter of 8.27 in (210 mm), weighing 242.5 lb (110 kg). Burnt-out velocity was 1,476 ft (450 m) per second. Thus far the R 100/BS was a relatively straightforward missile with no special characteristics and a fairly low maximum velocity. Two factors did, however, mark the R 100/BS as something special: the warhead and the missile firing system. The warhead, weighing 88.18 lb (40 kg), consisted of two parts, a large bursting charge and a 'canister' warhead consisting of 460 incendiary pellets forward in a large cone; the pellets were designed to cut through the fuel tanks of the target and set fire to their contents. The missile firing system was based on the use of a simple radar ranging device: as the missile was detonated by a time fuse, the pilot merely set the same time on the fuse and the radar ranger's associated computer; then as the pilot closed in for the attack and switched on the ranger, this measured the range accurately and fired the missile at just the right moment to ensure that the bursting charge was set off when the missile was the optimum 87 yards (80 m) from the bomber. The range of the missile was a useful 1,968 yards (1,800 m), keeping the launch aircraft well out of the range

of the 0.5 in (12.7 mm) defensive guns of the American bombers. The system was just about ready for operational use at the end of the war, it being intended that the Messerschmitt Me 262 should carry five and the Messerschmitt Me 410 six of the R 100/BS missiles. There can be little doubt that in the early stages of its operational employment the missile and its 'Oberon' firing system would have inflicted great damage on the American bombers, but the Allies would then have come up with a radar countermeasures device to ruin the accuracy of the ranging radar.

Effective as some of these and other unguided missiles may have been when fully developed, Germany realized that the best solution to the Allied bomber threat lay not with unguided but with guided missiles. With considerable inventive genius, therefore, the Germans set about developing the world's first effective air-to-air guided missiles, one of which had reached an advanced stage of development at the end of the war: the Kramer X-4 'Ruhrstahl' or 'Ruhr Steel'. Fitted with swept cruciform wings and tail, the X-4 was 82.68 in (2,100 mm) long, with a maximum body diameter of 8.66 in (220 mm) and a wingspan of 33.86 in (860 mm). The *Ruhrstahl* was powered by a liquid-propellant BMW 109-548 rocket, providing 22 seconds of 309 lb (140 kg) thrust. This was enough to propel the 132.28 lb (60 kg) missile at a maximum speed of 559 mph (900 kph) and to a range of 3,171 yards (2,900 m). The X-4 was controlled in flight by aerodynamic spoilers operated through twin wires (each 0.2 mm in thickness and 6,015 yards/5,500 m in length) trailed from bobbins on two of the wingtips. Along these wires the controller in the aircraft sent the commands to steer the missile into the target, where the 44.09 lb (20 kg) warhead would detonate with impressive results.

Japan also was severely hit by the American bomber offensive, and tried a number of methods other than gunfire in the campaign against the bombers. The most important of these techniques was air-to-air bombing (on opposite courses), but such efforts were still virtually useless even by the end of World War II in August 1945. Bombing had been considered as an anti-bomber weapon right through the 1930s by Japan. In 1939 the Type 99 No 3 Mark 3 bomb was introduced: weighing 83 lb (37.65 kg), the bomb was detonated by a tail fuse after the weapon had dropped a preset distance, the bursting charge firing 144 phosphorous incendiary pellets in a cone downwards and forwards, the lethal range being 82 yards (75 m) below the detonation of the bomb. The Type 2 No 3 Mark 1 was based on the same design, but was considerably larger: 551 lb (250 kg), firing 759 incendiary pellets over a lethal range of 219 yards (200 m). The Type 2 (1942) was to have been replaced in 1946 by the Type 5 (1945) No 25 Mark 29, which also weighed 551 lb (250 kg). The later bomb, however, had 1,100 incendiary pellets weighing 102 lb (50 kg). As an alternative to dropping the weapon, the pilot was provided with a cockpit switch to detonate the bomb and the whole aircraft, for *kamikaze* missions.

Of course, while the fighters were trying to shoot down the bombers, the latter were exerting their utmost efforts to ruin the formers' efforts. Such efforts could consist of evasive manoeuvres to throw off the opposing pilot's aim, electronic counter-measures of one kind or another to try to confuse or jam the enemy's own electronic aids (especially in night operations), and return gunfire.

At the beginning of World War II, most medium bombers were armed with a few hand-held machine-guns for defensive purposes, the most common mounting being a simple pillar or ball-and-socket unit, with rotating ring mounting the next most frequently encountered type. The trouble with such mountings was that the slipstream of aircraft moving at 200 mph (322 kph) or more made it difficult to manoeuvre the weapon, especially for fine movements in azimuth. The way forward had been shown by aircraft such as the Martin B-10, which had an enclosed cockpit for the nose gunner, protecting him from the worst of the slipstream, but still leaving him with the task of manhandling his weapon and turret.

Clearly, therefore, what was needed was a powered turret: the first such turrets provided the gunner inside them with means of making coarse

movements in elevation and azimuth by means of electric motors, and the last fine movements by hand. Typical of this type of turret was the DL131, armed with a single 0.512 in (13 mm) MG131, fitted to aircraft such as the Dornier Do 217E. The trouble with such turrets, though, was that it took some time for them to get into action, and the need to follow a rapidly moving fighter could not be met adequately by a combination of electrical and manpower.

Early in the war, as a result, there began to appear fully powered turrets, with electrical, hydraulic, or electro-hydraulic drives, such as the British Fraser-Nash and Boulton-Paul, and American Sperry turrets. These had two types of drive, fast for quick movement in elevation and azimuth, and slow for fine laying once the general bearing of the target had been reached. The fast drive allowed traverse at up to 50° per second, and elevation at up to 30° per second; while the slow drive was accurate to within $\frac{1}{4}°$ for the actual engagement of the target. Such a turret was the Sperry No 645473E electro-hydraulically powered unit fitted in the dorsal position of the Boeing B-17: this was armed with a pair of 0.5 in (12.7 mm) Browning M2 machine-guns with 500 rounds per gun, and weighed 1,000 lb (453.6 kg) complete except for the gunner, but including the gunner's armour. The guns themselves were fed

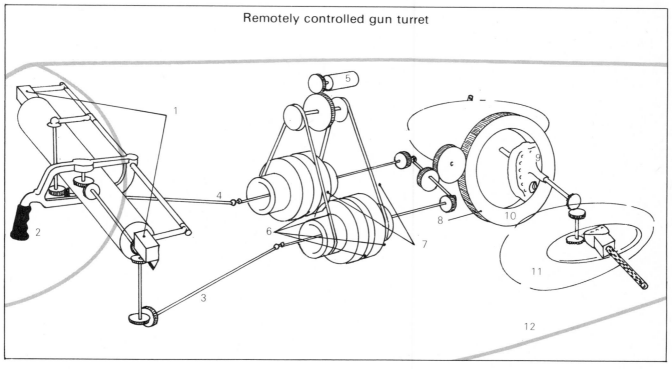

Remotely controlled gun turret

1. reflector gunsight
2. control grip
3. elevation and traverse angle linkage
4. elevation angle linkage
5. motor
6. friction drums (continuously rotating)
7. belt drive (schematic)
8. elevating ring
9. gear box
10. elevating and traversing ring
11. gun barbette
12. fuselage

The German *fernbetätigte Drehlafette* (FDL) 131 remotely controlled gun barbette system was used on the Messerschmitt Me 210 and Me 410 fighter-bombers to control one 13-mm (0.51-in) MG131 machine-gun on each side of the rear fuselage. The guns were controlled by the wireless operator/gunner in the rear part of the single cockpit enclosure, using one of the two reflector sights on the sides of his cockpit. By moving his handle, the gunner moved the sight on the target and this moved the relevant gun onto the right bearing (between 2° inboard and 45° outboard) and elevation (+/−75°) by clutching-in one or both of the rotating friction drums.

electrically, and the ammunition was electrically fired. The turret itself was capable of 360° traverse at 45° per second, and the guns of elevation from 0° to 85° at 30° per second.

With the gunner, such a turret probably weighed 1,200 lb (544.3 kg), and other turrets weighed considerably more. The Sperry No 645849-J ball turret used in the ventral position of the B-17 and the Consolidated B-24 was also armed with two Browning M2 machine-guns and 500 rounds per gun: it was 44 in (1,117.6 mm) in diameter, and weighed 1,290 lb (585.14 kg) with the gunner's armour but without the gunner. All-up weight for the turret was probably in the order of 1,425 lb (646.38 kg).

Such turrets needed to be large, weighty items principally to contain the gunner as well as the guns, ammunition and mechanical apparatus. Thus the need to carry nose, dorsal, ventral and tail turrets, as well as a number of other machine-guns firing from ports in the fuselage played a considerable part in the designer's calculations. All the weight needed to be lifted, at the expense of bombload or fuel, and the turrets themselves inflicted a severe drag penalty which could be overcome only by increased power and fuel consumption.

The solution to this problem would naturally have been to get rid of the turrets, but operational requirements demanded gun defence for bombers, many of which carried between eight and 13 machine-guns, with an average of perhaps 500 rounds per gun, and up to six gunners. The best compromise, therefore, appeared to be remotely-controlled turrets, which had a number of advantages. The gunner had the best possible field of vision, for he could be located in the optimum position rather than in the turret; the turret could also be located where its field of fire was greatest, for it was lighter and produced less drag than its manned counterpart. It could thus be located where tactical considerations, rather than merely aerodynamic considerations, dictated. It was also smaller, so that considerations of gunner-accessibility and limited fuselage width did not apply so severely; the weight distribution of the aircraft was improved by locating the gunner near the centre of gravity, with consequent improvement in aircraft manoeuvrability. Reduced weight and drag meant better performance; smaller turrets meant less need for turret motive power; and lastly the separation of the gunner and his turret meant that there was less chance of the gunner's vision being affected in combat by muzzle flash from his guns.

All in all, therefore, the combination of armament in a barbette, remotely controlled by a gunner with a first-class field of vision in a different part of the fuselage, offered advantages. First off the mark with such an armament system were the Germans, who introduced two FDL131 barbettes on the Messerschmitt Me 210 fighter of 1941. One of these barbettes was located on each side of the fuselage just aft of the wireless operator/gunner's cockpit, and contained one 0.512 in (13 mm) MG131 machine-gun with 450 rounds of ammunition. Power was pro-

vided by a 1½ hp electric motor, and each MG131 could be traversed 40° independently of the other, and elevated/depressed through 70°. The barbettes weighed 450 lb (205 kg) together without ammunition, and covered a far greater field of fire than could have been managed by a turret. Though the Me 210 was a failure, the FDL131 barbettes were not, being developed into the excellent FDSL barbettes used on the Me 410 with 500 rounds per gun.

Other German aircraft had remotely-controlled barbettes, but the World War II aircraft with the most advanced and successful armament installation of this type was undoubtedly the Boeing B-29, which featured a defensive gun system designed by the General Electric Corporation. This had five barbettes (tail with two Browning 0.5 in/12.7 mm machine-guns and one M2 20 mm cannon, rear dorsal with two Brownings, forward dorsal with four Brownings, rear ventral with two Brownings and forward ventral with two Brownings) controlled from five stations (positions in the tail and nose, and astrodomes just in front of the radar dorsal barbette and on each side of the fuselage behind the wing-root fairings). The system in its simplest form provided the B-29 with the most powerful and effective defensive armament used by any World War II bomber, but went far beyond this in providing for alternative control of several barbettes. The tail gunner controlled only his own guns; the two gunners in the waist astrodomes controlled basically the rear ventral barbette, but could also control the tail guns and the forward ventral barbette; the gunner in the rear dorsal astrodome controlled all the other gunners tactically, because of his position, and controlled physically the rear dorsal barbette (not controllable by any other gunner) with secondary control of the forward dorsal barbette; and the gunner in the nose controlled the forward ventral and dorsal barbettes. Extensive provision was made for the handing over of control from one gunner to another, an electric interrupter gear was fitted to prevent any gun from shooting into the aircraft, and a computer corrected the training of the guns to allow for the parallax of a gunner with a slightly different angular perspective.

So far as the weapons used for defensive purposes by bombers were concerned, there was a rapid increase in numbers and calibre as the war progressed. The Heinkel He 111H-2 of 1939 had three (later six) 0.312 in (7.92 mm) MG15 flexible guns, which was standard armament for the period except for the Lioré et Olivier Leo 451 which had two machine-guns and a 20 mm cannon, and the Mitsubishi G3M2 Model 22 which had three machine-guns and one 20 mm cannon; the Junkers Ju 88A-4 of 1941 had three 7.92 mm MG81 and two 0.512 in (13 mm) MG131 machines, or seven 7.92 mm MG81 machine-guns; the Boeing B-17G of 1943 had 13 0.5 in (12.7 mm) machine-guns; the Boeing B-29 of 1944 had 12 0.5 in (12.7 mm) machine-guns and one 20 mm cannon; and the Avro Lincoln of 1945 had four

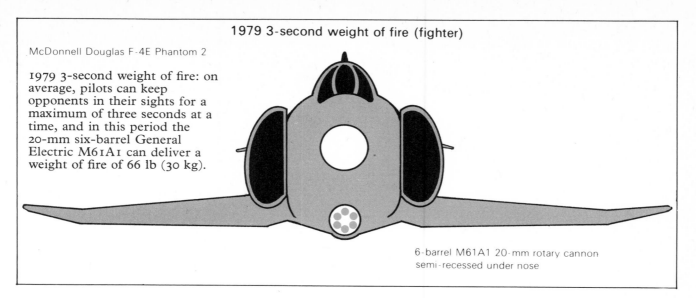

1979 3-second weight of fire (fighter)

McDonnell Douglas F-4E Phantom 2

1979 3-second weight of fire: on average, pilots can keep opponents in their sights for a maximum of three seconds at a time, and in this period the 20-mm six-barrel General Electric M61A1 can deliver a weight of fire of 66 lb (30 kg).

6-barrel M61A1 20-mm rotary cannon semi-recessed under nose

0.5 in (12.7 mm) machine-guns and two 20 mm cannon. In general, the Germans and Japanese armed their bombers with heavy machine-guns and cannon, the Americans and Russians with heavy machine-guns, and the British with medium machine-guns.

At the beginning of the war, most bomber guns were provided with ring and bead sights, but as the war progressed, reflector sights became common in turrets, and at the end of hostilities, the Americans had begun to introduce gyro gunsights on a large scale, as had the British to a slightly lesser extent.

The guns themselves were basically similar to those used in other aircraft as part of the fixed armament, with the addition of manual triggers, grips and other additions to suit them for flexible or turret use. There were, though, some weapons intended specifically for flexible or turret use.

The Germans produced the 0.312 in (7.92 mm) Rheinmetall MG15 specifically as a flexible aircraft gun. It was 42.91 in (1,090 mm) long and weighed 17.86 lb (8.1 kg), firing a 0.92 ounce (26 gram) round with a 0.45 ounce (12.8 gram) bullet at a muzzle velocity of 2,510 ft (765 m) per second at the rate of 1,250 rounds per minute. The design of the weapon originated in 1934, and the weapon was in widespread service by 1939. Feed was from a 75-round double drum, and the operation of the gun was completely mechanical.

Rheinmetall-Borsig started the development of the more ambitious 0.312 in (7.92 mm) MG81 as a flexible aircraft gun in 1938. Firing the same round as the MG15, the MG81 was only 35.04 in (890 mm) long and weighed 14 lb (6.35 kg). Despite the short barrel length, muzzle velocity was 2,904 ft (885 m) per second, and rate of fire 1,600 rounds per minute. Unlike the MG15, the MG81, which was electro-mechanically operated, was belt fed. The basic weapon also appeared as the MG81Z (*Zwilling* or twin), a double-barrel weapon with the prodigious rate of fire of 3,000 rounds per minute.

The Rheinmetall MK101 was an obsolete 30 mm cannon used, apparently, only in a few Dornier Do 24T flying-boats. The weapon was 103.94 in (2,640 mm) long and 306.44 lb (139 kg) in weight, had a muzzle velocity of 3,051 ft (920 m) per second, and was capable of firing at the rate of 260 rounds per minute.

Japan also produced specialized weapons for flexible use, the Imperial Army and Navy each having their own types. Early in the war, the Imperial Army used as its standard light flexible gun the 0.303 in (7.7 mm) Type 89 (1929) gas-operated machine-gun. This was fed from a 69-round drum magazine, weighed 20 lb (9.07 kg), was 42½ in (1,080 mm) long, and fired at the rate of 750 rounds per minute with a muzzle velocity of 2,444 ft (745 m) per second.

The Type 98 (1938) machine-gun was a licence-built copy of the German 0.312 in (7.92 mm) MG15, and was quite widely used on army aircraft. Other weapons used in turrets or on flexible mounts on army aircraft were the Type 1 (Ho-103) 0.5 in (12.7 mm) machine-gun, the Ho-1 version of the Type 97 20 mm cannon, and the Ho-5 (Type 1) 20 mm cannon, all of which could be used in modified form as fixed weapons.

The Imperial Navy's standard light flexible machine-gun was the 0.303 in (7.7 mm) Type 92 (1932) machine-gun, derived from the British Lewis gun. The weapon was fed from 47- or 97-round drum magazines, was 18½ lb (8.4 kg) in weight, 39 in (990 mm) long, and fired at the rate of 1,000 rounds per minute with a muzzle velocity of 2,500 ft (762 m) per second. Like the army's Type 98, the navy's Type 1 (1941) 0.312 in (7.92 mm) machine-gun was basically the German MG15. It was 42½ in (1,080 mm) long, weighed 15 lb (6.8 kg), and fired at the rate of 1,000 rounds per minute with a muzzle velocity of 2,592 ft (790 m) per second.

With the type 2 (1942) machine-gun, of 0.512 in (13 mm) calibre, the Imperial Navy had its first belt-fed flexible machine-gun. The weapon was based on the German MG131: it was 46.2 in (1,174 mm) long, weighed 37½ lb (17 kg), and fired 900 rounds per minute with a muzzle velocity of 2,461 ft (750 m) per second.

Of the major powers, the USA and USSR used derivatives of their fixed weapons as flexible and turret-mounted machine-guns, the Russians installing 20 mm ShVAK cannon in some aircraft. This was generally the policy of the British, also, but at the beginning of the war a number of Vickers GO (gas-operated) or 'K' guns were in use. Designed as a replacement for the Lewis gun, the Vickers GO gun was an effective, drum-fed weapon that fell foul of changing requirements and the fall from favour of drum-fed weapons. Weighing $19\frac{1}{2}$ lb (8.845 kg), the 0.303 in (7.7 mm) GO had a rate of fire of 1,050 rounds per minute, and was fed from 60- or 96-round drums.

Up to the end of World War II, the gun had been without serious rival as the basic air-to-air weapon. German experimental work in the programme designed to produce an effective bomber weapon, though, had opened up several new possibilities in the design of guns and in the realization of effective air-to-air missiles, both guided and unguided.

Immediately after the end of the war, the victorious Allies started an intensive analysis of captured German experimental weapons, combined with an exhaustive study of German designers and extensive examination of documents, plans and the like. The results were not long in coming.

It would be hard to overestimate the profound effect that the MG213 series cannon had on Allied cannon designers. The design of the weapon had started in 1942 as a collaborative venture between Mauser and Krieghoff, under the design leadership of Dipl. Ing. Lindner. Although the weapon showed promise, various problems were encountered, and design and development work ceased in 1943. In 1944, however, the introduction of the revolving feed mechanism designed by Dr. Maier of the Mauser company led to the revival of the concept. The chief trouble now was that the barrel had an extremely short life thanks to the high rate of fire and gas pressure of the weapon. Barrel life was eventually raised from 150 to 359 rounds fired without break, and this was the stage reached with the weapon when the war ended. Allied designers were profoundly impressed with the MG213 in both its 20 and 30 mm forms.

In the short term, the weapons with which they had won the war seemed adequate to the Allied nations, the British continuing to rely on the 20 mm Hispano Mark 5, the USAAF (later USAF) with the 0.5 in (12.7 mm) Browning AN-M3, and the Russians with the 20 mm ShVAK, quickly supplemented by 23 mm NS (Nudelmann-Suranov) and 37 mm Nudelmann cannon. Of the world's major air forces, only that of the US Navy saw fit to upgrade its armament, the first generation of postwar aircraft having a quartet of 20 mm cannon in place of the earlier six 0.5 in (12.7 mm) machine-guns. But with the widespread introduction of jet engines immediately after the war, aircraft performance began to increase so rapidly that World War II gun armament would not suffice.

Here the example of the MG213 found a use, and in the early 1950s there appeared a number of 20 and 30 mm guns based on the concept pioneered in the German cannon: the American 20 mm M-39, the British 30 mm Aden, the French 30 mm DEFA (supplanting the 20 mm Hispano-Suiza HS404 and 30 mm HS603) and the Russian 30 mm NR-30 (Nudelmann-Rikter) cannon. The NR-30 very rapidly supplemented the 23 mm NS and NR (Nudelmann-Rikter), and 37 mm N cannon in the mid-1950s, especially in primary fighter aircraft.

Apart from the NR-30, the two most prolific members of this family since World War II have been the British Aden and the French DEFA 30 mm cannon. The Aden was developed jointly by the Armament Development Establishment (now the Royal Armament Research and Development Establishment) and the Royal Small Arms Factory at Enfield Lock (hence the name, from ADE and Enfield). Mounting is simple, with mounting points at the front and rear of the cradle holding the barrel and chamber unit, and the mechanism of the weapon is very safe. Gas tapped off from the barrel operates a slide which controls the revolving breech cylinder and ammunition feed sprockets, and the weapon cannot fire unless the cylinder is locked, with a round correctly positioned in line with the barrel. The current weapon is the Mark 4, which is $64\frac{1}{2}$ in (1,638 mm) long overall (barrel $42\frac{1}{2}$ in/1,080 mm) and weighs 192 lb (87 kg). This has a muzzle velocity of 2,590 ft (789 m) per second, and a rate of fire of 1,200 to 1,400 rounds per minute. The cocking of the weapon is effected pneumatically, and firing electrically. High explosive and armour-piercing rounds are currently available, and an armour-piercing incendiary round is under development. The French DEFA 553, the latest model of the line, is very similar to the Aden Mark 4, though lighter and with a slightly lower rate of fire (1,200 rounds per minute), but with provision for automatic recocking in the air. Ammunition is entirely interchangeable with that of the Aden. The model of the DEFA gun currently under final development is the DEFA 554, which weighs 187.4 lb (85 kg) and has a rate of fire of 1,800 rounds per minute. In general the DEFA cannon have the same method of operation, and the same safety features, as the Aden.

Two other European aircraft cannon are currently in service or about to enter service, the 27 mm weapon for the Panavia Tornado multi-role aircraft from the Mauser company of Oberndorf, and the Swiss Oerlikon 30 mm Type KCA cannon. The Mauser weapon, developed in conjunction with Diehl (ammunition) and Dynamit-Nobel (propellant and primer), was designed with five main requirements in mind: high muzzle velocity, great accuracy and reliability, identical ballistic characteristics for all types of ammunition, reliable operation of the fuse at large impact angles, and very small recoil distance. All these factors appear to have been incorporated in the definitive IKWA-Mauser cannon for the Tornado. The gun weighs 22.46 lb (100 kg) and is 90.94 in (2,310 mm) long overall, and was designed to be capable of firing armour-piercing high explosive incendiary, high explosive tracer, high explosive incendiary practice and target practice discarding-sabot rounds.

The Oerlikon Type KCA also used the Mauser revolving cylinder principle, but is unusual in firing a round having a propellant charge/projectile weight ratio of about 2:1, instead of the more usual ratio of about 3:2, giving a higher muzzle velocity despite the use of a heavier than usual projectile. The revolving cylinder has four chambers. Overall length is 77.8 in (1,976 mm) and weight 275.58 lb (125 kg). Each round weighs 1.98 lb (900 grams) complete, with the projectile weighing 12.72 ounces (360 grams), and such rounds are fired at the rate of 1,350 rounds per minute with a muzzle velocity of 3,379 ft (1,030 m) per second. Both the rate of fire and muzzle velocity figures are distinctly impressive, and perhaps foreshadow the way that future single-barrel gun development will move. The effect of such performance is that the gun is equally suitable for the air-to-air and air-to-surface roles, and is provided with ammunition accordingly.

The other major producer of cannon for air-to-air use is the United States of America. After the end of World War II, the Colt company designed the excellent Mauser-derived M-39 20 mm cannon, which was built by Pontiac and armed several types of American aircraft in the mid-1950s. In its definitive M-39E version, the gun had an unusually high rate of fire, in the order of 1,500 rounds per minute, and a muzzle velocity of 3,400 ft (1,036 m) per second, which the Americans considered to have marked the practical limits of aircraft gun development: a larger calibre would be useful for greater destructive power, but the reduction in rate of fire

would be unacceptable, American tactical doctrine, as always, stressing the importance of the number of strikes over the effectiveness of individual hits.

Although the Americans considered in the mid-1950s that the guided missile would soon come to replace the cannon as primary aircraft armament, they instituted Project Vulcan to investigate the possibility of higher rates of fire by a reversion to one of the oldest machine-gun principles, that used in the Gatling guns of the 1860s and 1870s: a number of barrels clamped together round a common axis, and fed by a breech rotated by an independent motor, with fixed cam followers loading, cocking, firing and emptying each barrel in turn. In the M61 Vulcan cannon, designed by the Aircraft Equipment Division of the General Electric Corporation, six barrels are clamped together near the muzzle, about two-fifths of the way up the barrel, and by the breech, and attached to the front of the breech rotor, which rotates anti-clockwise in a stationary housing. Within the breech mechanism, the cam followers operating the bolt mechanism of each barrel are actuated by an elliptical slot machined into the wall of the stationary rotor housing. As well as allowing an extremely high rate of fire, the Gatling-type mechanism is extremely reliable, and prolongs barrel life by a considerable margin.

The prototype T171E3 weighed 265 lb (120 kg) and produced a rate of fire of 7,200 rounds per minute (20 rounds per second per barrel, or 1,200 rounds per minute per barrel). However, the production M61A1, which is externally powered except in the GAU 4 variant (using gas tapped from four of

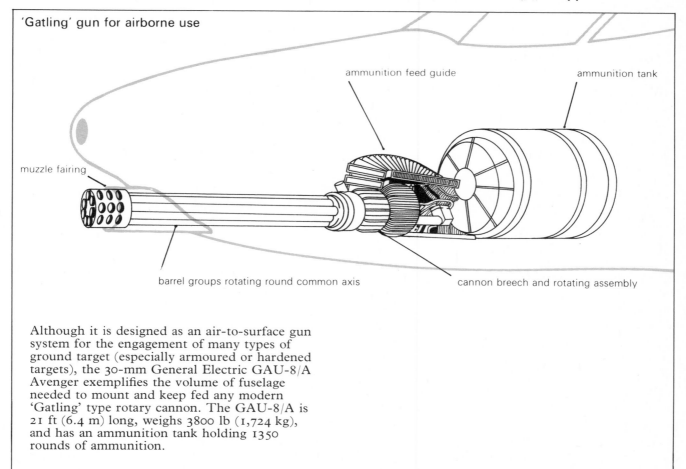

'Gatling' gun for airborne use

ammunition feed guide

ammunition tank

muzzle fairing

barrel groups rotating round common axis

cannon breech and rotating assembly

Although it is designed as an air-to-surface gun system for the engagement of many types of ground target (especially armoured or hardened targets), the 30-mm General Electric GAU-8/A Avenger exemplifies the volume of fuselage needed to mount and keep fed any modern 'Gatling' type rotary cannon. The GAU-8/A is 21 ft (6.4 m) long, weighs 3800 lb (1,724 kg), and has an ammunition tank holding 1350 rounds of ammunition.

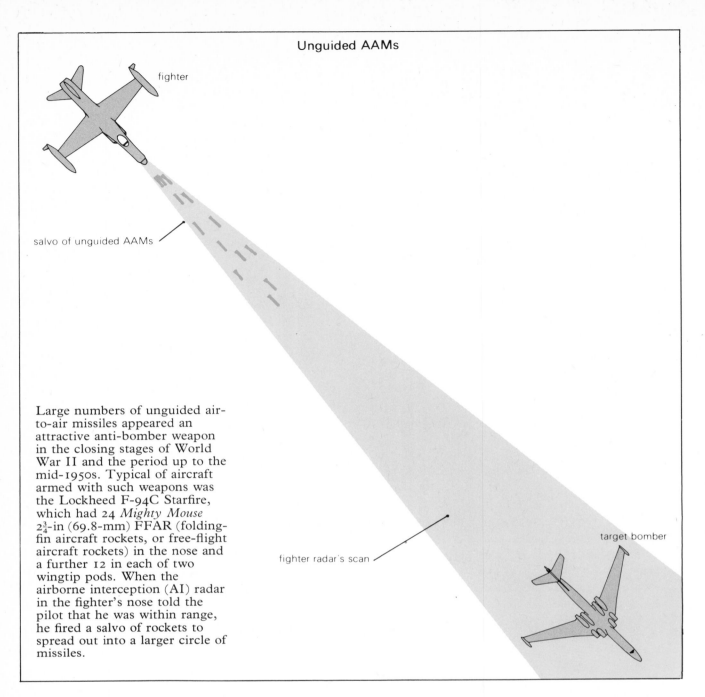

fighter

salvo of unguided AAMs

fighter radar's scan

target bomber

Large numbers of unguided air-to-air missiles appeared an attractive anti-bomber weapon in the closing stages of World War II and the period up to the mid-1950s. Typical of aircraft armed with such weapons was the Lockheed F-94C Starfire, which had 24 *Mighty Mouse* 2¾-in (69.8-mm) FFAR (folding-fin aircraft rockets, or free-flight aircraft rockets) in the nose and a further 12 in each of two wingtip pods. When the airborne interception (AI) radar in the fighter's nose told the pilot that he was within range, he fired a salvo of rockets to spread out into a larger circle of missiles.

the six barrels), has a standardized rate of 6,000 rounds per minute. The rotor motor requires about 20 hp, and though the standard drive is hydraulic, both mechanical and electric drives have been developed. The whole weapon is 73.82 in (1,875 mm) long and weighs 264.55 lb (120 kg). It takes 0.3 second to spin the barrels up to maximum rate, and 0.5 second to stop them, and the maximum possible rate of fire is 6,600 rounds per minute. The standard electrically-fired ammunition is of 20 mm calibre, weighing 8.834 ounces (250 grams) complete, and fires its 3.534 ounce (100 gram) projectile with a muzzle velocity of 3,400 ft (1,036 m) per second. A linkless feed system is used, its size, weight and other characteristics varying with the aircraft or pod in which the M61A1 is fitted.

With its aircraft of the 1950s intended primarily for air-to-air missile armament, the USAF thought in terms of podded Vulcans carried on external weapon pylons if necessary. When the need for gun armament was revealed by the Vietnam conflict in the 1960s, the podded method was tried and proved

useful, but not the best way to use the highly accurate Vulcan. Part of the trouble was that the considerable recoil force of the weapon (3,990 lb/1,810 kg) made the pod shudder slightly. Many user aircraft were therefore modified to accept a Vulcan internally, with highly beneficial results. Among current types equipped with this formidable weapon are the General Dynamics F-111, the Lockheed F-104 Star-fighter, the LTV (Vought) A-7 Corsair II, the Mc-Donnell Douglas F-4 Phantom II, the Republic F-105 Thunderchief, as well as the latest generation of fighters such as the F-14, F-15, F-16 and F-18.

Variations on the theme include the M197 20 mm three-barrel, the XM188 30 mm three-barrel, the M134/GAU 2B/A 0.3 in (7.62 mm) six-barrel Minigun, and other experimental air-to-air weapons, all designed by General Electric. The same principle is used in a number of air-to-ground weapons such as the Hughes XM230 30 mm Chain Gun and the General Electric XM-214 0.219 in (5.56 mm) machine-gun.

Another interesting weapon, used mostly in the

ground-attack role by the McDonnell Douglas A-4 Skyhawk but also capable of air-to-air application, is the Hughes Mark 11 Model 5 twin-barrel gun and its associated Mark 4 Model 0 pod. The Mark 11 Model 5 gun consists of five major assemblies: the breech, the receiver, the revolver cylinder, one Mark 19 Model 3 barrel and one Mark 20 Model 3 barrel. Air-cooled, the gun is operated by a combination of gas tapped from the barrels and gun recoil. Electrically-fired ammunition is fed into the eight-chamber revolver cylinder from two belts, while at the same time the gun fires two rounds, ejects the cases of the previous two rounds, and rams the forth-coming two rounds. Unlike the M61A1, this 20 mm weapon reaches its full rate of fire almost instantaneously (0.003 second). The gun is $78\frac{1}{3}$ in (1,990 mm) long with its loader, weighs 240 lb (108.86 kg) complete, has two basic rates of fire (700 and 4,200 rounds per minute), and has an average recoil of 2,500 lb (1,134 kg).

The Russians have the GSh-23 twin-barrel gun (3,000 rounds per minute) and a six-barrel 23 mm cannon. The other main type of weapon used for air-to-air fighters since World War II has been the missile, either unguided (early) or guided (later). With aircraft speeds increasing so rapidly in the years immediately after the war, as new types

powered by turbojets entered service, most air forces realized that guided missiles of the X-4 type, with guidance commands transmitted through wire by a controller in the launch aircraft, were impractical. Therefore an entirely new type of guided missile, containing its own seeking warhead package, had to be developed, using either the heat (infra-red) emissions of the target's jet engine or the radar reflections of the target as the source on which to home. Inevitably, such a process would take time, especially as miniaturization of the type necessary to produce an air-to-air missile of reasonably small proportions and weight was still very much in its infancy.

In the short term, therefore, unguided missiles seemed to offer the optimum solution: small, but highly lethal, such missiles could be carried in considerable numbers and launched in salvos against the target, the flat, high-velocity trajectory of the missiles giving a good success rate. Although the concept had originated with the Russian RS-82, the postwar idea was derived more closely from the German R4M missiles.

Among Russian missiles of this type are the S-5, with a diameter of 2.165 in (55 mm) and capable of use in the anti-tank, decoy, anti-aircraft and anti-personnel roles depending on the warhead fitted

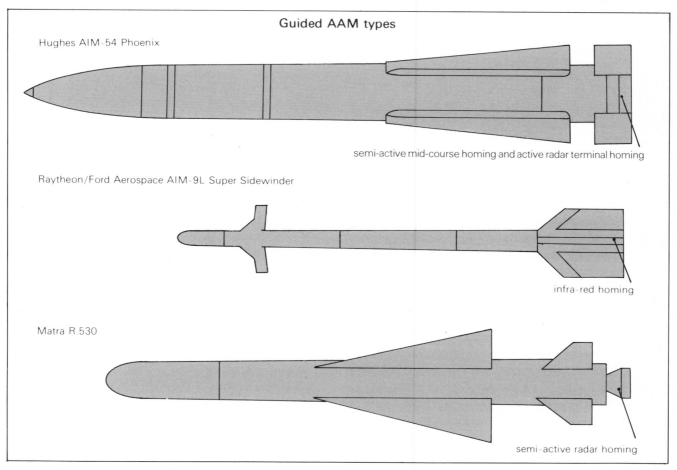

Guided AAM types

Hughes AIM-54 Phoenix

semi-active mid-course homing and active radar terminal homing

Raytheon/Ford Aerospace AIM-9L Super Sidewinder

infra-red homing

Matra R.530

semi-active radar homing

Guided air-to-air missiles (AAMs) fall into three main categories, depending upon their method of guidance. (*Top*) is the Hughes AIM-54 Phoenix long-range weapon, which has semi-active radar homing for the cruise phase of its flight and active radar terminal homing (detonation being by proximity or infra-red fusing). (*Centre*) is the Raytheon/Ford Aerospace AIM-9L Super Sidewinder dogfighting missile which has conical-scan infra-red homing. (*Bottom*) is the Matra R.530 all-aspect missile which has alternative infra-red or semi-active radar homing heads. (The three types are therefore IR, which homes on the target aircraft's heat emission; active radar, which homes on radar reflections from the target aircraft generated by radar pulses from the missile; and semi-active radar, which homes on radar reflections from the target aircraft.)

(fired from 8, 16, 19 or 32 tube launchers of 2.44 in/ 57 mm internal diameter with the designations UV-8-57, UV-16-57, UV-19-57 and UV-32-57); the M-100 of 5.39 in (137 mm) diameter and weighing 34.39 lb (15.6 kg); and other types with diameters of 6.3, 7.48, 8.35, 8.66, 9.45 and 12.8 in (160, 190, 212, 220, 240 and 325 mm), used for ground-attack work.

The Americans produced a similar type of missile, the $2\frac{3}{4}$ in (69.85 mm) Mighty Mouse, which formed the primary armament of fighters such as the Lockheed F-94 Starfire (48 rockets in the nose and two wingtip pods), the Northrop F-89 Scorpion (42 rockets in two wingtip pods), the North American F-86D Sabre (24 rockets in a retractable 'bin' under the cockpit), the Avro Canada CF-100 (104 rockets in two wingtip pods), and the Convair F-102 Delta Dagger (24 rockets in the weapons bay). The Mighty Mouse, more properly called the FFAR (Folding-Fin Aircraft Rocket), packs a very considerable punch, but suffers from the inherent disadvantage of all unguided missiles, in that it cannot alter course if the target manages to spot the attack and take immediate evasive action. In its original role as a salvo-launched missile for defence against heavy bombers operating in tight boxes, however, the Mighty Mouse could have been effective. The 2.75 in FFAR has now been relegated to the ground-attack role, where it has proved devastating. The LAU series of pods is used to carry the FFAR: the LAU-3A/B carries 19 rockets, -59A 7 rockets, -61A 19 rockets, -68A 7 rockets and -69A 19 rockets, while the M157/A/B carries 7 rockets as does the M159/A/B/C. The FFAR is also widely used in its ground-attack role by a number of the USA's allies.

Among the other nations to develop air-to-air rockets were the United Kingdom (2 in/50.8 mm folding-fin rocket) and France. The latter's MATRA 2.68 in (68 mm) SNEB rocket was developed as an air-to-air and air-to-surface rocket with a number of warheads suiting it to different roles. The model intended for air-to-air use is the 251P, which is 33.35 in (847 mm) long and weighs 9.48 lb (4.3 kg). The rocket's velocity is 1,790 mph (2,880 kph), and its blast warhead weighs 2.3 lb (1.05 kg). Other types of the widely used SNEB rocket are discussed in the air-to-surface armament section.

Such unguided missiles were only an interim measure, and were replaced in the middle of the 1950s by the first service examples of air-to-air guided missiles. These have since undergone an enormous amount of development, making them extremely formidable weapons. Air-to-air guided missiles fall into two main categories, depending on the type of guidance principle used: active homing guidance, in which the missile itself contains the means of illuminating the target and the relevant receiver; and passive homing guidance, in which the missile contains a receiver for the target's natural radiation. There is also semi-active homing guidance, a halfway system in which the missile contains a receiver for radiation from a target illuminated by a source other than the missile itself. For air-to-air

purposes, the two most useful types of radiation are infra-red (heat) and radar reflection.

Unlike the unguided missile, which is committed to a dynamic course so long as its motor burns, and then a purely ballistic course derived from its shape and mass, the guided missile is capable of 'decision making' after it has left the launch aircraft. The missile's sensors try to keep a constant watch on the target, and alter its course to ensure its arrival in the vicinity of the target. To this end, more modern missiles have been fitted with more sensitive sensors, improved computing ability and more advanced aerodynamics. These improvements allow them to follow an aircraft taking evasive tactics or trying to blot or confuse the missile's sensors with decoys and electronic countermeasures.

Two missiles, the Raytheon AIM-7 Sparrow and the Naval Ordnance Test Station AIM-9 Sidewinder, have been in production during most of the air-to-air guided missile's history, and provide an illuminating history of air-to-air guided missiles in the development of their various marks. Other missiles, such as the Hughes AIM-4 and -26 Falcon, have been in service as long, but have not undergone quite so many modifications in the constant search to keep the missile abreast of the opposing technology.

The Sparrow was first considered at the end of World War II, and the first prototype examples of the Sparrow I began test firings in 1949. The missile entered service in the early 1950s, and proved an immediate success with its relatively long range and semi-active radar homing. In 1958 the current Sparrow III entered service to improve on the performance and all-attitude attack capabilities of earlier AIM-7C and -7D, the -7A and -7B not having been operational models. The AIM-7E is controlled by a continuous-wave semi-active radar homing package, is 144 in (2,895 mm) long, 8 in (203 mm) in diameter, 40 in (1,016 mm) in span across the wings, and weighs 450 lb (204 kg). Powered by an Aerojet Mark 52 Model 2 or Rocketdyne Mark 38 Model 4 single-thrust solid-propellant rocket, the AIM-7E has a speed of Mach 3.7 and a range of 15 miles (25 km). To go with its more effective seeker head, the AIM-7E had a 66 lb (30 kg) continuous rod HE warhead in place of earlier models' HE blast/ fragmentation warhead. Fusing is either impact or proximity.

The AIM-7E-2 variant is a slightly improved model with plug-in fins requiring no tools for fitting or removal, and enhanced dogfighting capability.

Derived from the AIM-7E is the AIM-7F, which entered production in 1976: this has the same dimensions as the AIM-7E, but weighs 500 lb (227 kg). Performance is maintained at the same figures as the lighter AIM-7E by the use of the more powerful Hercules Mark 48 Model 0 or Aerojet Mark 65 Model 0 dual-thrust solid-propellant rocket. The missile is also designed for greater dogfighting agility, with the ability to manoeuvre in pursuit of aircraft pulling 7g manoeuvres. It is in the electronics,

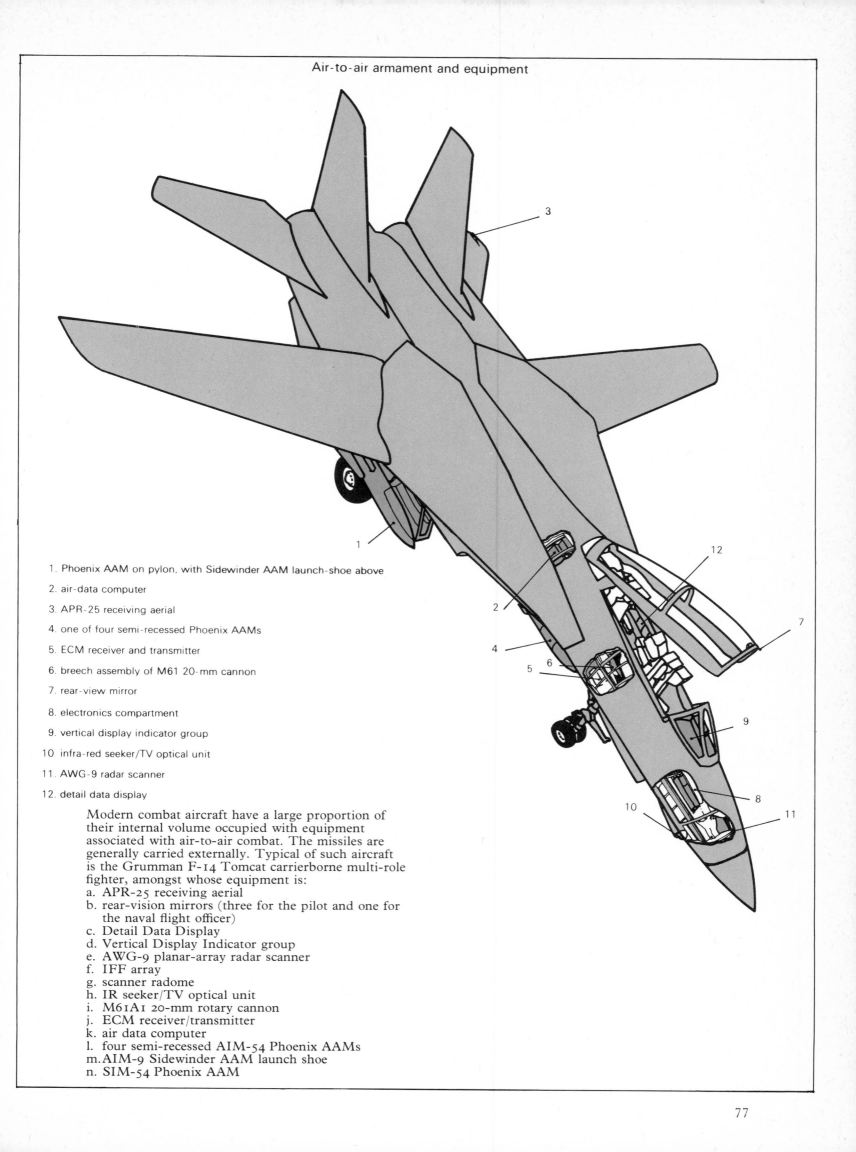

1. Phoenix AAM on pylon, with Sidewinder AAM launch-shoe above

2. air-data computer

3. APR-25 receiving aerial

4. one of four semi-recessed Phoenix AAMs

5. ECM receiver and transmitter

6. breech assembly of M61 20-mm cannon

7. rear-view mirror

8. electronics compartment

9. vertical display indicator group

10 infra-red seeker/TV optical unit

11. AWG-9 radar scanner

12. detail data display

Modern combat aircraft have a large proportion of their internal volume occupied with equipment associated with air-to-air combat. The missiles are generally carried externally. Typical of such aircraft is the Grumman F-14 Tomcat carrierborne multi-role fighter, amongst whose equipment is:

a. APR-25 receiving aerial
b. rear-vision mirrors (three for the pilot and one for the naval flight officer)
c. Detail Data Display
d. Vertical Display Indicator group
e. AWG-9 planar-array radar scanner
f. IFF array
g. scanner radome
h. IR seeker/TV optical unit
i. M61A1 20-mm rotary cannon
j. ECM receiver/transmitter
k. air data computer
l. four semi-recessed AIM-54 Phoenix AAMs
m. AIM-9 Sidewinder AAM launch shoe
n. SIM-54 Phoenix AAM

though, that most of the AIM-7F's superiority to the AIM-7E is to be found. All solid-state electronics are used; the lock-on to the target is improved even in the presence of 10-dB look-down clutter; and the continuous-wave radar has pulse-doppler compatibility. Range is slightly superior to that of the AIM-7E at 28 miles (44 km), and the lethality of the missile had been increased by fitting an 88 lb (40 kg) continuous-rod HE warhead with better fusing arrangements. Although the electronic counter-countermeasures capability of the AIM-7F is limited as a result of its conical-scan seeker, a monopulse seeker has been tested successfully and will be fitted retrospectively as well as in later models. The net effect is that the AIM-7F is a highly effective all-attitude missile capable of all-altitude operation. The Sparrow III, in its AIM-7E/F version, forms the basis of the British Hawker Siddeley Dynamics Sky Flash missile, which has proved exceptionally capable, even in snap-down and snap-up firings.

The AIM-9 Sidewinder is altogether a different type of missile, being intended initially only for pursuit-course attacks, and so fitted with an infra-red seeker head that locks on to the hot exhaust of a turbojet engine from the rear, its most 'visible' angle. The Sidewinder was developed very cheaply and quickly, and can lay undoubted claim to the title of being the most cost-effective missile yet produced. Designed by the Naval Ordnance Test Station (now the Naval Weapons Center), the Sidewinder was test-fired for the first time in 1953 as the AIM-9A. The type entered large-scale production with minimal modifications as the AIM-9B Sidewinder 1A at Philco (now Ford Aerospace) and General Electric, and entered service in 1956. More than 60,000 examples of the AIM-9B were made between 1955 and 1962. The AIM-9B is $111\frac{1}{2}$ in (2,832 mm) long, 5 in (127 mm) in diameter and 22 in (559 mm) in span across the tail. The missile weighs 165 lb (74.84 kg) and is powered by a Naval Propellant Plant solid-propellant rocket, giving the AIM-9B a speed of Mach 2, a range of 1,100 yards (1,006 m) at sea level, and an operating altitude between sea level and 36,000 ft (10,973 m). The warhead weighs 25 lb (11.34 kg) and is of the high explosive blast type, fitted with a proximity fuse. The AIM-9B has also been made in Germany with a FGW *Modell* 2 seeker head. This uses cooled infra-red detectors to increase their sensitivity and so improve performance in adverse conditions or bright sunlight.

The AIM-9B Sidewinder 1A was followed by the AIM-9C Sidewinder 1C and AIM-9D Sidewinder 1C, which were derived from the AIM-9B with basic improvements to the seeker head, and entered service in 1965. The missiles are $114\frac{1}{2}$ in (2,908 mm) long, 5 in (127 mm) in diameter, and 25 in (635 mm) in span across the fins. Weight is 185 lb (83.9 kg), but a more powerful engine, the Rocketdyne Mark 36 Model 5 solid-propellant rocket, gives a speed of Mach 2.5 and a range of over 2 miles (3.7 km). A proximity-fused HE blast warhead is used. The main difference between the AIM-9C and AIM-9D lies in

their seeker heads, the former having a Motorola semi-active radar head and the latter a Philco or Raytheon infra-red head. The Motorola head can operate either on the ECM activity of the target, or on target reflections from an illuminating radar. The AIM-9D has a continuous-rod warhead with impact and proximity fuses.

Next model of the AIM-9 series was the AIM-9E, basically an improved version of the AIM-9B with a better infra-red seeker head and other modifications to improve low-altitude performance, hence the alternative designation Sidewinder LAP. Power is provided by a Thiokol Mark 17 solid-propellant rocket. All AIM-9Es are probably updated AIM-9Bs.

The AIM-9G, -9H and -9J are all basically similar. The AIM-9G has a vacuum tube and the Sidewinder Expanded Acquisition Mode system, which helps to give the missile, based on the AIM-9D, a considerably enhanced lead-acquisition capability. The AIM-9H is a 1970 version of the AIM-9G for the US Navy, with solid-state electronics and provision for close range dogfighting: the target can be acquired off the aircraft's boresight, the seeker head (fitted with SEAM) has faster angle tracking rates, and minimum range has been reduced. The AIM-9H is 113 in (2,870 mm) long, 5 in (127 mm) in diameter and $24\frac{3}{4}$ in (629 mm) in span across the fins. Launch weight is 190 lb (86.2 kg), and though speed remains the same at Mach 2.5, range has been increased to between 6.2 and 11 miles (10 to 18 km). The AIM-9J is an improved version of the AIM-9E, itself a modified version of the initial AIM-9B Sidewinder. The same infra-red seeker head as that in the AIM-9E is used, but high-power servo controls are used for the modified long-span canard control surfaces near the nose of the missile to improve dogfighting ability by a considerable margin. All AIM-9Js were produced between 1977 and 1978 by conversion of surviving AIM-9Bs. There is also a modified version of the AIM-9J, built from scratch as the AIM-9J-1. This has solid-state electronics and the same fuse as the AIM-9L, and has the ability, only just appearing in infra-red seeking missiles, to attack from any angle. Some AIM-9J-1 missiles are converted AIM-9Es and AIM-9Js, and all are scheduled for delivery between 1978 and 1980.

The latest version of the Sidewinder, and the first 'third-generation' model of the basic design, is the AIM-9L Super Sidewinder. This is designed for all-aspect dogfighting missions, and is, in effect, a new design using the same configuration and dimensions as earlier models. Dimensions, weight, performance figures and some other details are the same as those of the AIM-9H, but the AIM-9L is powered by a Rocketdyne/Bermite Mark 36 Model 6 solid-propellant rocket. The one feature which distinguishes the AIM-9L from its predecessors is the double-delta, rather than triangular, shape of the canard planes, which are also of greater span than the canards of earlier models. Operated by powerful servo controls, these foreplanes give the AIM-9L exceptional dog-

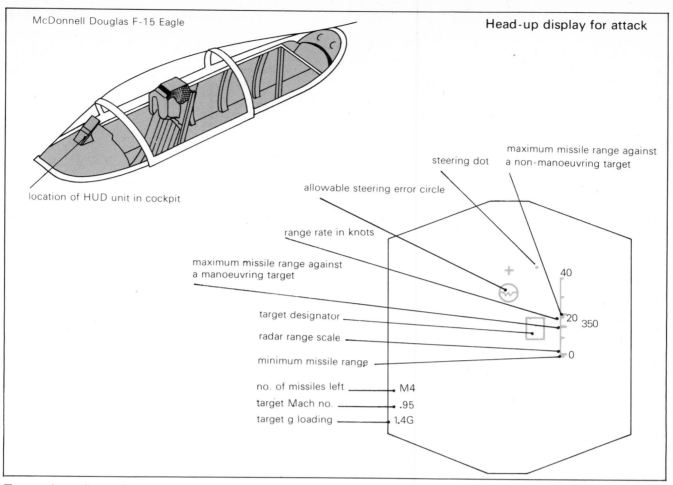

McDonnell Douglas F-15 Eagle

Head-up display for attack

location of HUD unit in cockpit

steering dot

maximum missile range against a non-manoeuvring target

allowable steering error circle

range rate in knots

maximum missile range against a manoeuvring target

target designator

radar range scale

minimum missile range

no. of missiles left — M4

target Mach no. — .95

target g loading — 1.4G

40

20 350

0

For modern air-to-air and air-to-ground combat at high speed there has been developed a means of providing the pilot with attack/flight information in simple form, reflected on a glass behind the windscreen. This is generally known as a head-up display (HUD). In the example here, showing the location of the unit in the cockpit of a McDonnell Douglas F-15 Eagle, the following information is displayed, the pilot having rejected the radar search mode and normal scales in favour of the radar tracking mode and a symbolized display of attack information:

1. on the left, the printed matter informs the pilot that he has four missiles available on his external pylons, that the target is moving at Mach 0.95 and that it is also pulling 1.4 g.
2. the symbolic displays indicate course, target, range and allowable steering error, while the figure between the target designator box and the radar range scale indicates the range rate in knots.

fighting capability. Internally, the seeker head is totally new: though still an infra-red seeker unit, it features AM-FM conical scan with increased sensitivity and tracking stability.

Other air-to-air missiles carried by US aircraft are the Hughes AIM-4D Falcon with an HE warhead and infra-red homing, the AIM-4 AIM-4E/F Super Falcon with HE warheads and continuous-wave semi-active radar homing, the AIM-4G Super Falcon with an HE warhead and infra-red homing, the AIM-26B Falcon with an enlarged HE warhead and semi-active radar homing (the AIM-26A Nuclear Falcon had a 1.5 kiloton nuclear warhead), and the McDonnell Douglas AIR-2A Genie with a 1.5 kiloton nuclear warhead but no guidance.

Other missiles for the air-to-air role used round the world are: the French Matra R.511 semi-active radar air interception missile, the Matra R.530 semi-active radar/infra-red all-weather all-aspect missile, the Matra Super 530 electro-magnetic homing improved-performance version of the R.530, and the Matra R.550 Magic infra-red close-combat dogfighting missile; the Israeli Rafael Shafrir infra-red high-performance interception missile with good dogfighting capabilities; the Italian Selenia Aspide

semi-active radar multi-role missile; the Japanese Mitsubishi AAM-1 infra-red interceptor missile; the British Hawker Siddeley Dynamics (now part of British Aerospace) Firestreak infra-red rear-hemisphere pursuit missile, Red Top infra-red all-aspect interception missile, and Sky Flash semi-active radar, all-weather, all-aspect dogfighting missile; and the Russian AA-1 to AA-8 missiles.

The most advanced air-to-air missile currently in service is the Hughes AIM-54A Phoenix. This is a long-range high-performance missile designed for use on the F-111B but now used only on the Grumman F-14 fleet defence aircraft of the US Navy. All modern missiles make extensive use of radar in the initial stages of any combat, to detect, plot and identify all aircraft in the vicinity. The aircraft's onboard weapons system/tactical computer then controls the 'acquisition' of the target, selecting the right type of target within the performance parameters of the missiles carried (in the more sophisticated aircraft, at least two), locking the missile's seeker head onto the given target and launching the missile at the optimum interception range and attitude.

The combination of these factors and an advanced

missile has reached, currently, its highest form in the missile system of the Grumman F-14 Tomcat: the Hughes AWG-9 fire control and armament system (also known as the airborne missile control system) in conjunction with the Hughes AIM-54A Phoenix missile. The AWG-9 system is a highly effective and versatile system capable of controlling the launch of Sidewinder and Sparrow missiles, and the use of the M61A1 rotary cannon.

The AWG-9 radar system is based on the use of a 36 in (914.4 mm) radar scanner, which is unusual in being a slotted flat plate rather than the more common parabolic type. This is apparently less susceptible to certain types of jamming than a parabolic antenna of the same diameter, has a higher gain, and can mount IFF (identification, friend or foe) equipment for simple assessment of possible targets. For long-range search the AWG-9's pulse-doppler search mode is used, providing range/rate information at ranges in excess of 125 miles (201 km) for targets with a radar cross-section of 50 sq ft (4.645 m^2), about the size of an average fighter. The planar antenna array allows great flexibility in this search, both in elevation and azimuth, and has excellent look-down capability to detect targets against ground 'clutter'. The range-while-search mode can also be used, providing the onboard digital computer with accurate range and bearing inputs. For assessments of multiple targets, one of the AWG-9's most important accomplishments, the track-while-scan mode is used. This can detect and track multiple targets at ranges in excess of 60 miles (97 km), allowing the aircraft to engage six with missiles fired from a range of 55 miles (88.5 km). In the track-while-scan mode the AWG-9's computer assesses all the targets available and decides their 'threat priority number' based on their ranges, closing speeds and course in relation to the radar scan volume. The computer can store the information about the most threatening 24 targets for comparison with later information.

The longest firing range is for a single missile, using the pulse-doppler single-target track mode. This locks on to the target at more than 80 miles (129 km), and provides the computer with range, range/rate and bearing data for the launch of one missile at over 65 mile (105 km) range. In addition to this velocity/track capability, the AWG-9's pulse-doppler single-target track mode also has a jam angle track facility to provide rate and bearing information on targets using electronic countermeasures. This mode also 'slaves in' the electro-optical (infra-red) sensor subsystem, which has superior angular resolution of single/multiple blips.

For closer ranges, the radar has normal pulse mode availability instead of pulse-doppler operation. In this mode, the radar provides the Control Data Corporation high-speed, large-memory general-purpose digital computer with range and range/rate inputs, and closes a 'tracking gate' round the target.

Control of the AWG-9 weapons system is entrusted to the F-14's naval flight officer, seated behind the pilot. This officer is provided with information from the radar and infra-red sensors (the latter able to discriminate closely grouped targets which the radar might identify as a single target, or to continue high-altitude surveillance while the radar is tied up with low-level tracking) on a 5 in (127 mm) detail data display, while computer-processed information is available on the 10 in (254 mm) tactical information display, which can also show information received by the computer from other aircraft or ships by means of the Mark 4 tactical data link. The tactical information display provides the naval flight officer with tabulated information and recommandations on target priority, which the officer can override, and indicates the optimum time for missile launch.

The AIM-54 Phoenix is 13 ft (3.96 m) long, 15 in (381 mm) in diameter, and 36 in (914 mm) in span across the wings. Launch weight is 985 lb (446.8 kg), and power is provided by a Rocketdyne Mark 47 Model o or Aerojet Mark 60 Model o long-burn solid-propellant motor, giving the AIM-54 a speed in excess of Mach 4, a flight time of 3 minutes at this speed, and a range of more than 130 miles (209 km). The warhead is of the continuous-rod HE type, weighing 132 lb (64.5 kg) and detonated by impact, doppler, Bendix infra-red or Mark 334 proximity fuses. The AIM-54 has a complex, but very effective guidance sequence: for a long-range mission the missile's initial course is preprogrammed by the aircraft computer; at the mid-course point semi-active radar is switched on, and the missile homes on target reflections produced by the aircraft's radar, or on the electronic countermeasures radiation of the target; in the terminal homing phase the seeker head guides the missile with pulse-doppler active radar.

The Phoenix is highly manoeuvrable, largely as a result of its low drag and rear-mounted control surfaces, and has performed 17g manoeuvres in pursuit of a target pulling 6g.

The capability of the AIM-54/AWG-9 combination can be showed by the results of a test launch of six missiles in November 1973: in the course of 38 seconds six missiles were fired at six targets over a range between 30 and 50 miles (48.3 and 80.5 km); two Lockheed QT-33 drones were destroyed by the unarmed missiles, while a subsonic Teledyne Ryan BQM-34A and supersonic Teledyne Ryan BQM-34E were damaged by direct hits, and the last two missiles failed to score, one suffering an internal failure and the other being unable to follow its BQM-34 target when the latter malfunctioned. Other tests have revealed the AIM-54's ability to intercept at altitudes in excess of 80,000 ft (24,384 m) below 50 ft (15.25 m), targets flying at Mach 2.7, targets up to 10 miles (16 km) apart, and targets within 300 yards (274 m) of each other.

The current models are the AIM-54A initial production variant and the AIM-54B improved model with greater reliability, digital guidance equipment and sheet metal aerodynamic surfaces. Currently under development is the AIM-54C, with improved ECCM capability.

Between the Wars

Supposedly the 'war to end all wars', World War I was immediately followed by a number of conflicts of varying sizes and in varying parts of the world. The main protagonists of World War I, however, immediately set about demobilizing their vast armed forces, and cutting back all manner of expenditure on matters military. Thus France, Great Britain, Italy and the United States had by the early 1920s reverted to relatively small peacetime forces, equipped with aircraft left over from the war, or developed in the closing stages of that conflict. With money in very short supply as a result of a postwar financial retrenchment, the armed forces had to accept that for some time to come their equipment would have to remain substantially unaltered, while the few resources of the military were channeled into research and development. This applied most strongly to the air services, where the pace of technological advance was the swiftest: it was clearly beyond the financial reach of most air forces to develop new combat aircraft and then purchase them in significant numbers, so most countries opted for the development of a few advanced types, to keep up with the latest technological advances, while equipping the forces initially with World War I types, and then with limited numbers of aircraft of a more advanced nature.

Air operations played a not inconsiderable part in the course of the Russian Civil War (1917–1922), in which the Bolshevik regime ('Reds') strove to secure its position in Russia against the counter-revolutionary efforts of the 'Whites', supported by their 'interventionist' allies. The two main theatres to see air activity of a more than sporadic nature were in the north, where a British contingent had arrived in Murmansk in May 1918 to prevent Allied

stores to Russia falling into Red hands and to prevent the Germans from using the port as a U-boat base, and in the south, where the opening of the Dardanelles after the surrender of Turkey allowed British, French and American forces to arrive to support the local White forces.

In the north, an RAF detachment co-operated with White units, which all used British equipment as well as remnants from the Tsarist air service, in an advance from Murmansk to Archangel, which fell in August 1918. However, it was in the south that the main air fighting occurred, for here British bomber and fighter forces supported the effort of Denikin's White forces to drive up the Don river on Moscow from the Black Sea coast. The RAF units, equipped with de Havilland bombers and Camel fighters, at first had an easy and successful time of it, harassing the Red forces on the ground with machine-gun fire and bombs. Gradually, though, the strengthening Red air force began to make its presence felt, most of its aircraft being relics of the Tsarist service. At least two RAF pilots claimed five victories in the sector, and one Red pilot may have shot down as many as 13 White and allied aircraft. The 'interventionist' forces gradually pulled out as a result of political pressures at home, leaving the numerically superior but hopelessly inefficient and divided White armies to be slowly beaten by the Reds.

While still involved in their civil war, the Reds became involved in a war with newly independent Poland, which had seized various Polish speaking areas of Russia proper during 1918 and 1919, and then come to blows with the Ukraine, which had taken the opportunity in the confusion reigning towards the end of World War I to declare itself independent of Russia. During April 1919 the Poles had

launched a major offensive into the Ukraine with the help of Polish troops trained in and equipped by France during World War I. By this time the Poles had 40 aircraft, and soon received another 110 French aircraft as well as ordering about 400 more aircraft from France, Great Britain and Italy. However, before the Poles could consolidate their position in the Ukraine, the Reds invaded the country, and faced with two evils, the Ukrainians sided with the Poles, thereby bringing Poland and Soviet Russia into direct confrontation.

In April 1920, the Poles launched an offensive into the Russian-occupied Ukraine, with Kiev as the main objective. The Poles had some 130 aircraft, deployed mainly in the north and south, while the Russians had about the same number of aircraft, with about one-third of them, manned by the best pilots, in the centre-north sector from which they planned to launch their offensive on Warsaw. The Poles were first off the mark, with General Josef Pilsudski's southern forces attacking on 25 April 1920 and taking Kiev on 7 May. Here the Poles ran out of logistical backing, which would have enabled them to strike the left rear of the main Russian build-up under Marshal Mikhail Tukhachevsky. A week after the fall of Kiev, these main Russian forces drove forwards on Warsaw, while cavalry forces under General Semyon Budenny pinned Pilsudski and drove on Lvov. There was initially little that the Poles could do, especially in the air where serviceability rather than combat losses had reduced Polish strength to about 30 aircraft. Russia had perhaps less aircraft, for the same reason. However, at Poland's darkest hour, supplies of new aircraft began to arrive, notably Bristol F 2B Fighters from Great Britain. These were

Bristol F 2B Fighters, despite their World War I provenance, soldiered on into the early 1930s in roles such as reconnaissance and light bombing for policing remote areas of the British empire, such as the north-west frontier of India, Iraq, Sudan and other areas of Africa.

thrown into the fray immediately, and had an important part in the checking of Budenny's cavalry thrust in the south: between 16 and 18 August 1920, about 15 Polish aircraft flew nearly 200 sorties, firing 27,000 rounds of machine-gun ammunition and dropping 17,637 lb (8,000 kg) of bombs. Meanwhile, further north, Pilsudski had counterattacked the Russian centre and broken through with the aid of a few more aircraft. The Russians, having outrun their supplies and with their lines of communication cut to pieces, fell back in disorder as far as Brest-Litovsk.

With both sides exhausted, a temporary lull fell, to be ended on 12 September 1920 as the Poles once again pushed forward to the north and south of the Pripet Marshes. Hostilities finally ended with an armistice on 12 October, and by the Treaty of Riga on 18 March 1921 the Russians ceded all the territory claimed by the Poles. During this war to secure the independence of Poland, air fighting had been minimal, both sides concentrating their efforts on ground-attack work.

For the victors of World War I, faced with the task of trying to re-establish the economies of their countries on the basis of peacetime requirements, financial cuts in the budgets of the armed forces seemed only reasonable. To the commanders of the armed forces involved, most cuts seemed to be excessive, and so any and every means of justifying a fuller budget was seized. During the 1920s and early 1930s, such opportunities for the air forces arose from the need for 'imperial policing', which could be achieved by aircraft and a small number of troops more efficiently and swiftly, and thus more economically, than a larger number of troops without air support. Such 'policing' came to play an increasingly important part in the work of the air forces of countries with imperial holdings or mandates in North Africa, the Middle East and other sparsely populated and underdeveloped parts of the world. Yet the notion was not a novel one in the 1920s, for even before World War I the French and Spanish had used aircraft in their pacification of North Africa, the Italians had found use for aircraft in a similar role in Libya, and the British had used aircraft to keep in check dissident Mesopotamian and Persian tribesmen.

However, these operations may be regarded as exploratory, and the first proper use of aircraft for policing occurred in the 3rd Afghan War (1919). Six squadrons of British aircraft were used to provide reconnaissance and ground-support for the army units making the punitive expedition into the country, and missions were flown against concentrations of tribal levies.

At the same time, British aircraft were also involved in suppressing Arab revolts in Iraq and Persia. In Iraq alone, between 1919 and 1920, the army deployed 120,000 men and the RAF some four squadrons of De Havilland 9A bombers. About 100 tons (101.6 tonnes) of bombs were dropped, and many thousands of rounds of machine-gun ammunition fired by the RAF, for the loss of 11 aircraft to small-arms fire, and damage to another 57 aircraft. Yet the activities of the aircraft, which bestowed considerable tactical flexibility on the British effort, were recognized as being vital in the suppression of similar revolts. Accordingly, in 1922 the RAF, under the local command of Air Vice-Marshal Sir John Salmond, assumed overall control of Iraq. The concept of 'air policing' then began to show its real virtues as a method of keeping the peace, and British aircraft played an important role in North-West India, Iraq, Transjordan, Sudan and other trouble spots in the area.

Other countries to use aircraft in a similar fashion were the French and Spanish in North Africa, where the revolt of the Moroccan leader Abd-el-Krim was defeated in Spanish Morocco in 1926, and in French Morocco at the end of 1934. In both these campaigns, in which the colonial powers co-operated with each other, widespread use was made of aircraft in an effort to whittle down the rebel leader's forces and penalize those who dared to join him.

During the same period, moreover, the Italians came to rely heavily on the punitive aspect of air policing in their constant trouble with dissident elements in Libya and Italian Somaliland. Whereas the Spanish and French had used mainly two-seater aircraft such as the Bristol F 2B Fighter, the De Havilland 4 and 9 bombers, the Breguet 14 and the Potez 25. The Italians, on the other hand, made use of two-seaters such as the Fokker C.V and the Meridionali Ro 1, but also of three-engined bomber/transport types such as the Caproni Ca 101 and 133.

The USA also indulged in 'colonial' policing operations, to support regimes friendly to the US and to try to maintain stability in the notoriously unstable central American and Caribbean republics: the Dominican Republic (1919–1924), Haiti (1915–1934) and Nicaragua (1925–1933).

Throughout the 1920s and early 1930s, therefore, imperial policing by aircraft played an important part in maintaining and even improving air forces' positions in relation to their countries' armies and navies. However, it should be noted that in many ways such air operations were counterproductive: in local terms, because bombing and machine-gunning of suspected hostile villages and camps raised great resentment against the colonial power; and in overall terms, because many air forces became convinced of the value of dual-purpose aircraft such as bomber/transports and reconnaissance/light attack types.

During the 1920s, the theory that strategic bombing would be the arbiter of the next war slowly gained ground thanks to the efforts of men such as Sir Hugh Trenchard, who had become Chief of the Air Staff again on 11 January 1919, and General Giulio Douhet. The notion was fostered assiduously by its proponents, aided by the sensational press looking for 'scare stories', by the success of the limited

bombing carried out in the period, by films such as *Things to Come* in the 1930s, and then by the total success of bombing raids such as that against Guernica in the Spanish Civil War (1936–1939). Yet the only air force to commit itself entirely to the concept during the 1920s was the RAF, under the tutelage of Trenchard. What the prophets had ignored, as operations in World War II were to show, was that their assumptions were just about valid, assuming the bombers could get through to drop a heavy weight of bombs accurately on their targets. World War II was to show that the fulfilment of this requirement was extremely difficult.

The technical progress made during the 1920s was epitomized by the service introduction in 1931 of two fighters capable of more than 200 mph (322 kph), the Hawker Fury and the Nakajima A2N. Thus the 13 years since the end of World War I had been marked by an increase of about 60 mph (97 kph) in the top speed of fighters, largely attributable to the development of more powerful engines using better fuels and driving more efficient propellors. For the rest, design philosophy and armament remained largely unchanged, though structures had been 'translated' into metal, and the standard twin-gun armament featured weapons of increased reliability. Shortly after this, a variety of modern bombers began to appear, featuring monoplane design, retractable undercarriages and a number of other aeronautical improvements such as variable-pitch propellers, flaps, enclosed cockpits and gun turrets for the defensive

armament. Typical examples are the Boeing B-9, the Martin B-10 and the Tupolev TB-3 (ANT-6). Thus the 1930s witnessed a leap forward in aircraft design as the technical lessons of the 1920s were fully absorbed and turned into hardware. By 1936 modern bombers were the equal of first-generation monoplane fighters, but then the advent of the second generation monoplane fighters (such as the German Messerschmitt Bf 109, the British Hawker Hurricane and Supermarine Spitfire, the French Dewoitine D.520, the Italian Macchi MC.200 *Saetta*, the US Curtiss P-36 and the Japanese Mitsubishi A6M and Nakajima Ki-43) once again raised fighter performance above that of bombers, and set the technical scene for the air combat typical of the first stages of World War II.

Most of the 1920s had been characterized by an absence of 'formal' war, an illusion that was rudely shattered by a number of increasingly savage conflicts in the 1930s. What was more disturbing to

In the early period between the wars, there was considerable stagnation in the design of more advanced aircraft, with only limited conceptual advances over the machines of World War I. Typical of the bomber types of the early 1930s was the Boulton Paul P.75 Overstrand.

the combatants of World War I was that these wars seemed to move ominously closer to home as the decade progressed. A war began on 19 September 1931 between China and Japan, or rather between China and the Japanese Kanto Command, which controlled part of Manchuria as a 'province' of the Imperial Japanese Army. Alleging that China had tried to cut the rail line connecting Mukden and Port Arthur, a Japanese possession, the Kanto Command moved quickly to seize the rest of Manchuria, which was in Japanese hands by February 1932. In the war, the Chinese forces had been completely outmanoeuvred and outfought by the Japanese, whose air element, consisting mostly of Nieuport 29 fighters, Salmson A2 reconnaissance aircraft and Kawasaki Type 88 reconnaissance bombers, played an important part in providing the Kanto Command with accurate reconnaissance information and in destroying the few Chinese Potez 25 reconnaissance aircraft that had not been captured by the Japanese. Thereafter the air units of the Kanto Command played a useful role in strafing the Chinese ground forces. After its seizure, Manchuria became the puppet Japanese state of Manchukuo.

All that the Chinese could do to strike back at the Japanese was boycott Japanese goods, an effective weapon as China was Japan's main trade outlet. The Japanese therefore landed an expeditionary force at Shanghai in January 1932 in an effort to reopen this major centre of trade, and the action was marked by short-lived but extensive use of Japanese carrierborne aircraft for the support of the land forces, a clear portent of what the Japanese would be able to achieve in World War II with a far larger carrier force. The Shanghai operation was over on 4 March 1932, and though the Chinese had shot down three Japanese aircraft with ground fire, the Japanese had lost no aircraft in air combat, though shooting down at least three. With the Japanese presence in Shanghai finally confirmed after a determined resistance by the local Chinese forces, the boycott of Japanese goods was lifted. However, for the next five years the tension between China and Japan built up steadily.

Closer to home was the Italian invasion of Abyssinia, which started on 3 October 1935 when Italian motorized forces struck from Italian Somaliland, supported by about 320 aircraft: about 240 bombers and reconnaissance aircraft (Caproni Ca 101, 111 and 133, Meridionali Ro 1 and Savoia-Marchetti SM.81) supported by 80 fighter aircraft (IMAM Ro 37 twin-seat and Fiat CR.20 single-seat). Against this large and fairly modern force the Abyssinians could deploy only a few obsolescent types that were crashed by mercenary pilots or shot up on the ground by the Italians. The *Regia Aeronautica* thus had a free hand in the air, the bomber/transports ferrying troops and bombing without hindrance, and the fighters being used for reconnaissance and strafing.

Of far greater significance, and even closer to home, was the Spanish Civil War (18 July 1936–28 March 1939). Both

sides deployed a miscellany of obsolete aircraft at the beginning of the war, the Nationalists having fewer of the aircraft but most of the pilots. Main types were the Nieuport-Delage NiD.52 sesquiplane fighter, the Breguet 19 reconnaissance bomber and Vickers Vildebeest reconnaissance bombers, plus a number of Fokker bomber/transports. Sporadic air fighting of an insignificant nature started almost at once, but it was only with the arrival of foreign support for each side that the pace of operations speeded up: the Nationalists were supported by Germany and Italy, the Republicans by Russia, France and a number of sympathetic governments, plus many private individuals of socialist, or perhaps antifascist, persuasion.

First to arrive were the Germans, 20 of whose Junkers Ju 52/3m bomber/transports played a decisive role at the end of July and the beginning of August by airlifting some 13,500 troops and 573,196 lb (260,000 kg) of supplies from North Africa to metropolitan Spain, and thereby preventing the quick suppression of the Nationalist revolt by the government.

During August 1936 the Germans supplied more Ju 52/3m bombers, and a number of Heinkel He 51 biplane fighters, while the Italians sent Savoia-Marchetti SM.81 bomber/transports and Fiat CR.32 biplane fighters, the last to be the most important Nationalist fighter, in numerical terms, of the whole war. Both fascist states also supplied aircrew and groundcrew in growing numbers, as well as ground combat and support elements. Both Germany and Italy saw the Spanish War as a chance to help another fascist state into existence, as well as to test their new weapons and personnel in realistic combat situations. Russia also wished to test her latest weapons and untried aircrew in combat, but although the Republic government had basically the same political leanings as the Soviet regime, the latter insisted on payment in gold for all material aid. Russian and French aid began to arrive in Spain during September 1936, and the intensity of operations immediately began to grow.

At first the Nationalists, though outnumbered, had enjoyed a successful campaign in their drives towards Madrid. However, the increasing efficiency of the Republican troops, allied with aid from France and Russia, began to turn the tide late in 1936. In the air, the most notable factor was the clear qualitative superiority of the Russian aircraft, the Tupolev SB-2

twin-engined monoplane bomber, and the Polikarpov I-15 and I-16 biplane and monoplane fighters. The I-15 was the equal of the CR.32, but decidedly superior to the He 51, and the I-16 was better than both Nationalist fighters. The immediate result was that the Republicans gained control of the air, enabling their bomber forces to help slow the Nationalist advance. The He 51 was relegated to ground-attack work, where it proved surprisingly efficient, and German and Italian air commanders called for newer combat aircraft from home. The Germans responded in early 1937 with the Messerschmitt Bf 109 monoplane fighter, which became by far the best fighter used in the

King George V inspects Handley Page Heyford night bombers at the RAF station at Mildenhall in Suffolk on 6 July 1935. The Heyford was obsolescent when it entered service, and was the RAF's last biplane heavy bomber. It had the highly unusual features of a fuselage suspended from the upper wing, and the bomb bay located in the special deep-ended centre-section of the lower wing.

Spanish Civil War, with the Ju 87 dive-bomber and the Dornier Do 17 and Heinkel He 111 monoplane medium bombers. The Italians, satisfied with the performance of the CR.32, sent in two new monoplane bombers, the Savoia-Marchetti SM.79 and the Fiat BR.20. This combination of advanced bombers, faster than the Republican fighters, meant that the Nationalists were able to strike almost at will into the Republican rear areas, the most celebrated, or perhaps infamous, being the destruction of Guernica on 26

April 1937 by a wave of He 111 bombers, followed by a wave of Ju 52/3m bomber/transports.

The balance in the air was restored to a certain extent by the arrival of more Russian fighters, notably later marks of the I-16, so that 1937 may be regarded as a fairly evenly balanced year in the air: each side was generally able to secure air superiority over its own offensives, but the Nationalists had an edge in their possession of a better medium bomber force.

During 1938, though, the balance

tipped decisively towards the Nationalists as the Germans and Italians continued to pour aircraft and men into the country, and the Russians realized the hopelessness of the Republican situation, as well as their inability to purchase further aid with hard cash, and so began to tail off the amount of aid supplied to the Republicans. By the end of 1938 the Nationalists were in an unbeatable position, and although the Republicans held out for some time more with fanatical courage and determination, the end was inevitable. Indeed, the Germans and Italians pulled out large portions of their combat forces, leaving General Francisco Franco y Bahamonde's Nationalists to complete the campaign in 1939.

Most important of all, though, were the long-term results of the air war outside Spain, for it was the conduct of air operations in this war that conditioned the tactical thinking of many of the major combatants of World War II, notably Germany, Italy and Russia, the three countries that had been most deeply involved in operations over Spain.

Russia had dispatched her latest types to Spain, and these had on the whole performed creditably. However, most of the aircraft were what might be described as 'first-generation 1930s state of the art' aircraft, that is the first generation to make full use of the technological advances of the 1920s and early 1930s. Certain shortcomings had become clear despite this, and a new generation of aircraft was immediately set in hand. Unfortunately for the Russians the fruits of the programme would not be ready in quantity until 1942. The Russians had also appreciated the magnificent support furnished to the ground forces by the aircraft of Germany's *Legion Condor*, and this confirmed them in their opinion that large air forces were essential, but that they should be subordinated to the tactical requirements of the ground forces, a view increasingly held in Russia since dalliance with heavy bombers in the late 1920s and early 1930s.

Germany had seen the Spanish Civil War as a golden opportunity to test the men and machines of her new *Luftwaffe*, which had existed in clandestine form ever since World War I, but had been revealed publicly only in 1935. The deficiencies of the *Luftwaffe's* first-generation aircraft had been clearly seen, but the performance of later types, such as the Bf 109, the Do 17, the He 111 and a number of other types tested in small numbers, had convinced

the Germans that their aircraft were all that were required for the forthcoming war. What they had failed to take into account, though, was the fact that their potential enemies were already preparing designs that would render the current German types obsolete by the early 1940s, and that Germany should accordingly give high priority to the development of the next generation of combat aircraft.

Italy was perhaps the country that did least well out of the Spanish Civil War, so far as lessons for the future were concerned. Ignoring the fact that their bombers had operated mainly in an environment of air superiority, and that their main fighter, the CR.32, had done no more than hold its own against first-generation monoplane fighters, the Italians felt that they were well provided with modern aircraft for future operations. Other aircraft of more modern design were in the final stages of preparation, but the Italians felt that their manoeuvrability would keep them out of trouble, and that the armament of only two machine-guns was adequate against modern aircraft. They ignored the fact that the latest fighters being produced by other countries placed greater emphasis on climb, speed and rate of turn than on manoeuvrability, that twin guns had been replaced by batteries of up to eight machine-guns or a combination of cannon and machine-guns, and that armour protection and self-sealing fuel tanks were becoming standard.

These lessons were there for all to see, and even the blindest should have been alerted to these and other factors, such as the high quality of Japan's air forces, by a resumption of war in China during 1937, and by hostilities between Japan and Russia along the Mongolian border in 1938 and 1939. Full-scale war flared up between China and Japan on 7 July 1937, though there had been a succession of clashes between 1934 and 1937. This time the Japanese had decided to launch a

The Messerschmitt Bf 108 Taifun was designed in 1933 as a four-seat liaison and touring aircraft. The one shown here illustrates clearly some of the design features of its successor on the Messerschmitt drawing boards, the Bf 109: angular wings of relatively little area, narrow-track outward-retracting main undercarriage legs, cleanly cowled engine and braced horizontal tail surfaces.

decisive offensive to take the key areas of China, after a faked 'incident' outside Peking. At the time the Imperial Army air service had some 500 aircraft in 10 squadrons, the Imperial Navy about 400 aircraft in 30 squadrons. Substantial quantities of these were committed early in the campaign, though the Japanese did not get things all their own way even with their latest aircraft, foreign instructors having done much to raise the standards of the Chinese air force. In August 1937, for example, some 54 of the navy's latest long-range bomber, the Mitsubishi G3M, were shot down in three raids over China, clear indication that even the latest aircraft were vulnerable on deep-penetration missions unless escorted; and on 17 August, the navy suffered a further blow when 11 of 12 biplane torpedo-bombers were shot down near Shanghai.

Realizing that they had underestimated the Chinese, the Japanese rushed into the theatre their latest fighter, the monoplane Mitsubishi A5M, which immediately turned the scales in favour of the Japanese. However, the Chinese were also reinforced, for on 29 August 1937 they signed a non-aggression treaty with Russia, by which they received 400 I-15 and I-16 fighters, as well as two SB-2 bomber squadrons and four fighter squadrons manned by Russians. However, not even these could prevail against the excellent fighters of the Imperial Navy air service, which dominated the air war over China in these early stages. By the onset of winter, most of the Russian fighters had been shot down, freeing the Japanese bomber force to wreak havoc on Chinese cities.

Altogether more difficult for the Japanese was the Nomonhan Incident with Russia, which started in May 1939 when Mongolian nomads crossed into Manchukuo (as Japan's puppet state in Manchuria was named) and the Kanto Command decided to teach them a lesson, a fact to which the Russians objected, not least because of the bitter border clashes between the two countries between July and August the previous year over the possession of Changkufeng Hill. The border area around the Khalkin river was in dispute, but the Japanese moved up major ground forces, with air support, to clear the Russians from the area. Combat experienced and well equipped, the Japanese at first pushed the Russians back, the army air arm proving itself decidedly superior to that of the Russians: on 27 May 1939, during the first air battle, the Japanese shot down seven I-16 fighters, and another 42 on the following day. The Russians built up their forces quickly, and counterattacked in June, pushing the Japanese right back. Japan's 120 aircraft were outnumbered, but the Nakajima Ki-27 proved itself generally superior to

Above: *The model of the Bf 109 entering service in 1939 was the E series.* Below: *The Polikarpov I-16.*

the Russian fighters, which seem in general to have lost 10 of their own number shot down for every Japanese fighter destroyed in the air.

The Russians were still building up their air strength, and on 27 June the Japanese launched a pre-emptive strike at their airfields, claiming 99 Russian aircraft in the air and another 111 on the ground, for only five of their own aircraft shot down. There is almost certainly a quantity of exaggeration, both deliberate and unintentional, in the Japanese claims, but it is still possible to discern that the Japanese were having very much the better of the air war, a trend that continued into July. During this month, the Japanese claimed 560 victories for the loss of only 31 of their own aircraft. In August, though, the Russians brought in newer aircraft with superior protection and armament, as well as pilots trained in the new tactics adopted since Russia's experience in the Spanish Civil War. The tide thus turned very much the other way, with the exhausted and outnumbered Japanese aircrew being decimated even as they strove to protect the crumbling ground forces below them.

At times the Japanese were still able to strike heavy blows against the Russians, but the latter were concentrating on the provision of good tactical support for their armies, and this the Japanese were not able to prevent. Before a decisive military solution should be reached, an agreement brought hostilities to an end on 16 September 1939.

More momentous events were taking place during this time to the west in Europe, as German ambitions led to the invasion of Poland on 1 September 1939 and the outbreak of World War II.

Tactical Air Power
in Europe and North Africa World War II

The initial line-up at the beginning of World War II placed Germany on one side, opposed by Poland, France and Great Britain, these being joined by Denmark, Norway, the Netherlands and Belgium when these countries were invaded in April and May 1940. Italy joined Germany in June 1940, while Yugoslavia and Greece were brought into the Allied fold by the Axis invasion of April 1941. Finally, Russia joined the list of Germany's victims in June 1941; Bulgaria, Hungary and Romania threw in their lots with Germany, and Finland co-operated with Germany in an effort to regain the territory lost to the Russian invasion of November 1940.

The war was of German making, and her forces were relatively well prepared for the outbreak of hostilities, although they were not as large as many senior commanders would have liked, Hitler having earlier told them to prepare for a war that would not start before 1942.

Two main concentrations of ground troops, spearheaded by armoured formations, were to strike into Poland from the north-west and north, and from the south-west. The object of this strategy was to break through the Poles' main defences, encircle and destroy the main fighting forces, and then mop up the rest of the country by pushing on to the east to link up with the Russians. By arrangement, the Soviet army was to invade eastern Poland shortly after the Germans had successfully secured most of the western half of the country.

The German ground forces were supported by two *Luftflotten* (air fleets) of the *Luftwaffe*, with 648 twin-engined bombers, 219 dive-bombers, 30 ground attack aircraft, 210 fighters and 474 reconnaissance aircraft, supported by a large number of liaison, transport and other aircraft. Not-

The Junkers Ju 87, almost universally known as the Stuka, *was a principal contributor to the success of German arms in the period between 1939 and 1941.*

able is the large number of reconnaissance aircraft, clear indication of the importance attached to the primary task of support for the ground forces, and the use of 219 dive-bombers. This was to be the first occasion on which large numbers of dive-bombers had been used operationally, though the type had seen limited service elsewhere. The concept was American: World War I fighters had proved useful ground-attack aircraft with their light bombs, and this concept had been extended in the early 1920s by the carriage of a greater bomb-load.

The pattern of air operations over Poland by the *Luftwaffe* typified that force's use of its tactical potential in all German *Blitzkrieg* campaigns up to the

end of 1941, and was geared closely to the needs of the ground forces, though the air force had certain tasks of its own to ensure that the opposing air force was effectively neutralized. Loosely escorted by fighters, the medium bomber force had as its primary objective the elimination of the enemy's airfields and items such as bridges on the enemy's main lines of communication. Swift blows against these two types of target were intended firstly to catch the Polish air force on the ground and so destroy it before it could make its weight tell; to destroy the airfields so that aircraft already aloft had no base to which they could return, and to tempt the Polish fighters into combat with the tactically superior German fighters; and secondly to

The Heinkel He 111 medium bomber was the best such aircraft in widespread service with the Germans in 1939, having proved its capabilities in the Spanish Civil War.

disrupt the whole pattern of the Polish defence by making it difficult for weight to be switched from one area to another, and for reserves to be moved up to the line.

While the level bombers attacked these targets well to the rear of the battle zone, it was the task of other fighters, and the dive-bombers, to cut the Polish lines of communication immediately behind the front, and to eliminate the main centres of Polish resistance by means of concentrated bombing, in which they would be joined by the level bombers once they had destroyed their primary objectives. In these areas the roaming fighters would attack targets of opportunity with gun fire.

Over the battlefield itself, the remain-ing German fighters provided cover to prevent the Polish air force from making any real contribution to the defence, and to destroy any Polish fighters attempting to get among the German bombers heading for their targets behind the front. At the same time they attacked targets of opportunity, and aided the ground-attack aircraft and remaining dive-bombers to clear the way for the armoured forces by attacking and eliminating Polish centres of resistance, artillery positions and AA sites that might engage other German aircraft.

After these primary tasks had been achieved, the German concept continued, all available air forces would contribute to the land battle except where they might be needed for special tasks such as the complete elimination of the Poles' road and rail network, telephone communications system, power supply, munitions industry, and main civilian areas in a final attempt to force the enemy to sue for terms.

The concept was an excellent one, but as always in war, to a very great extent dependent on what the enemy would do. In the Polish campaign, the *Luftwaffe* was able to provide the army with good support right from the start, and to create havoc in the Poles' lines of communication. However, the elimination of the Polish air force proved a difficult task, with the result that the Poles were able at times to use their aircraft, especially their obsolescent PZL P-11 gull-winged fighters, to good effect. The bomber force, whose two main aircraft were the PZL P-23 and PZL P-37 single- and twin-engined machines, was also able to play its part occasionally. But as always in modern war, in which every aspect is interdependent with a number of others, the German attacks on the Poles' lines of communication finally began to pay dividends as the Poles' early warning system failed on 7 September. The immediate result was that the Polish fighters lost many chances to intercept, and the Germans began to catch more enemy aircraft on the ground, though the first fully effective bombing attack on an airfield did not occur until 14 September, when 17 bombers were destroyed at Hutnicki airfield.

By the time the Russians invaded on 17 September the war of movement in the west was all but over, and all that survived were fortified localities such as Warsaw, Modlin, Lvov and Brest-Litovsk. Realizing the hopelessness of the situation after the invasion by the Russians, the remnants of the Polish air force evacuated to Romania and internment, some 116 survivors of the fighting managing to get away.

With most of Poland holding out so defiantly, the German high command decided on special measures to end Polish resistance because the German overall plan called for the forces in this theatre to be moved west for the planned campaign against France and the Low Countries. On 13 September, therefore, the *Luwt-waffe* started a series of devastating raids on Warsaw, which culminated on 25 September with an attack by 240 Ju 87 dive-bombers, followed by 30 Ju 52/3m transports. Out of the latter were shovelled tons of incendiaries, and by the evening Warsaw was a mass of flames and rubble. Facing starvation and typhoid, the Polish capital surrendered on 27 September, with Modlin, across the Vistula river from Warsaw, surrendering on the next day. This ended effective Polish resistance, though isolated pockets continued to hold out until 5 October.

Although France and Great Britain had declared war on Germany to support Poland, the two Allies provided the Poles with no real assistance apart from a minor French offensive in the Saar and some sharp air battles over the French/German border, the protagonists being reconnaissance machines and fighters. During September, for example, the French admitted the loss of four aircraft but claimed to have downed 27 German aircraft, and probably 10 more. This lack of any real air effort is largely attributable to the prewar scare about the terrible efficiency of bombers: neither side wished to resort to this weapon, whose use would inevitably bring about retaliatory bombing. The one exception to this general rule was that both sides considered naval installations and warships to be fair targets, and so there developed a small-scale but lively interchange of raids on such targets, the RAF making its first raid on 4 September and the *Luftwaffe* its first raid against British ships on 16 October.

During December 1939, the RAF was forced to revise its long-cherished belief in the capabilities of modern bombers in daylight raids when three raids by Vickers Wellington medium bombers against German naval installations on the coast of the Heligoland Bight were severely handled by the fighter defences. The first raid got off relatively lightly, but in the second raid five out of 12 bombers were disposed of by the German fighters. This was enough to worry the Air Staff, though not unduly.

However, on 18 December a force of 24 Wellingtons was dispatched to bomb Wilhelmshaven, which had been the target for the second raid, only four days earlier. On 18 December the weather was perfect for flying, and the Wellington formation was intercepted by the defending Bf 109 and Bf 110 fighters: two of the British bombers had already turned back with engine trouble, and of the remaining 22 Wellingtons 12 were shot down and another three crash-landed on returning to England. This was an effective loss rate of 68%, and the British realized that unescorted bombers could not operate by day when faced by adequate fighter defences. Accordingly, the policy of the RAF for long-range bombing became one of night operations for the rest of the war, with a few notable exceptions.

Germany's next move, undertaken at very short notice, was the seizure of Denmark and Norway to protect Germany's northern flank and allow German shipping free access to the iron ore port of Narvik. Here the *Luftwaffe* showed itself to be a force of great tactical flexibility, the bombers and fighters effectively neutralizing much of their opponents' first-line

Above: *The view from the nose of an He III.* Below: *Armourers tow a 1102-lb bomb.*

defences with gun fire and bombs, and the transport fleet flying in a large number of men to occupy key positions right at the beginning of the campaign on 9 April 1940.

The *Luftwaffe* immediately moved onto occupied airfields for the prosecution of the Norwegian campaign, Denmark having capitulated almost immediately. Neither Denmark nor Norway had been able to offer any real air resistance to the Germans, and so it was left to the RAF, operating from extemporized airfields in central and northern Norway, to try to check the Germans in conjunction with the land forces. However, the presence of overwhelming German fighter strength, despite heavy losses, made it all but impossible for the British tactical bomber force to play a significant part in operations. Eventually, the campaign turned on the ability of each side to move supplies and men by sea, and a lively air war against shipping developed.

By this time, though, the centre of operations had moved to the west, where on 10 May 1940 the Germans launched their long-expected attack against France; Belgium and the Netherlands also falling under the German hammer in the process. Expecting a virtual repeat of the German invasion of 1914, its right wing sweeping through Belgium and northern France before wheeling left to pass to the west of Paris, the Allies had concentrated their forces in northern France, so that they could move forward to the assistance of Belgium at the apposite moment. Their right, the Allies felt, was adequately protected by the French Maginot Line of static fortifications. The Germans had indeed contemplated such an offensive, until a suggestion by *Generalleutnant* Erich von Manstein, at that time a staff officer, persuaded Hitler to adopt an idea of great strategic genius: the main armoured thrust would be launched through the 'impassable' Ardennes to strike through the weakly held Sedan sector, just north of the Maginot Line but south of the main Allied mobile forces, and then push on to the English Channel coast to cut the Allied armies in two before mopping up each part individually. The Allied movement in Belgium at the time of the German invasion, before Germany's intentions became clear, played right into the hands of the German plan.

The result was inevitable, and although the Germans suffered heavy losses right from the start, they were able to undertake and fulfil all the tasks required of them

by the army. The skill and willingness to improvise that characterized German aircrews throughout the war was reflected in the general success of the airborne and air-landing operations undertaken by the *Luftwaffe's* airborne arm. These involved glider landings, paratroop drops, assault landings from transport aircraft, and even the landing of troops from floatplanes beside riverine targets. These airborne landings had been planned for Belgium and the Netherlands to reduce the number of ground troops that would otherwise have been needed, and although they were only partially successful, they were greatly aided by the *Luftwaffe's* total command of the air over the Low Countries. The Belgians and Dutch did at times manage to shoot down numbers of German aircraft, but their small numbers and considerable losses meant that the German command of the air was little challenged in overall terms.

The main air battle, however, was over France, where the weight of the German bomber force was concentrated. As in the Polish campaign, a major strike against Allied airfields featured prominently, but not altogether successfully, only about 60 Allied aircraft being caught on the ground and destroyed. This failure to eliminate a major proportion of the Allied air strength before the onset of the battle proper meant that the Germans now had to fight an energetic war in the air to achieve their objectives. During the first day's air battles, the Allies claimed the destruction of some 90 German aircraft for the loss of 20 fighters. During the night they started a limited and unsuccessful attempt to slow the German advance by bombing their lines of communication. Though these battles of the first day had been extensive, both sides were to an extent probing the other's defences, and the air activity of the second day was consequently far more intense, especially when the Allies tried to bomb the bridges over the Albert Canal near Maastricht. These had been taken the previous day by German airborne assault as the main means of advance by the German armoured force in the area. Nearly the whole of the Belgian Fairey Battle light bomber force, plus its escorting fighters, were shot down by German flak and fighters. So important did this German-held crossing point appear to the Allies at the time, that during the afternoon of 11 May and the morning of 12 May British and French bombers were thrown into the battle with the similar results. Indeed, the raid of 12 May lost all

the bombers sent out, complete with their volunteer aircrews.

The Germans had not as yet shown their hand, though the Allies began to appreciate what was impending on 13 May, when II and VIII *Fliegerkorps* launched a concentrated and beautifully executed attack on the French positions defending the Meuse crossings south of Sedan, the chosen point for the crossing of the main German armoured force. Some 310 medium and 200 dive-bombers wrought havoc on the French positions, and the German crossing went ahead against minimal opposition.

It is no exaggeration to say that these crossings were the key to the German campaign in France, a fact keenly appreciated by the Allied high command. Accordingly,

Above: Groundcrew at work on a Messerschmitt Bf 110 heavy fighter, which proved only relatively successful. **Below:** *The 13-mm dorsal gun position of a German bomber.*

14 May was punctuated with a number of determined, but eventually hopeless, attacks by Allied bombers. The Germans had larded the district with heavy concentrations of flak guns, and numerous fighters patrolled the areas. The British committed about 120 aircraft, of which 70 were shot down (including 36 of the hapless Fairey Battles), and the French lost more than 40 aircraft also attempting to destroy the German bridges to no avail. Throughout, the German ground forces were able to push across and drive deep into the heart of northern France. At the same time, the old quarter of Rotterdam was razed by a German raid: the threat of the raid had been designed to persuade the local Dutch commander to surrender, and such an undertaking had been received by the German commander just before the raid was due. Unfortunately, a failure in German signal procedures then prevented the raid being cancelled. By the end of 14 May, the Belgian and Dutch air forces had ceased to exist as fighting entities, the Dutch having lost nearly all their aircraft and the Belgians 120 aircraft to ground attacks and another 39 in air combat.

By now, the battle of attrition in the air had so weakened the French and British air units in France that the Germans were at last able to implement their air tactics almost without hindrance. France desperately appealed to Britain for another 10 squadrons of fighters, but at the urging of Air Chief-Marshal Sir Hugh Dowding, air officer commanding-in-chief of Fighter Command, Churchill at first refused, though subsequently relenting to the extent of wasting another six squadrons of Hawker Hurricanes in the now futile battle for France. Dowding had realized that the squandering of aircraft in France would serve no purpose but the weakening of Fighter Command for the battle that would inevitably take place over England after the fall of France.

Meanwhile, the Germans had driven their 'Panzer corridor' from Sedan to the English Channel between 13 and 21 May, splitting the Allies in two and necessitating the British evacuation from Dunkirk. Then, with the German ground net tightening round the Allied perimeter at Dunkirk, Hitler was persuaded by Hermann Göring, the commander-in-chief of the Luftwaffe, that it was senseless to risk the precious armoured forces in the boggy country around Dunkirk. Instead, the ground forces should be halted, the destruction of the Allied beach-head then being undertaken by the bombers of the

Bomb damage after a German raid near the Old Bailey criminal courts in London.

Luftwaffe. The result was Germany's first setback of the war, as exhausted German crews, whose aircraft were reaching a high degree of unserviceability and operating from bases too far to the east, battled poor weather to get to the beach-head, only to be met by fresh British fighters.

With the elimination of the Allied 'pocket' to its north-east, the bulk of the German armies along the line of the Seine river could, from 5 June, return to the systematic destruction of the remaining French forces. Under cover of almost unopposed bombers and fighters, the Germans soon drove deep into France bringing a French call for an armistice on 21 June. By 25 June 1940 the fighting had ended, and the Germans were in possession of most of France to the north of a line between Bordeaux and Lyons.

Britain, under the dynamic leadership of a new prime minister, Winston Churchill, since 10 May 1940, was in no mood to call for terms. And so the Germans were faced with the prospect of having to launch a seaborne invasion of a country possessing a navy far superior to their own. While the army and the navy bickered on how best to undertake this formidable task, the Luftwaffe was to eliminate the RAF as an effective force, by destroying its airfields and aircraft, and the factories that could supply new aircraft, as a preparation for the invasion.

Göring confidently expected that the British would surrender – once the full power of the Luftwaffe became apparent to the British people. Primarily, though, the task of the Luftwaffe was to eliminate the RAF so that the German aircraft could devote their attentions to the protection of the invasion convoys once the invasion started. The Germans blundered in assessing the morale of the British people, the strength of the RAF, the reserves of aircraft available to Fighter Command, and the British possession of a radar-aided ground-controlled interception system, which would allow Fighter Command to make the most economical use of its numerically inferior force. Also ignored by the Germans were the facts that the RAF would be operating over its own country, thus shortening its lines of communication whereas German pilots would have to nurse crippled aircraft back across the English Channel to France and the Low Countries, and that large proportions of Fighter Command were fresh, having been husbanded for this very purpose by Dowding.

The first phase of the Battle of Britain (10 July–7 August) took the form of German attacks on British coastal shipping and ports to tempt Fighter Command into battle on terms advantageous to the Luftwaffe. German tactics proved superior, but the British held their own and concentrated on building up strength and experience for the main battle ahead. Overall Fighter Command lost 169 aircraft, the Luftwaffe 192 and another 77 damaged.

The second phase (8–23 August) featured German attacks on radar stations and forward fighter bases in southern England. Some attacks were made from Scandinavia, but the range prevented single-seat fighter escort, and such raids were severely handled by Fighter Command. In the south, though, the attacks of Luftflotten II and III were by 15 August causing Fighter Command severe problems as pilot fatigue reached critical proportions. Inexplicably, then, Göring instructed his crews to abandon attacks on the vital radar stations, giving Fighter Command the respite it needed. Losses in this phase totalled 303 for Fighter Command and 403, plus 127 damaged, for the Luftwaffe.

The third phase (24 August–6 September) concentrated German efforts on the main centres of fighter production and the inland fighter bases. The strong bomber forces were well escorted by fighters, so

The two main RAF fighters of the Battle of Britain were the Supermarine Spitfire (left) *and the Hawker Hurricane* (main picture), *both powered by Rolls-Royce Merlin engines and armed with eight 0.303-in (7.7-mm) Browning machine-guns. In numbers of aircraft destroyed the Hurricane proved superior, though note must be taken of the fact that the Spitfires' primary responsibility was the German fighter escort, while that of the Hurricanes was the German bomber force.*

Britain was over and the Germans had been repulsed, at least temporarily. Hitler, however, was concerned that the war should still be taken to the recalcitrant British. So the great *Blitz* of night bombing began in November 1940, continuing up to May 1941. This was a new type of air war: on one side were the bombers, trying to find their targets in the dark by means of ever improving navigational aids, and then to inflict serious bomb damage on that target with relatively few losses to themselves. On the other side was the defence, trying to hide the target with decoys, or divert the attackers with ever more sophisticated electronic devices to jam or distort their electronic aids, and to cut down enemy bombers with AA fire

Above: German groundcrew prepare to load a reconnaissance camera into a Bf 110. Right: A Hawker Hurricane IID, armed with a pair of 40-mm cannon.

that British fighters tempted up to intercept could be dealt with while their airfields were comprehensively destroyed. While the Supermarine Spitfires concentrated on the German fighters, the Hawker Hurricanes tackled the German bombers; the Bf 110 long-range fighter proved vulnerable to both British fighters. The Germans were suffering heavily, but despite Dowding's well timed rotation of exhausted squadrons, the fatigue factor was coming to play a decisive part in Fighter Command's ability to continue. On 24 August, though, a German bomber had inadvertently dropped some bombs on the outskirts of London. Churchill ordered a 'retaliatory' raid on Berlin, and on the next night 29 out of 81 Bomber Command aircraft dispatched managed to drop a few bombs on Berlin. Incensed, Hitler immediately ordered the *Luftwaffe's* current plans to be abandoned in favour of massive raids against London. Paradoxically, this was just what Britain needed, as it lifted the weight off Fighter Command. Losses in the third phase amounted to 262 Fighter Command aircraft, and 378 Luftwaffe aircraft, with another 115 German aircraft damaged.

The fourth phase of the battle (7–30 September) consisted of massive bomber raids against London by day, with strong fighter escort. This was just what Fighter Command needed, for the streams of German aircraft heading for a known target presented the defence with an ideal target. Moreover, the German fighters could linger over London only a few minutes before fuel shortage forced them to turn back. The battle reached its

climax on 15 September, and on 18 September Hitler decided to postpone the invasion of England. So costly were the daylight raids, the last major example of which took place on 27 September, that the Germans decided on a policy of hit and run raids to keep Fighter Command off balance while the night '*Blitz*' of Britain's industrial centres was prepared. Fourth phase losses were 380 Fighter Command, and 435 *Luftwaffe*, with another 161 German aircraft damaged.

The last phase of the Battle of Britain proper (1–31 October) consisted of German fighter-bomber and intruder missions over southern England. Damage caused was minimal, and Fighter Command recovered swiftly from its earlier ordeals. German losses in this phase were 325, and another 163 damaged, while Fighter Command lost 265 aircraft.

The Battle of Britain was Germany's first major defeat in World War II, and brought home to *Luftwaffe* commanders the truth that they had so forcibly inflicted on countries such as Poland, Norway and the like: that it is impossible to undertake a massive task with minimal forces; or more specifically, in the case of the *Luftwaffe*, that it is impossible to win a strategic battle with forces designed only for tactical operations. Time and time again. the *Luftwaffe* had shown the stupidity of pitting even the most modern bombers against fighters unless the agressor has total air superiority. This the Germans most decidedly did not have during their ill-advised daylight bombing campaign against London.

By 31 October 1940 the Battle of

and more effective night-fighters fitted with airborne interception radar.

Throughout the winter of 1940–1941, the German bombers raided targets in southern and central England. The first really damaging raid took place on 14 November 1940, when *Kampfgruppe* 100 acted as pathfinder force for another 437 bombers in a raid on Coventry, whose centre was totally destroyed. Bomber Command tried to hit back, but lacked navigational aids and could rarely muster more than 100 aircraft. Right up to 1942 British navigation by night was poor in the extreme, for the British had never placed the same emphasis on night flying and navigation as had the Germans.

London continued to be the Germans' favourite target, and during the winter the city was hard hit on several occasions, the campaign reaching its climax in the period between 19 February and 13 May 1941, when Britain was extremely hard hit. German losses were in the order of 3.5%, which was quite low, but then from 14 May onwards, the mass raids were replaced by nuisance raids to harass the British.

Although it was not clear at the time, the reason for the end of the *Blitz* was not the growing number of successes by the British night-fighter arm, which had shot down 96 German bombers, but Germany's switch to the east of many of the forces in France and the Low Countries. For Hitler had at last determined that, despite his aversion to a two-front war, the time had come for Germany to settle with Russia, though first Yugoslavia and Greece must be overrun to bolster Germany's southern flank and aid the Italians, who had entered the war on Germany's side on 10 June 1940.

At this time the Germans also had to reinforce the Italians in North Africa, where Italy's substantial land and air forces were receiving rough treatment at at the hands of the British forces in Egypt. From February 1941 German land and air forces began to arrive in the theatre, and there developed a seesaw campaign between Egypt and Tunisia as first one side, then the other acquired superiority. At first the Germans were able to dominate the air war thanks to superiority in men and machines – in the process developing an ace who has many claims to being World War II's greatest. Hans-Joachim Marseille. Marseille flew only against the Western Allies, and in a career terminated by a fatal accident on 30 September 1942 he shot down no less than 158 aircraft. A superb deflection shot, Marseille, on 1 September 1942, shot down 17 Allied aircraft in one day.

Nevertheless, as the war progressed, Germany's qualtitative lead was whittled away, and the Allies were able to pour into North Africa far greater numbers of aircraft than the Germans and Italians combined.

Two particular features of the air war in this theatre deserve special mention: the maritime air war, and the development of Allied tactical air power. Because of its geographical location, British Egypt had to be supplied round the Cape of Good Hope unless the supply convoys could run the gamut of Axis sea and air power from Gibraltar via Malta to Alexandria. Thus the key to the Mediterranean was Malta, lying off the southern extremity of Italy, neatly astride the Axis supply lines to North Africa. Despite determined Axis efforts, Malta never fell, and became a bastion of British light naval and submarine forces, as well as maritime strike aircraft. There thus developed, during 1942 and 1943 especially, a savage maritime air campaign as the British aircraft on Malta strove to aid the submarines (and such surface units as ventured from Gibraltar and Alexandria on occasion) in decimating the convoys ferrying supplies to North Africa. Thus Malta ceased to be a

linchpin in the British supply route to become a thorn in the Axis lines of communication. Maritime strike aircraft, notably Bristol Beauforts and Bristol Beaufighters, finally proved too much for the Axis' resources, and towards the close of the North African campaign in late 1942, the forces under *Generalfeldmarschall* Erwin Rommel were starved of all types of supplies. Yet to do this, Malta had to survive some of the worst bombing in the war, with her people near to starvation and her protecting fighters all but overwhelmed by sheer numbers in the air, or grounded for lack of fuel. The island was kept going by the occasional convoy that managed to get through, plus air reinforcements flown in from aircraft-carriers.

In the North African campaign proper, the Germans at first used their tried and tested tactical methods, which once again proved highly efficient so long as they had air superiority. Gradually, though, the motley of obsolete types with which the British had started the war in the area gave way to increasing numbers of new aircraft. Essentially a fast-moving campaign, the North African war gave Allied air com-

manders the opportunity to develop tactics for ground support far superior to those of the Germans, with a heavy weight of bombs and tank-destroying cannon fire available at relatively low levels of army command – thanks to an efficient radio network. Increasingly, the Axis forces found themselves deprived of the scanty supplies reaching the ports of North Africa by the depradations of the Allied tactical bomber force, which savaged the Axis lines of communications almost at will in the second half of the campaign. On the battlefield they were subjected to attacks from other Allied tactical bomber units while being mercilessly pounded with bombs, rockets and gun fire from fighter-bombers. The Axis armoured forces came in for special attention from fighter-bombers and tank-busting aircraft armed with heavy cannon and rockets. Thus by the close of the campaign in May 1943, the Allies had developed a powerful tactical air force superior in all respects to that of the Germans. Most of this force was later used in the Italian campaign, while the 'know-how' returned to Britain for the development there of similar forces for service in the North-West European campaign of 1944 and 1945.

Hitler had decided that despite the continued resistance of Great Britain, Russia would be invaded by German forces in May 1941. He was then sidetracked for a fatal six weeks by Mussolini's call for aid in the Italian campaign in Greece and his own desire to deal with Yugoslavia. In conjunction with three Italian armies (the 2nd in the Fiume peninsula, and the 9th and 11th in Albania) and the Hungarian 3rd Army,

Above: Italian aircrews were generally inferior in training compared with their Luftwaffe *and RAF counterparts.* Below: *A Bristol Beaufighter strike fighter in Malta.*

the German 2nd Army was to strike into northern Yugoslavia, the *Panzergruppe* von Kleist was to strike into central Yugoslavia, and the 12th Army was to push into southern Yugoslavia and then on into Greece. The hapless Yugoslavs were over-run between 6 and 17 April, and the Greeks between 6 and 27 April. Against the combination of modern German ground forces, supported by powerful *Luftwaffe* units, there was little that the Yugoslavs and Greeks could do, despite British assistance to the latter.

Air support for the Axis onslaught was provided by the 1,200 aircraft of *Luftflotte* IV, supported by 650 aircraft of the *Regia Aeronautica*. As usual, the *Luftwaffe's* primary task was the support of the ground forces. But as it was known that Yugoslav mobilization would take a few days, it was decided to launch a *Terrorangriff* (terror attack) on Belgrade with all available air units right at the beginning of the campaign to shatter morale and incapacitate the government and army high command.

Yugoslavia's air force was small but useful, and perhaps the most effective of her armed forces, and mustered some 210 fighters and 170 bombers, plus a number of other types. For two days right at the beginning of the attack, therefore, the Yugoslavs were able to offer a realistic defence of their capital, and it was not until their fighter arm had been ground down by the size of the *Luftwaffe* forces opposing them that the Germans were able to operate freely over Belgrade. Then the Yugoslav capital was crippled in a series of massive attacks, and Yugoslav resistance crumbled in the face of the Germans' fast-moving attacks.

Much the same situation prevailed in Greece, though the Hellenic air force was not as modern as that of Yugoslavia. With British air aid, the Greeks put up a stiff but hopeless resistance. The campaign was notable for the usual first-class assistance from the *Luftwaffe*, and the death of Britain's highest scoring ace of the war, Squadron Leader M. T. St J. Pattle, whose score was at least 50 aircraft shot down, possibly more.

To cap their seizure of Greece, the Germans planned to take the island of

The Douglas Boston III, known to the USAAF as the A-20C Havoc, had a relatively unspectacular war, but emerged with a considerable reputation for strength, versatility and hitting power with guns and bombs. Other versions were used as night fighters and night intruders, compared with the original role of attack bombing.

Crete by airborne assault reinforced from the sea. Though the Allied defence was numerically stronger, the nature of the assault came as a tactical surprise, and after some very bitter fighting, the 11-day battle came to an end with the evacuation of the Allied survivors on 31 May 1941. Yet the invasion cost the *Luftwaffe* 271 Junkers Ju 52/3m transports, and some 6,453 men, though this severe loss was balanced by catastrophic losses by the Royal Navy (three cruisers and six destroyers sunk, plus three battleships, one aircraft-carrier, seven cruisers and four destroyers damaged, one battleship and three cruisers severely).

The Balkan adventure was to cost Germany dear, for it had imposed a six-week delay on Operation 'Barbarossa', the invasion of Russia. This was to be the last campaign in which the tactical expertise of the *Luftwaffe* dominated, and remains a classic example of how tactical air power may be employed to best advantage.

The German offensive was to strike with utmost speed, and was supported by the 1,400 aircraft of four *Luftflotten*. To meet

mediocre quality. The aircraft were even lined up neatly on forward airfields, presenting the Germans with ideal targets.

The invasion started with a massive German raid on 31 Russian airfields by 637 bombers escorted and supported by 231 fighters. Caught unawares, the Russians offered negligible resistance and lost very large numbers of aircraft on the ground, the Germans losing only two aircraft. Thereafter the *Luftwaffe* roamed time and time again into Russian airspace, destroying aircraft in the air and on the ground, most damage being done by the level bombers and single-engined fighters. The dive-bombers and twin-engined fighters, meanwhile, supported the armoured columns as they began their thrusts deep into Russia in a campaign marked by a number of brilliantly executed enveloping or 'pincer' movements. The scale of the campaign, and the success of the *Luftwaffe*, may be clearly seen from the fact that on the first day the Russians are estimated to have lost almost 1,500 aircraft on the ground and 322 in the air for minimal German losses. The Russians did indeed

delivery of large numbers of new aircraft. At first, production of the older types had to be restarted merely to keep the air force supplied with machines to fly, but these were soon superseded in mass production by types such as the Ilyushin Il-2 ground-attack aircraft, the Ilyushin Il-4 medium bomber, the Lavochkin LaGG-3 fighter, the Petlyakov Pe-2 medium bomber and multi-role aircraft, and the Yakovlev Yak-1 fighter. Concentrating on the mass production of a few basic types, the Russians soon built up an enormous output of these and a few other aircraft types. Modifications to the basic type were unusual, and then of so fundamental a nature as to warrant an alteration in designation. A case in point was the Lavochkin La-5, which entered production in 1942, and was basically the LaGG-3 redesigned to use the 1,640 hp Shvetsov ASh-82FN radial in place of the 1,100 hp Klimov M-105 inline.

This was still in the future during the first weeks of the German offensive, as the ground forces cut to pieces all opposition and the *Luftwaffe* gained and exploited total air superiority. The continuing scale of the air war is easily appreciated: in the first seven days of hostilities the Russians lost some 4,990 aircraft to the Germans' 179. By the end of the month the Germans were closing in on Minsk, forcing the Russians to ever more desperate measures, such as the commital of large bomber forces without fighter escort, providing the German fighters with magnificent scoring opportunities.

From September onwards the tally of Russian aircraft downed began to decline, the Russians being unable to put as many aircraft into the air as they were running out of men and machines to sacrifice. Nevertheless, the pace of the air war continued, the Germans taking every opportunity to aid their ground forces and to attack Russian targets such as Moscow, which was raided for the first time on 22 July, and attacked whenever possible after that in an effort to demoralize the Russians.

The number of aircraft lost by the Russians in the period between 22 July and 5 December 1941, the period of the German offensive that eventually became bogged down and then frozen in the dreadful winter of 1941–1942 in front of Moscow and Leningrad, will probably never be known. Estimates for the period between 22 June and 20 November range from 6,400 (Russian sources) to 15,877 (German sources).

By far the most successful attack aircraft of the war was the Russian Ilyushin Il-2 Shturmovik, *which was armed with cannon, machine-guns, bombs and rocket projectiles.*

this force, the Russians had up to 15,000 operational aircraft throughout the Soviet Union, with perhaps 7,000 of them in European Russia, controlled by 23 air divisions allocated to army formations as support forces. Despite the Russians' numerical superiority, though, it was the Germans who were superior in experience, tactical doctrine and the element of surprise.

The Germans swept forward on 22 June 1941, with complete tactical surprise and greatly aided by the fact that the Russians had deployed the bulk of their armies and air units well forward. Most Russian aircraft were obsolete (the new types designed since the Spanish Civil War having yet to enter service), and their crews were of

try to strike back, but of the nine bombers dispatched to attack targets in East Prussia, five were shot down by German fighters.

This was only the beginning of an air campaign that destroyed most of the aircraft deployed in western Russia by the Soviet Union. In an odd way, however, this proved a blessing in disguise, for though the Red air force could not offer its reeling ground forces any real support in the terrible retreat before the Germans, it neatly disposed of most of Russia's obsolete aircraft, and urged the aircraft industry to magnificent efforts in the removal of large numbers of factories to the relative safety of the area to the east of the Urals, and then the rapid service

Strategic and Tactical Air Power
in Europe World War II

It was during the winter of 1941–1942 that many German military men began to realize the difficulties in which they were placed. Great Britain was still in the war, and was being reinforced at an increasing rate by the United States of America, brought into the war by Japan's attack on her Pacific Fleet at Pearl Harbor on 7 December 1941. Russia was still in the war, with a large proportion of her industries removed to the safety of western Siberia, and her will to resist undeterred by Germany's undoubted victories of 1941. The precariousness of the German situation had become clear as the Allied blockade began to tell, and the deficiencies of German planning became apparent: there were no winter uniforms for those in Russia, aircraft had not been prepared for winter operations, and production, even of now elderly designs, was falling behind requirements while the newer aircraft types needed to combat the latest generation of Allied aircraft were not forthcoming. This last factor was to play an increasingly important part in the *Luftwaffe's* operations as the war continued. After starting with a technically superior air force, by 1942 the *Luftwaffe* was operating at technical parity, and from 1943 onwards would begin to feel the worst effects of technical inferiority. There were, of course, exceptions such as the great Focke Wulf Fw 190 fighter, and technical masterpieces such as the Messerschmitt Me 262 jet fighter, but there were no new ground-attack and bomber aircraft worthy of mass production, the whole of German planning before the war having dreamt of quick successes in lightning campaigns.

The Russians, as their newer types entered service, began to make their presence felt in the air during early 1942. In general, though, the *Luftwaffe* retained its air superiority in Russia thanks to the vastly superior skills of its pilots: men such as Gerhard Barkhorn, Erich Hartmann and Günther Rall in the fighter arm, and Hans-Ulrich Rüdel, one of the most famous and decorated Germans of World War II, operating in the bomber arm.

The way things were going was well illustrated during the period from February to May 1942, when a German corps was cut off at Demyansk near Lake Ilmen. Unable to support itself, the corps was wholly reliant on air transport for the

Above: *Focke-Wulf Fw 200* Condor *maritime patrol bombers of KG40.* Below: *Britain's heavy bomber, the Short Stirling.*

supply of food and ammunition, and for the evacuation of the wounded. The *Luftwaffe* responded to this need, but it was not until 19 May that ground forces broke through to relieve the six isolated divisions.

The loss of aircraft during this operation severely hampered the *Luftwaffe's* aircrew training programme, for the aircraft were used for this purpose when not needed at the front; and the mere fact that the Russians had been able to cut off so large a force for so long a time boded ill for the German army. Unfortunately, the success of the Demyansk airlift served to confirm the less realistic senior *Luftwaffe* commanders in the view that they could always undertake such operations. How wrong they were was demonstrated towards the end of 1942 when the German 6th Army was cut off at Stalingrad, and Göring blithely assured Hitler that the isolated forces, two and a half times as large as that cut off at Demyansk, could be supplied by air. The 6th Army needed at least 500 tons of supplies per day, and two bases were set up for the effort: Tatsinsk-

aya, with 320 Ju 52/3m and Ju 86 transports in 11 *Gruppen*; and Morosovskaya, with 190 He 111 bomber/transports in two transport *Gruppen* and six bomber *Gruppen*. The effort was hopeless: Russian flak and fighters were rife, the weather was vile, and the airfields both inside and outside the Stalingrad perimeter were at the mercy of the Russians. Between 25 November 1942 and the garrison's surrender on 2 February 1943, the *Luftwaffe* supplied an average of only 100 tons per day. Aircraft losses totalled 490 by 31 January 1943. It should be noted that while the *Luftwaffe* was trying to save the 6th Army at Stalingrad, it was also trying to build-up and supply the Axis bridgehead in Tunisia (seriously threatened by the advance of the 8th Army from the east after its victory at El Alamein) and the 1st Army from the west, after the successful Allied landings in French North Africa. The African airlift achieved its short-term objectives, but only at heavy cost.

It is, perhaps, significant that the African operation was only necessary because the strike aircraft and naval forces of Malta had made it all but impossible for the Axis powers to move men and *matériel* into the theatre by sea. This closing stage of the North African war was also notable for the most devastating use yet by the Allies of their new tactical air power. On 24 March 1943, carefully timed waves of fighter-bombers struck the Axis artillery positions covering the Tebaga Gap on the western flank of the Mareth Line, barring the 8th Army entry into Tunisia. Completely crushed by the attack, the German artillery and anti-tank guns could offer no resistance when the 8th Army moved through.

During 1942, the Germans had kept their tactical air superiority over Russia, but by 1943 this was precarious in the extreme, the Russians being able to secure general air superiority, which the Germans could break locally by the introduction of forces brought in from less threatened sectors of the front. In July 1943 the Germans made their last bid to secure the strategic initiative from the Russians in the Battle of Kursk, the world's largest ever armoured battle, in which two German forces tried to pinch out the Russian salient centred on Kursk. The land battle ended in victory for the Russians, and in the air there occurred the most costly air battle ever waged.

The Germans planned to open their offensive with a pre-emptive strike on the Russian airfields with 800 bombers es-

corted by 275 fighters. The bombers were a mixture of level bombers, dive-bombers and Henschel Hs 129 ground-attack aircraft. However, the Russians were fully aware of the German plans, both ground and air, as a result of information from a still unidentified spy in the German high command, and planned their own pre-emptive strike with some 450 aircraft, their object the German bombers forming up for their own attack. Technically unsophisticated, the Russians had failed to take into account the German possession of radar: '*Freya*' sets picked up the oncoming Russians, and while the bombers took off and circled well out of the way, the German fighters tore into the unwieldy masses of Russian bombers. About 120 bombers went down in this first attack, and during that day the German fighters claimed another 312 victories, plus 205 on the following day. The local superiority of the Germans was assured, and their bombers were able to play an important part in the battle, the Hs 129s proving most effective. It appears that the Germans were just on the brink of victory when the news of the Allied landings in Sicily persuaded Hitler to call off the offensive, allowing the Russians to turn near defeat into crushing victory.

New aircraft such as the Lavochkin La-5 and Yakovlev Yak-9 fighters were now appearing in great numbers, and from this time on the Russians assumed almost total control of the air over the

Eastern Front, allowing their devastating bomber and ground-attack forces to play a decisive part in the defeat of the Germans and their satellites. The German position was weakened by the gradual withdrawal of fighter units to defend Germany from bombing raids, and to provide tactical cover for the German forces in Italy and North-West Europe. Shortly after the Allied invasion of France, for example, the Eastern Front was so denuded of fighters that when the Russians launched a huge offensive against Army Group 'Centre' (on 22 June 1944), the Germans had only 40 fighters with which to try to halt the efforts of five Russian air armies with 7,000 aircraft, all of them used tactically. By the end of the year the position had been partially stabilized, but the essentially defensive nature of Germany's task was indicated by the fact that the Eastern Front was allocated only 11 *Jagdgruppen* and 16 *Schlachtgruppen*, but no major bomber forces. During 1945, with pilot and fuel shortages crippling its efforts still further, the *Luftwaffe* could do nothing to halt the Red Army which was supported by massive and highly efficient tactical air forces.

Apart from tactical operations that sapped the German strength on the Eastern Front, the other major problem facing Germany was the need to combat the growing threat posed by Allied heavy bombers in their strategic campaign against German cities, industries and the

Left: *Mosquito bombers under construction at the main de Havilland works at Hatfield. With the Junkers Ju 88 the Mosquito can claim to be the most versatile aircraft of World War II.* Above: *The Mosquito T.3 was used to train pilots new to the type.*

armed forces from 1942 onwards.

The origins of the strategic campaign against Germany lay in the prewar British dalliance with the concept of strategic bombing, and the later American adoption of the concept of 'hemisphere' defence of the continental United States, which had led to the development of four-engined heavy bombers of considerable range. With the fall of France and the inability of Great Britain to take the land war to Germany for some years to come, it was inevitable that the decision was made to take the war to Germany by means of bombing.

In the short term, the RAF was severely hampered by the inability of its crews to navigate to the target by night with sufficient accuracy to inflict serious damage, and by the inadequacies of the bombers then in service, with the notable exception of the Vickers Wellington. Thus the first concrete indication of the scale to which RAF Bomber Command's effort was to grow was the introduction early in

1941 of the force's initial four-engined night bomber, the Short Stirling. The type made its first raid on 10–11 February 1941, with an attack on Rotterdam. The Stirling was not a very successful bomber, for the carriage of a heavy bomb load entailed short range and low ceiling, and it was soon joined and then supplanted by the Handley Page Halifax, which had the honour of conducting the RAF's first four-engined bomber raid on Germany on 12–13 March 1941. The Halifax had been preceded into service by a twin-engined heavy bomber, the Avro Manchester, potentially an excellent aircraft let down by the unreliability of its Rolls-Royce Vulture engines. Even before this had occurred, though, plans had been made for a four-engined version, the Avro Lancaster, which entered service at the end of December 1941, and soon proved itself to be the best heavy night bomber of World War II. With these three four-engined types in service, the RAF was able to phase out of primary bombing duties

types such as the Handley Page Hampden and Armstrong Whitworth Whitley. One other type was to feature prominently in the bombing campaign: the marvellous de Havilland Mosquito twin-engined multi-role aircraft, built largely of balsa and other woods. Entering service in July 1941, the Mosquito soon acquired a reputation for reliability and performance equalled by few other aircraft types.

The campaign against Germany was due to start in the first half of 1941, but was delayed by a decision to use Bomber Command in a series of raids against the German battle-cruisers *Gneisenau* and *Scharnhorst*, which had arrived in Brest harbour after a successful sortie into the Atlantic in March 1941. However, the offensive against the Ruhr and Rhineland started on 11 June with the first of 20 raids, all totally useless thanks to bad navigation.

The *Luftwaffe* had realized earlier that such a campaign would be forthcoming, and that even if its effect was at first small,

The Avro Lancaster was developed from the unsuccessful twin-engined Manchester, and was the best heavy night bomber of World War II, serving in large numbers from the beginning of 1942. The type's main tactical disadvantage was lack of ventral defensive armament.

operational experience would soon improve the impact of the heavy bombers. Therefore a night-fighter force had already been set up, *Nachtjagdgeschwader Nr 1* being formed in June 1940 to counter the first Allied probing raids. By September 1943 there were to be six *Nachtjagdgeschwader* with 24 *Gruppen*, and in the subsequent part of the war a number of other units were raised. Thus the German night-fighter force at peak strength numbered some 700 aircraft, six searchlight regiments and more than 1,500 radar stations. The force's first and most important commander was Josef Kammhuber. It was Kammhuber who devised the night-fighters' first tactical system using the 'Himmelbett' system of radar-controlled interception 'boxes', and these began to take a heavy toll of the RAF bombers raiding Germany. Between May 1940 and July 1941 the RAF lost 543 aircraft, about half of these to the still evolving night-fighter organization.

As more four-engined bombers entered service, the basic strength of Bomber Command naturally grew, but more than 150 aircraft were rarely committed to a single raid, and successes were non-existent. During the autumn of 1941, the situation began to improve as a new radio navigation aid, 'Gee', was introduced. The Germans ceased flying night intruder missions over England, and priority was allocated to cities rather than oil refineries as the primary objective of the bombers. The change in priorities occurred on 8 July. To balance this, though, losses increased to a greater extent than the improvement in the success rate: between August and November 1941 Bomber Command lost just over 5% of bombers sent out. In November, therefore, the bombing of Germany was temporarily suspended to allow extra training of the whole force and to allow new aircraft to be introduced in large numbers. However, the real change in the impact of the British night bomber effort can be dated to February 1942 and the appointment of Air Marshal Arthur T. Harris to be air officer commanding-in-chief of Bomber Command. Harris was concerned with 'area bombing' (in which bombs were dropped in large numbers on a given area of a city, irrespective of whether or not civilians also lived in the area. He had the

ear of Churchill, and was able to operate Bomber Command almost as an independent force. The object of area bombing was to cripple the German war-making potential by destroying factories and the homes of the civilian workers usually located in the same area. Perhaps it might have been better to limit the RAF's efforts to the factories, for, as Albert Speer has pointed out, continued attacks on key industrial targets such as the U-boat yards in Bremen could have ended the war one year sooner. In the event, too much of the RAF's bomb tonnage landed on civilian areas causing needless suffering while the factory areas escaped with too little damage. Moreover, as the British had learned during the *Blitz*, civilians can learn to live with even the heaviest of bombing; and industries vital to the German war effort were dispersed to less exposed sites so that the bombing failed to halt the German war machine. It cannot be denied, though, that the British bombing did hit the Germans hard and, while it failed in its basic purpose of breaking the will of the German people and destroying their war industries, it did slow down the rate of production in very many factories, and occasioned considerable dislocation as the factories were moved to dispersed sites.

The bombing campaign moved from strength to strength, and was marked by several important milestones. On the night of 31 May–1 June 1942, Bomber Command made its first '1,000-Bomber Raid' against Cologne, but only by pulling aircraft and crews out of operational training units and other formations to make the magic number. Thus great damage was caused to Cologne, though 41 bombers were lost to fighters and flak.

During June 1942, two major raids were dispatched against Essen and Bremen, with small results because of poor weather. During the month, though, 4,800 sorties were flown, and 212 bombers lost, a rate of just over 4.4%. It was a clear indication that Bomber Command and the German night-fighter arm had started on a seesaw war of technical and tactical superiority, the most important factor of which was the development of new electronic aids.

During the middle of the year, the USAAF had been building up its main bomber forces in England and, on 17 August 1942, 12 Boeing B-17 Flying Fortresses devastated the marshalling yards at Rouen in northern France in the first of the Americans' daylight raids, designed to cripple Germany by destroy-

Above: *Designed as a night bomber, the Lancaster was occasionally used with success as a low-level day bomber.* Below: *Air Chief Marshal Sir Arthur Harris, AOC-in-C.*

The Boeing B-17 Flying Fortress was numerically the most important American bomber in the European theatre and it acquired an excellent bombing reputation. Illustrated is the definitive B-17G variant, with a chin turret armed with two 0.5-in (12.7-mm) guns.

ing small targets of a vital nature. Under the command of men such as Carl Spaatz, Ira Eaker and James Doolittle, the US strategic bomber forces set out to disprove the British assessment of day bombing. The Americans felt that concentrated three-dimensional boxes of B-17 and Consolidated B-24 Liberator bombers, armed with large numbers of heavy machine-guns, could throw up so great a weight of defensive fire that the German day fighters would not be able to shoot down significant numbers of bombers. This would allow the bombers of the 8th and other army air forces to penetrate deep into hostile territory and destroy Germany's ability to wage war by eliminating the key industries in her war economy. So was born the double bombing offensive, the RAF attacking German cities by night in an effort to break Germany's will and destroy urban areas, and the USAAF attacking vital industries by day in an effort to break Germany's ability to fight on. The Rouen raid con-

firmed the Americans' hopes, more than 50% of the bombs dropped falling on the target. Only a few fighters intercepted, causing no losses.

Small though it was at the time the general effect of the American effort was reflected in the German decision to step up day fighter production at the expense of night fighters, a clear indication that the Germans realized the vulnerability of their key industries to the ever-growing US day bomber effort. From then on the joint American/British day/night bomber offensive would overtax the Germans' defensive capabilities.

At the beginning of 1943, the primary objectives of the US effort were U-boat pens and yards, and the German aircraft industry. The 8th AAF had 155 bombers, against which the Germans could match 200 fighters. Bomber Command, meanwhile, continued its offensive against German cities with 740 four-engined bombers and 25 Mosquitoes, opposed by 390 night-fighters. At this time, the

efficiency of the British bombers was improving thanks to the introduction of the latest navigation aids, 'Oboe' and 'H₂S', and special marker bombs for use by the RAF's specialist 'Pathfinder Force' established in 1942.

Five major raids were launched against targets in the 'Battle of the Ruhr', between March and July 1943, by Bomber Command, but industrial production was not affected seriously. In all, there were 43 raids in the battle: 18,000 sorties resulting in the loss of 872 bombers, with another 2,126 damaged, an effective loss rate of some 4.85%. Bomber Command's highest total losses of the war occurred in June, when 275 bombers were lost and a further 662 damaged. It seemed, though, that Bomber Command had finally achieved its object with the devastation of Hamburg in four raids between 24 July and 2 August: 3,095 night bomber sorties, plus 235 daylight sorties in two USAAF raids, caused enormous damage on the ground, killing more than 50,000 civilians and

A North American P-51 Mustang fighter escorts Boeing B-17Gs of the 381st Bombardment Group on an 8th Air Force mission over northern Europe.

making homeless another 800,000. The most damaging of the raids was that of 27 July, when a 'firestorm' was created by the mass use of incendiary bombs: more than 40,000 were killed in the self-sustaining inferno of the firestorm.

The 8th AAF had moved on to attack targets in Germany, meanwhile, and had suffered its first significant defeat on 26 April 1943. Some 107 bombers tackled the Focke Wulf factory in Bremen, but lost 15 aircraft and another 48 damaged. However, the fact that the American threat was felt to be an important one is indicated by the German withdrawal of fighter units from other fronts for the day defence of the *Reich*, making the task of the Allies in Russia and in the Mediterranean somewhat easier.

The threat of the German fighters was confirmed in the 8th AAF's first large defeat on 17 August 1943, during the double attack on the ball-bearing factories at Schweinfurt and the Messerschmitt works at Regensburg. Though great damage was caused, the Americans lost 59 of the 363 bombers sent out, with many more damaged. This rude lesson was confirmed on 14 October, when Schweinfurt was again raided. Some 291 bombers set off, and though again the target was badly damaged, the Americans lost 60 bombers with another 138 damaged, a loss rate of 20.6%. Clearly such losses could not be sustained, and it was brought sharply home to the Americans that unescorted daylight raids against defended targets were impossible. But unlike the British,

who had opted for night raids, the USAAF only temporarily halted deep-penetration raids, until the first long-range escort fighter, the North American P-51 Mustang, arrived in quantity early in 1944. The other two fighters available, the Lockheed P-38 Lightning and Republic P-47 Thunderbolt, lacked the necessary range.

The British, having succeeded in the Battle of Hamburg, tried to repeat this in the Battle of Berlin, between 18 November 1943 and 24 March 1944. Harris thought that for the loss of only 500 aircraft, a combined British and American assault could so damage Berlin, its people and its industries, that the Germans would be forced to sue for peace. It must be admitted that this might have been a possi-

bility had the same success been achieved in Berlin as in Hamburg, had similar damage been inflicted on other German cities at the same time, and had not the country been under the control of so irrational a man as Adolf Hitler. Berlin was the object of 16 main raids involving 9,111 sorties, and 16 other 'nuisance' raids by 208 sorties, and the involvement of the USAAF was minimal. But the range was too great for an effective bombload to be carried, the German fighters were surmounting the effects of 'Window' (anti-radar reflecting chaff), and the flak defences were formidable: the result was an Allied defeat of considerable proportions. During the battle of Berlin, Battle Command had lost 1,146 bombers, an effective loss rate of 5.66%. The end of the Battle of Berlin and of the British strategic campaign against German cities at this time was marked by Bomber Command's heaviest single defeat, on 30 March 1944 in an attack on Nuremberg. Some 794 bombers caused relatively little damage, but lost 94 bombers shot down, 12 damaged beyond repair and 71 others less seriously damaged, the 294 German night-fighters involved causing most of the losses. This was a loss rate of 13.35%.

With the advent of the Mustang, the USAAF could once again start its deep raids into Europe, with the objective now being the elimination of the *Luftwaffe* by raids on Germany's aircraft factories, while the escort fighters decimated such *Luftwaffe* fighters as rose to intercept. The campaign started on 11 January 1944 with a defeat during a raid on Braunschweig after the bombers and their escort failed to link up in bad weather. Some 60 of the 667 bombers committed were lost to the German fighters. More successful though,

Three B-26 Marauders of US Far East Air Force on a bombing mission over Korea.

was the 'Big Week' between 20 and 26 February: 26 aircraft factories were attacked with some success in 3,800 US sorties, while losses amounted to only 228 bombers (6%) and 28 fighters, for the loss to the *Luftwaffe* of 355 of the 1,100 fighters available.

At the end of March 1944, control of the US and British strategic bomber forces passed to General Dwight D. Eisenhower for tactical use before the invasion of Europe on 6 June 1944. With strong Allied fighter escort for relatively short-range missions, the heavy bombers were able to carry maximum bombloads and attack by day against the decimated German fighter force, causing enormous tactical damage on German lines of communication in North-West Europe, and seriously hampering the build-up of German forces in the area. After the invasion the heavy bombers were used again for tactical purposes, twice blowing enormous holes through German defensive lines with a 'carpet' of bombs.

Thereafter the heavy bombers returned to their strategic roles, with the main emphasis as before, the USAAF attacking German aircraft strength in the air and on the ground, and Bomber Command tackling German cities. In fact, oil and energy production in Germany received a far higher percentage of the heavy bombers' attentions, and all manner of transport in Germany was cut to pieces in preparation for the Allied drives into that country. In March, April and May 1944 the Germans had lost 2,442 fighters in combat and another 1,500 to other causes, so the renewed American offensive met little resistance and succeeded in whittling away German strength still further. Even the belated introduction of great aircraft such as the Messerschmitt Me 262 jet fighter and the fascinating Me 163 rocket fighter could not stem the tide. By the end of 1944 Germany's armies were starved of fuel as production slumped and immense difficulties were encountered moving the fuel that had actually been produced.

Bomber Command's effort culminated in the destruction of Dresden with USAAF aid on 13–14 February 1945. The RAF's night raid, with 804 bombers, started an immense firestorm in the city, causing vast damage and killing tens of thousands of people. The city was the principal rail and logistic centre supplying the German Eastern Front and Soviet leaders wanted this complex knocked out. This was completed the next day in a raid by the 8th AAF.

In overall terms, it can be seen that the Allied joint bomber offensive did not gain

The Hawker Typhoon was conceived as a fighter, but came into its own as a heavy fighter-bomber in its Mark IB form. Its armament consisted of four 20-mm cannon in the wings, plus an underwing load of eight rocket projectiles or up to 2000 lb (907 kg) of bombs.

In its TF.10 form, the Bristol Beaufighter was perhaps the best strike fighter of World War II, playing an important part in the destruction of German coastal shipping in the North Sea with its four 20-mm cannon, seven 0.303-in (7.7-mm) machine-guns, one torpedo under the fuselage, and eight rocket projectiles or up to 1000 lb (454 kg) of bombs under the wings.

its true strategic objective, the elimination of the Germans' ability to prolong the war, until after the D-day landings, which many Allied air planners had hoped to render superfluous by strategic bombing in 1943 and early 1944. As it was, the relative weakness of the bomber forces and an unclear order of priorities in targeting meant that this chance slipped by. It must be emphasized though that worthwhile strategic results were achieved: German war production was increasingly tied to defensive rather than offensive weapons, the rate of production increase was slowed considerably, fighters were recalled from other fronts, large amounts of manpower and material had to be devoted to the anti-aircraft defences, considerable effort was used for the dispersion of key industries, and attacks on fortified areas such as the 'West Wall' tied down large numbers of men who could more profitably have been used for new formations needed in Russia.

So far as tactical air operations were concerned, it should be noted that during the period between 1941 and early 1944, the lessons learned in North Africa were carefully assimilated by the British and American air forces, and powerful tactical air units built up, largely with American bombers such as the Douglas A-20, the Martin B-26 Marauder and the North American B-25 Mitchell. By 1943, the Allies possessed highly effective tactical air forces based on such bombers, which were capable of carrying up to about 4,000 lb (1,814 kg) of bombs and were armed with both offensive and defensive guns, supported by powerful fighter-bombers such as the Republic Thunderbolt, Hawker Typhoon and other modified fighters, capable of carrying up to 2,000 lb (907 kg) of bombs or up to eight rockets, and armed with heavy machine-guns or four 20 mm cannons.

The medium bombers and attack aircraft proved decisive weapons of battlefield interdiction, while the fighter-bombers, supported on occasion by the medium bombers and attack aircraft, proved an invaluable weapon on the battlefield. This was amply shown in the battles of Mortain (7 August 1944) and of the Falaise Gap (13–19 August). At Mortain some 19 squadrons of RAF Typhoons were called in to stem a German armoured counterattack: in 294 sorties the RAF fighter-bombers dropped 80 tons of bombs and fired 2,088 rockets, knocking out a large number of armoured vehicles and halting the rest by destroying almost all the support vehicles on which they relied for ammunition and fuel. Much the same story can be told of the Falaise Gap action, where wave after wave of fighter-bombers and medium bombers decimated the Germans trying to escape Allied encirclement.

Also worthy of note was the part played by Allied aircraft in the maritime war, especially the defeat of the threat posed by German U-boats. The trouble was that early patrol aircraft such as the Lockheed Hudson and Avro Anson could operate only in coastal waters, and even long-range aircraft such as the Short Sunderland flying-boat could operate only relatively short ranges into the Atlantic from Newfoundland and Britain. Carrierborne aircraft eventually proved to be the answer, but these were not widely available until the advent of escort carriers in early 1943. Previously the 'gap' between the limits achievable by aircraft operating from each side of the Atlantic had been unclosable from the air.

Successes there were, however, especially after the introduction of air-to-surface vessel (ASV) radar during the late summer of 1940, and the introduction of effective weapons such as depth bombs and acoustic homing torpedoes. Aircraft were responsible for the destruction of 336 German, 16 Italian and 21 Japanese submarines (many in conjunction with surface forces), while 446 German, 69 Italian and 109 Japanese submarines were lost to other causes.

Allied aircraft also played an important part in the destruction of German and Italian merchant shipping, especially in the Mediterranean, the Bay of Biscay, the English Channel and the North Sea. The most important aircraft here were the Bristol Beaufighter, armed with cannon, rockets, bombs and torpedoes, and the de Havilland Mosquito, armed with cannon, rockets and bombs.

Derived from the Short 'C' class or Empire flying-boats, the Sunderland was Britain's best long-range patrol bomber. It played a significant part in defeating the threat of the German U-boats by the middle of 1943. The nose turret could be pulled back to make room for an anchor.

Air Tactics

True air war, in which both sides possessed aircraft, may be said to have started in 1914 with the beginning of World War I. Air fighting of a rudimentary nature started almost immediately after this, but with the carriage of weapons into the air generally frowned upon because of the inevitable loss of performance resulting from the weight penalty of of the gun, this early air fighting was sporadic, ill-organized (if organized at all) and almost entirely without results. So though there was an almost universal 'ban' on the fitting of machine-guns to aircraft, large numbers of other weapons were taken up: rifles, carbines, pistols, *fléchettes*, shotguns, grappling hooks and all manner of other unlikely weapons which could and did occasionally cause damage and inflict some casualties (and the very occasional death). But in the absence of adequate weapons, there emerged few tactics worthy of the name. Such tactics as there were resulted from the nature of the weapon used: *fléchettes* had to be dropped from above, so pilots strove to gain a position over their adversary; the optimum position for small arms fire was one of relative immobility in regard to the opponent, so pilots whose inclination had led them to such weapons were often seen flying alongside their would-be victim, potting away with a rifle while his opponent returned fire.

Later in 1914, though, improved performance and the need to deny the enemy the fruits of aerial reconnaissance, whose value had been amply proved in the first months of the war, led to a practical resurgence in interest about machine-guns as the primary armament of aircraft. By November and December 1914, therefore, the skies over the Western Front began to hear the ever more frequent sound of machine-gun fire. Mountings for such weapons were largely extemporized, but operational experience soon showed how these mountings could be modified for easier manoeuvring and reloading. At the same time tactics for air fighting began to acquire a measure of reality: the problems facing the early military aircrews were still legion, but most such aircrew were now in a position to see that at last they had practical armament of a kind, though it was by no means ideal, and that a study of elementary tactics would pay dividends not only in the winning of victories but also in the retention of their own lives.

Success in war is frequently attributed to an understanding and implementation of the variously defined and usually verbose 'principles of war'. There can be little doubt that an understanding of these principles is of great use in war, but for practical purposes, they can be summed up in the five words 'concentration in time and space'. Concentration in time gives the attacker speed and the element of surprise; concentration in space gives local superiority of forces and greater striking power. The combination of the two is a fairly good recipe for success, given that one's weapons, personnel and the like are a match for the enemy's.

With a few modifications this major principle was soon found to hold true in air combat. There was room for the headlong charge at the enemy, using speed and surprise in individual combats to fluster the opposing pilot and shoot him down before he could organize his defence; there was also room for careful stalking of a likely victim using all the 'cover' the sky can provide, so that he may be totally unaware of his danger until the moment bullets strike home. There was also the possibility of careful patrolling in large numbers, waiting for a loss of concentration on the part of numerically inferior opposition, or a diversion to aid the attackers by confusing the opposition, and there were many other ways in which the principle could be, and was, applied.

Early air tactics were essentially individual, evolved by pilots in the light of their own experiences and altered to suit the circumstances and the aircraft/armament installation they were using. A classic example of such tactics is provided by Captain Lanoe G. Hawker of No 6 Squadron, Royal Flying Corps. Hawker had been a keen advocate of aircraft armament for some time, and had always flown armed with a pistol which he would empty at any passing German aircraft. Then in June 1915, No 6 Squadron was issued with one Bristol Scout biplane, far superior in performance to the BE 2c reconnaissance/artillery spotting two-seaters which formed the principal equipment of the squadron. Greatly impressed with the capabilities of the Scout, Hawker immediately designed a Lewis gun mounting for the aircraft, angled out from the port side of the fuselage to fire past the left-hand edge of the disc swept by the propeller. This was the nearest Hawker could get to aligning his gun to fire along the aircraft's longitudinal axis, also the pilot's optimum line of sight straight forward, without mounting the gun above the upper wing where changing the ammunition drum was tricky. Having the gun on his left meant that Hawker could pilot with his right hand and fire the gun with his left.

On 25 July 1915, Hawker was on patrol between Passchendaele and Ypres in his armed Bristol Scout, and at about 1800 hours spotted a German two-seater below him, intent on its mission. Diving steeply, Hawker fired a 47-round drum at the two-seater, which turned and dived for safety deep behind its own lines. Undeterred, Hawker climbed again and resumed his patrol. Twenty minutes later another German two-seater appeared, this time over the Houthulst Forest. Again Hawker dived and fired, and again the German pilot in turn sheered off and dived for safety. But a British AA gun position in the area was able to report that the German aircraft had been forced down with its engine ruined by Hawker's gunfire. But the British pilot was not yet through, and about 40 minutes later spotted an Albatros two-seater at 10,000 ft (3,050 m) over Hooge. Hawker quickly climbed to 11,000 ft (3,353 m) and then swung down on the Albatros in a shallow dive from out of the westering sun. Hawker opened fire at a range of 100 yards (91.44 m), and the German aircraft immediately burst into flames,

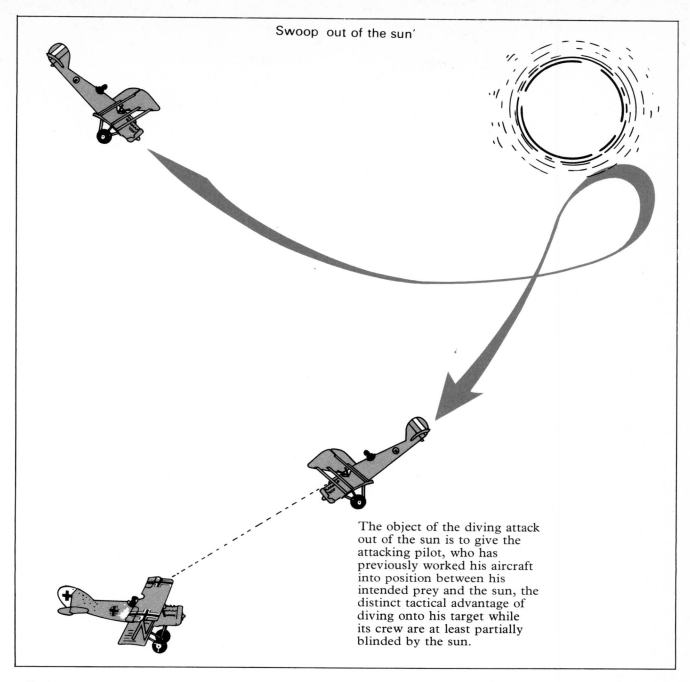

The object of the diving attack out of the sun is to give the attacking pilot, who has previously worked his aircraft into position between his intended prey and the sun, the distinct tactical advantage of diving onto his target while its crew are at least partially blinded by the sun.

rolled onto its back and crashed to destruction far below.

Here, then, were some of the basic elements of air tactics: a diving attack, to ensure a superiority of speed, careful consideration of conditions, to ensure surprise by diving out of the sun, and accurate shooting, no mean feat with a gun fitted to fire at an angle to the aircraft's line of flight. All three of Hawker's adversaries on that day had been armed with flexible machine-guns, and it was not surprising that Hawker was awarded the first Victoria Cross given for air combat. The award was gazetted on 24 August 1915, by which time the air war was beginning to alter dramatically.

The change had become inevitable on 1 April 1915, when Roland Garros introduced the era of true air fighting by shooting down his first aircraft, using a machine-gun capable of firing straight through the disc swept by the propeller. For although extraordinary pilots such as Hawker had the flying skill and intuitive shooting 'eye' to make use of devices such as the angled machine-gun, the average

pilot did not. The latter needed an aircraft with the gun aligned to fire directly forward, along the aircraft's line of flight and the pilot's parallel line of sight. Only thus was it possible to aim the whole aircraft at the enemy, and so fly the gun into position rather than have to make the difficult assessment of factors necessary to fly the aircraft into a position in which its angled machine-gun was at the correct bearing and elevation. Perhaps the single factor that marked 'ace' pilots from the more ordinary breed was their ability to come to the correct intuitive answer to the problems of deflection shooting, and so make the right allowances for the relative courses and speeds of the two aircraft involved, and aim off by the right angle (except in attacks from ahead or astern) to make their bullets and the target coincide in space and time. Such problems were greatly aided by the development of aircraft able to fire directly forwards, and even the ace pilots found such devices necessary once the era of true air fighting was under way: for whereas earlier fighting had taken place in an atmosphere of fairly leisurely flying, the introduction of effective armament led to an immediate increase in the use of aircraft manoeuvrability for evasive purposes. From late 1915, therefore, aircraft were designed with a far greater aerobatic agility, and the necessary structural strength (it was hoped) to execute the manoeuvres in safety. With aircraft jinking about in three dimensions at the merest hint of opposition, even the aces would have found it next to impossible to use an angled machine-gun effectively except in pursuit-course attacks.

On 1 April 1915, though, Roland Garros was finally in the right place at the right time and with the right weapon. A week of poor weather had kept most aircraft grounded, and the return of good conditions on this day meant that the air was relatively full of aircraft catching up on reconnaissance and returning to their normal tasks. Patrolling to the north of Buc, Garros spotted a flight of four Albatros two-seaters flying at 9,842 ft (3,000 m) over the front. None of the aircraft was armed with more than a carbine (rifles were relatively rare in the air because of their length). Seeing Garros flying towards them, the Germans paid little heed, for few aircraft weighed down by a machine-gun could operate at this altitude, and it was virtually unknown for a monoplane (Garros was flying a Morane-Saulnier Type L parasol-wing monoplane) to carry a machine-gun for offensive purposes. The surprise of the Germans must have been enormous as the French aircraft suddenly unleashed a hail of bullets through the turning propeller at one of their number. Garros fired three strips of Hotchkiss 0.315 in (8 mm) ammunition, and one of the German aircraft fell earthwards streaming flame, its pilot dead at the controls. Before his capture by the Germans 18 days later, Garros added two more confirmed victories and two unconfirmed claims to his total. Word of Garros' marksmanship and new weapon quickly spread along the front, and the German authorities were not slow to capitalize on their prize when Garros' aircraft fell into their hands on 19 April. As detailed in the air armament section, an effective gun synchronizer gear was quickly designed by the designers of the Fokker aircraft company, and rushed into service on the M.5k monoplane, which forthwith became the E.I. With this aircraft and the later E.II, E.III and E.IV the Germans ushered in the era of the true fighter aircraft.

If the weapon was adequate, early air tactics were not, and it was some time before the Germans became adept users of their new fighting aircraft, which were issued in ones and twos to *Fliegerabteilungen* operating two-seaters on the primary missions of artillery spotting and reconnaissance. The tactical doctrine of the day had progressed no further than the idea of providing such squadrons with a few fighting aircraft to escort them as they went about their tasks. Only later would there appear, as a result of the farsightedness of *Hauptmann* Oswald Boelcke, the rudimentary concept of air superiority, in which the fighters would be grouped together in homogeneous units for offensive purposes, acting on

their own so that maximum use could be made of the type's superior performance. The idea was to sweep the skies clear of enemy fighters, thus giving the German two-seaters total freedom to operate as they wished, and the German fighters the chance to get amongst the Allied two-seaters without hindrance from Allied fighters. The concept was entirely valid, if complete execution was impossible.

The initial lack of expertise can be seen in the first victory secured by *Leutnant* Max Immelmann, one of the two great aces to emerge from those flying the Fokker *Eindecker* fighters. On 1 August 1915 Immelmann, having made only two previous training flights on an *Eindecker*, set off about 10 minutes later than his commander, Oswald Boelcke, because he had first rushed to his two-seater when British machines bombed *Fliegerabteilung Nr* 62's airfield near Douai. Only when his observer, *Leutnant* Ehrhardt von Teubern, declined to fly in the poor conditions did Immelmann rush to the unit's second *Eindecker*. Chasing the British machines, Immelmann saw Boelcke attack and then break off, his gun jammed by a faulty round. But Immelmann was not deterred by the prospect of tackling 10 British two-seaters (though he did not know it at the time, they were all being flown as unarmed single-seaters to allow a bombload to be carried), and picked a machine straggling slightly as the object of his attack. But then Immelmann tried unsuccessfully to down the British machine: he sprayed the machine, so he thought, with several bursts fired from each side, from below and from dead astern, all apparently without effect. But then the British machine put its nose down in a steep glide and landed in a field behind the German lines. Immelmann landed beside the British aircraft, and found that the pilot had been wounded in the left arm. Immelmann had fired more than 100 rounds, but only from long range and some unrealistic angles, and was fortunate to secure his victory.

But experience soon taught the Germans better methods of getting the most out of their indifferent aircraft, Immelmann in particular soon proving himself a master of the new art. One tactic has since been associated with him – the 'Immelmann turn'. This involves the pilot of the attacking aircraft positioning his machine above and behind the prospective victim. The attacker then dives towards the target passing behind it and then using the speed built up in the dive to climb up past the target, raking the latter in the resultant firing pass. Continuing past the target, the attacker zoom climbs into the beginning of a loop, kicking the rudder bar over as the aircraft reaches the vertical, to reverse course and begin another diving attack on the target, should it still be flying, though the attack this time will be from the front. For its time the tactic was excellent, because it ensured that the attacker always had a speed superiority, and could continue his attacks until the target was shot down. As better armed Allied aircraft, with performance superior to the *Eindecker*, appeared the tactic became obsolete,

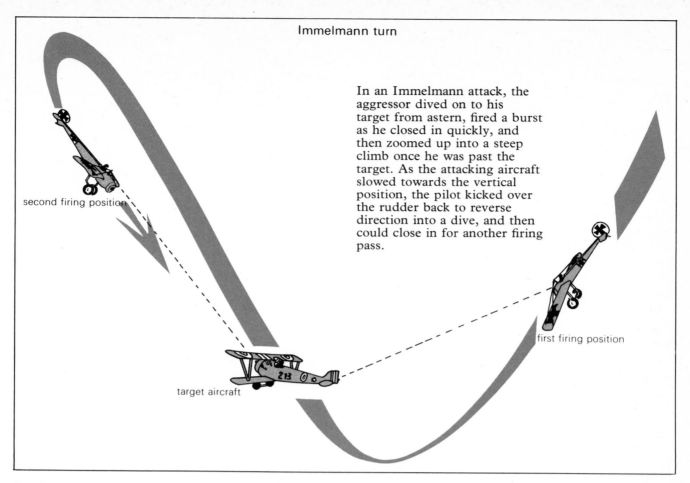

Immelmann turn

In an Immelmann attack, the aggressor dived on to his target from astern, fired a burst as he closed in quickly, and then zoomed up into a steep climb once he was past the target. As the attacking aircraft slowed towards the vertical position, the pilot kicked over the rudder back to reverse direction into a dive, and then could close in for another firing pass.

second firing position

target aircraft

first firing position

for the potential victim became the attacker if not dispatched in the first firing pass. It could climb after the Fokker as the latter began its zoom climb, and pick it off in a simple no-deflection shot as the German pilot lost speed and kicked over the rudder bar.

Oswald Boelcke also showed himself to be a superb combat pilot, generally superior to Immelmann. More importantly, however, he showed himself to be the world's first master technician of the air. Immelmann had excelled in individual combat, but Boelcke went beyond this, and while considering the requirements for victory in individual combat, also considered how best to achieve the right tactical position even before combat was joined. Frequently finding himself some distance from a likely target, Boelcke carefully used the sun and clouds to close in on his hopefully unsuspecting target so as to dispatch him without warning in one swift pounce. All too frequently, though, Boelcke found his stalk interrupted by another Allied aircraft, which then had him at a tactical disadvantage. Boelcke thus came up with the idea that has lasted to this day as a general tactical precept of air combat: a single aircraft is hopelessly vulnerable to attack whether it is on the offensive or defensive, and so the minimum tactical unit of fighting aircraft should be two. In such a unit, the leader would constitute the mid and cutting edge of the team, selecting the target and closing in for the kill, while the second pilot, or wingman, operating slightly behind and to one side of his leader, and usually at a slightly greater height, would protect his leader from attack by any intervening aircraft, the wingman's eyes serving as the leader's second pair,

leaving the leader to concentrate on the primary task of dispatching the target aircraft. This and other tactical principles and ideas formalized by Boelcke were adopted quickly by other German pilots, and soon became common to both sides. Boelcke also wrote down his principles, and these have become known as the 'Dikta Boelcke', still generally valid today.

During the spring of 1916, Boelcke and many other German pilots were concentrated in the region of Verdun for the great battle of attrition there, in which the German high command hoped to 'bleed France white'. To protect their own rear areas from the reconnaissance of French aircraft, the Germans instituted what became known as barrage patrols over the front line, elements of three aircraft patrolling the front to prevent any incursion into German airspace by French aircraft. Effective enough in its limited way, the system failed to shoot down significant numbers of French aircraft, for the reconnaissance machines and their escorts soon came to see that the German aircraft (both two-seaters and fighters were used) were 'policemen' on a beat, and could be avoided. Boelcke saw the inefficiency of the system, and his growing number of aerial victories were enough to persuade the authorities that his was a voice that should be listened to. In August 1916, therefore, at a time when the Allies had regained air superiority over the Somme battlefield and the Germans called off the great Verdun battle, homogenous fighter squadrons were at last formed by the Germans, following the example already set by the British and French. Only thus, Boelcke had reasoned, could the growing number of Allied fighters be tackled on equal terms, and the air war taken to the enemy by offensive patrolling, rather than merely waiting for 'trade' to come their way as had been the case with the barrage patrols.

It had been over Verdun, moreover, that the first major air battles had begun to occur, with the obsolescent Fokker monoplanes receiving rough handling by the French Nieuport 11 fighter, later joined by the redoubtable Nieuport 17. Such combats, in which a relatively large number of aircraft were involved, quickly became known as 'dogfights' and provided Boelcke with the stimulus to formalize his ideas on air fighting for the benefit of less experienced pilots. Firstly, each pilot must know about the construction of his aircraft, and the strengths and weaknesses of the design, so that he could get the best out of his machine and avoid getting into situations in which his opponent could exploit the weaknesses of the design. Secondly, he must know as much as possible about the strengths and weaknesses of any Allied aircraft he was likely to encounter. Thirdly, the pilot must be fully at home in his aircraft as a result of training and familiarization flights, so that the machine could be exploited fully without conscious thought, the full spectrum of aerial manoeuvres being second nature to the pilot. Fourthly, the pilot must know all about his armament, so that the right range and deflection could be selected simply, and jams and stoppages cleared quickly and without taking his attention away from more pressing matters. Fifthly, the pilot must develop the knack of seeing enemy aircraft without himself being seen, developing this knack of spotting opposing aircraft at a considerable range by constant practice in knowing how to search the sky and what to look for. Sixthly, the pilot must acquire the habit of 'taking in' uncons-

ciously the general progress of the whole multi-aircraft dogfight going on around the individual cambat in which the pilot was himself involved, so that a third party entering the duel could be spotted and allowed for, and no time wasted in assessment of the general situation after the end of an individual combat. Seventhly, the pilot was to become accustomed to flying in a regular position in the formation, so that teamwork was improved and each man could get used to flying with the same companions. Eighthly, the pilot must memorize a number of rendezvous points in the area, so that if the formation were split up, lost pilots could pick up the formation again by circling over the rendezvous point just under the clouds (aircraft over clouds being very easy to spot) until rejoined by others of the formation. Ninthly, formation was to be kept at all times, leaving the leader to spot the opposition while the others covered his and each others' tail by constant vigilance, unless another pilot spotted the opposition first and signalled the leader by moving ahead and waggling his wings before turning in the direction of the opposition. Tenthly, the leader would signal the best method of attack, using all advantages such as sun, cloud, haze and rain, but attacks would always be from above where possible. Eleventhly, once combat had been joined in a dogfight, it was every man for himself, but it was essential to keep a cool head and courting disaster to try to evade an attacker by the execution of copybook aerobatics such as loops and half-rolls.

Perhaps the most important thing that Boelcke told his pilots was the futility of smoothly executed, predictable evasive manoeuvres in combat. When attacked, he told his pilots, they should always turn into the attacker so that a circling combat would ensue: here it was essential for the pilot to keep his

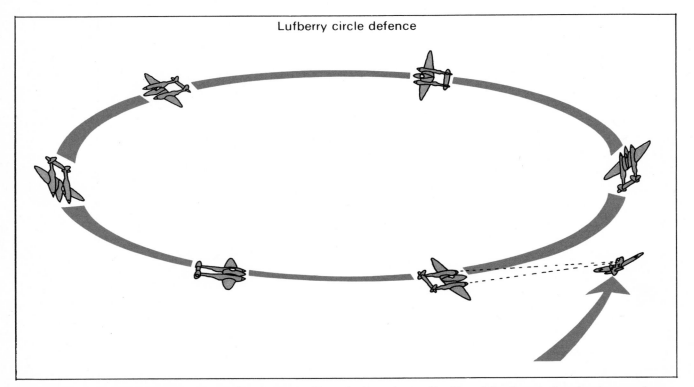

Lufberry circle defence

The Lufberry circle defence, named for the great French-American pilot Raoul Lufberry, involved a number of aircraft following each other round in a circle, so that any fighter attempting to get into a firing position on one aircraft's tail could be engaged by the pilot of the aircraft next astern.

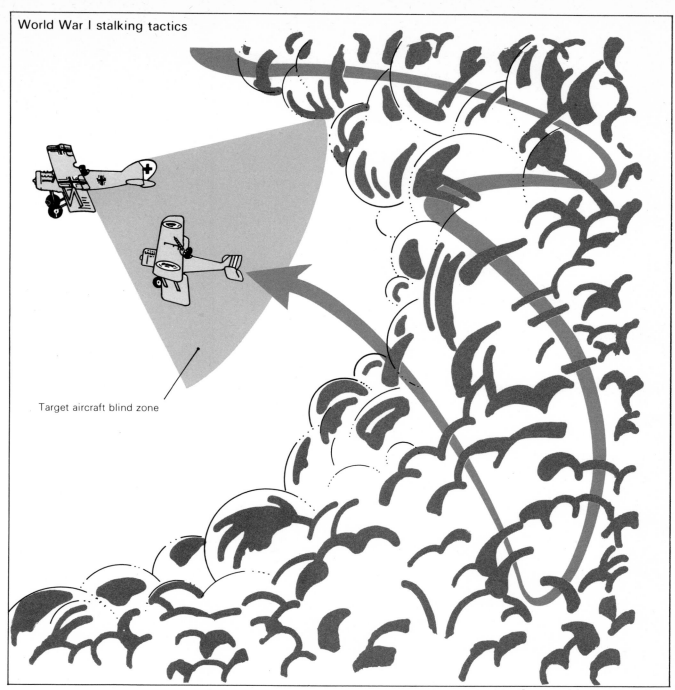

Target aircraft blind zone

The object of the tactics favoured by Albert Ball and other 'loner' aces of World War I was to stalk the target aircraft using cloud cover and any other natural camouflage, and so close right up under his tail, in the observer/gunner's blind spot. The attacker could then either pull up the nose of his aircraft and rake the target's belly at point-blank range in a no-deflection shot, or merely angle up the quadrant-mounted machine-gun on the upper wing, again to rake the target's belly in a point-blank no-deflection shot.

turn as tight as possible to try to close up on his attacker and dispatch him with an accurate burst of machine-gun fire. Vitally important in a turning fight, though, was perfect control so that height was not lost, for this inevitably gave the enemy the upper hand. Boelcke also stressed the manifest lack of sense in running from a fight with an aircraft of equal performance, unless some tactical consideration gave the pursued aircraft a considerable advantage – greater acceleration in a dive perhaps. But to be avoided at all costs were jinking movements, for the pursuer could always cut across the corner so formed and make up the necessary distance on the pursued aircraft.

From its small beginnings over Verdun in March and April 1916, dogfighting quickly grew in scope and geographical extent during the rest of the year, so

by the winter formations of perhaps 50 or more aircraft were often involved, and dogfighting became the air war 'norm'. There was still scope for individuals, however, in careful stalking attacks on lone reconnaissance machines, or small flights of unescorted two-seaters, or even on unwary fighters which could be dispatched quickly, allowing the attacker to dive to safety or to disappear into a cloud. It should be emphasized here, that though air combat is usually considered in terms of fighter *versus* fighter battles, this was not always the case. Even when used offensively, the primary function of the fighter is defensive: to prevent the enemy's fighters operating against one's own aircraft, and by destroying enemy aircraft to prevent them gaining the benefits of reconnaissance, bombing and spotting for the artillery. Seen in this light, combat against other fighters could only be a means to an end, the destruction of the enemy's offensive aircraft. The fighters' main target, therefore, were the so-called 'corps aircraft', two-seaters engaged in reconnaissance/artillery-spotting work, and later in the war the bombers/ground-attack aircraft which came to play an increasingly important part in the conduct of operations. The general principle held true in World War II, in which the fighters' main targets were the bombers, and still holds true today. In essence, the more damage an aircraft cause, both directly and indirectly, the higher its position on the defending fighters' list of priority targets. The pure fighter, with little offensive value as such, comes relatively low down on the list. Neat though this seems, however, in practice it was and is difficult to attack only the aircraft at the top of the priorities list, for there is every chance that enemy fighters will intervene.

Two-seaters were therefore the main target in World War I, and were at a disadvantage in attacks by fighters: the aircraft itself was generally not as manoeuvrable nor as high in performance as the fighter, and was usually worse armed; and the pilot of the two-seater was trained for his primary mission of reconnaissance and artillery-spotting rather than air combat. Nevertheless, some two-seaters could give a very good account of themselves, and although the standard armament of two machine-guns (one fixed weapon fired by the pilot, and one flexible weapon operated by the observer/gunner) meant that only one gun at a time could be brought to bear on the attacker (usually equipped with two guns from 1917 onwards), defensive fire could be thrown up in most areas except directly under the fuselage.

One of the arch exponents of the difficult task of individual stalking was Captain Albert Ball, one of Britain's major aces of World War I, and a supreme individualist in the air. Although by inclination a lone operator, Ball was capable of worsting an enemy force superior in numbers. An enthusiast in his work, he delighted in telling all of his accomplishments, in a way indicative of his youth (he was 20 in 1916). A letter to his parents reveals his attitude and capabilities:

'Really I am having too much luck for a boy. I will start right away, and tell you all. On August 22 (1916), I went up. Met twelve Huns.

'No. 1 fight. I attacked and fired two drums, bringing the machine down just outside a village. All crashed up.

'No. 2 fight. I attacked and got under machine, putting in two drums. Hun went down in flames.

'No. 3 fight. I attacked and put in one drum. Machine went down and crashed on a housetop.

'I only got hit eleven times in the plane's (wings), so I returned and got more ammunition. This time luck was not all on the spot. I was met by fourteen Huns, about fifteen miles over their side. My windscreen was hit in four places, mirror broken, the spar of the left (wing) broken, also engine ran out of petrol. But I had a good sport and good luck, but

only just, for I was brought down about one mile over our side . . .

'Oh, la, la. Topping, isn't it?'

Ball's favourite mount was the Nieuport 17, the type he was flying at the time of the extraordinary first-hand account above. This aircraft had provision for a Lewis gun firing over the upper wing, in the way pioneered by the Nieuport 11, also flown by Ball. It was the location of the gun, as well as the perfect handling characteristics of the aircraft, which attracted Ball: for all his enthusiasm, he was embued with enormous amounts of patience, and he often patrolled on the edge of the clouds, using his excellent eyesight to pick up lone German two-seaters at long range. With an uncanny intuitive ability Ball would then set off in lonely and circuitous pursuit, using all the cover he could, so as to come up on the enemy aircraft from dead astern and slightly under the tail, the gunner's blind spot. In this position Ball was able to close up right under the fuselage of his target, pull back the Lewis gun to an angle of about 45°, and rake the belly of the aircraft in a no-deflection shot almost certain to hit the engine, fuel tanks, pilot and observer. Ball finally disappeared in unexplained circumstances on 6 May 1917 after scoring 44 victories.

With the growing size of the air war over the Western Front, there gradually came to be no scope for individualists such as Ball. The last of the real individuals, the Frenchman *Capitaine* Georges Guynemer, was killed on 11 September 1917. But Guynemer was not an individual tactician like Ball, but rather a pilot who capitalized on good shooting ability combined with the tactical surprise of a headlong attack no matter what the odds. Such attacks had given Guynemer a good proportion of his 54 victories.

Though the days of the complete individualist were effectively over by the middle of 1917, submerged in the whirling dogfights between the so-called 'flying circuses' of the Germans (the elite *Jagdgeschwader* of four *Jagdstaffeln*, a logical increase in the size of the fighting formation advised by Boelcke for command by a single leader) and the Allied fighter squadrons, with upwards of 100 aircraft frequently involved, there was still scope for small, tight formations under an able leader. This was proved by the Allied ace of aces, *Capitaine* Rene Fonck, who scored 75 victories, just five short of *Rittmeister* Manfred, *Freiherr* von Richthofen's tally. Fonck was notable for his superb tactical positioning, precise flying and quite outstanding marksmanship, the latter resulting in such economy of ammunition that many of his claims were at first disbelieved. Perhaps the classic example of Fonck's skill occurred on 9 May 1918, when in two combats he shot down six German aircraft. He set off on his first patrol of the day, accompanied by two wingmen, at 1600 hours. Climbing as they headed for the front line in search of 'trade', the patrol spotted a reconnaissance two-seater escorted by a pair of two-seat fighters. Fonck immediately dived to the attack, and sent one aircraft down with a short burst that killed the pilot. Then giving the other German aircraft no time to gather their wits about them, Fonck immediately reversed course and sent another aircraft earthwards streaming flame. The third German aircraft had taken the brief respite afforded it by the destruction of its two comrades to turn back for the German lines in a steep dive. Yet Fonck was after in a moment, and within 45 seconds of the beginning of the engagement the last German had been destroyed, this time the aircraft falling apart in the air as a result of Fonck's fire. All three aircraft fell within 400 yards (365 m) of each other, eloquent proof of the cohesive speed of Fonck's attack. Yet the day was not yet over, and after a return to base for reammunitioning, Fonck was airborne again by 1730 hours accompanied by two different wingmen. At 1830 hours Fonck spotted a German two-seater some distance off. Dodging into cloud cover for an undetected approach, Fonck reappeared at exactly the right spot and shot down the two-seater before its crew had even realized they were under attack. At this point there appeared on the scene four Fokker and five Albatros fighters, and not even Fonck wanted to engage such odds. But there had long been in the French ace the desire to score five victories in one day, and this persuaded Fonck that a chance could be taken: he immediately pounced on the last Fokker and sent it down, relying on the fact that the Germans would not be expecting attack, but taking their time readying themselves for combat on their own terms. Fonck had scored his five victories and turned for home pursued by the eight German fighters. The leader of the formation managed to get slightly ahead of Fonck, who was flying a Spad S.13, and tried to turn him back towards the pack of German fighters. Fonck saw a small scoring opportunity and shot down the leader before making good his escape. It was a remarkable feat, and equalled by only three men in World War I: Captain William Claxton, Captain H. W. Woollett and Captain J. L. Trollope, all of the Royal Flying Corps. Unlike the Britons, however, Fonck repeated his sextuple victory on 26 September 1918.

Fonck was a keen advocate of the three-man V formation used by most Allied air forces from 1917 onwards. Such an arrangement, with the leader well covered by his wingmen, seemed to offer the best compromise between manageable size (in the days before air-to-air radio telephony, hand signals and prearranged wing movements had to be used for communication) and effective tactical disposition/fighting strength. Occasionally a fourth machine was added to one side of the V, and such three- or four-aircraft Vs, disposed three-dimensionally, were an effective method of deploying a squadron in flight, in three one-V flights.

By 1918, tactics had become fairly standard on both sides of the line, the three basic combat formations being the V described above, line and echelon. The line formation consisted simply of all the aircraft of a squadron in line abreast, with the

leader at one end of the line. The echelon formation again placed the squadron in a line, in this case stepped backwards and upwards as though on a ladder, with the leader at the bottom. In such a formation the tail of the man in front and below could be watched by the man behind, while the rear aircraft was flown by a seasoned veteran unlikely to be caught napping by an attack out of the sun. The most important variation on these standard dispositions was the *Juncksche Reihe* or Junck's Row, developed by *Leutnant* Werner Junck, the commander of *Jagdstaffel Nr* 8 from March 1918. This formation was an adaptation of the basic echelon, with the stepped-up line disposed diagonally across the sky. The great advantage of the Junck's Row formation was that the whole line could manoeuvre three-dimensionally with less chance of aerial collision than would otherwise have been the case.

Perhaps the perfect fighting disposition, so far as World War I was concerned, was that evolved by No 84 Squadron, RFC from the beginning of 1918 onwards. The three flights of the squadron, each with five aircraft, were echeloned upwards and backwards with between 1,500 ft (457 m) and 3,000 ft (914 m) between the flights. The flight at the bottom led, and was normally the first into action, the other two flights circling above to ensure that no German top-cover fighters could intervene in the dogfight below, and only assisting the first flight when necessary. Wherever possible, some fighters were left 'upstairs' to prevent the British fighters from being 'bounced'. The concept was further expanded in 1918 to the use of three or more squadrons: at low level would be a squadron of Sopwith Camels to harass the German ground forces with machine-gun fire and light bombs, and protect the low-level corps aircraft as they went about their business. At about 14,000 ft (4,267 m) would be a squadron of SE 5a fighters to guard the Camel unit from surprise attack, and also to deter German fighters from trying to intercept Allied reconnaissance and bomber aircraft on their missions. Right at the top of the stack would be a squadron of Bristol F.2B Fighters, twin-seat fighters with excellent performance at altitude, operating at about 18,000 ft (5,486 m) to prevent the best German fighters from diving out of the sun on any of the lower formations.

The tactical methods devised and used by fighter pilots for both offensive and defensive purposes were numerous, yet one tactical disposition was ideally suited to the capabilities of two-seaters, and was widely used by all combatants. This was the 'Lufberry circle', named after the supposed inventor, Raoul Lufberry, who had been born in France of French parents who then emigrated to the USA. Lufberry joined the Foreign Legion and served in the French bomber force before returning to train and then fly with the Americans until his death on 19 May 1918. The tactic named after Lufberry consisted of a number of two-seaters circling round an imaginary common point when under heavy attack. In this way it was impossible for any

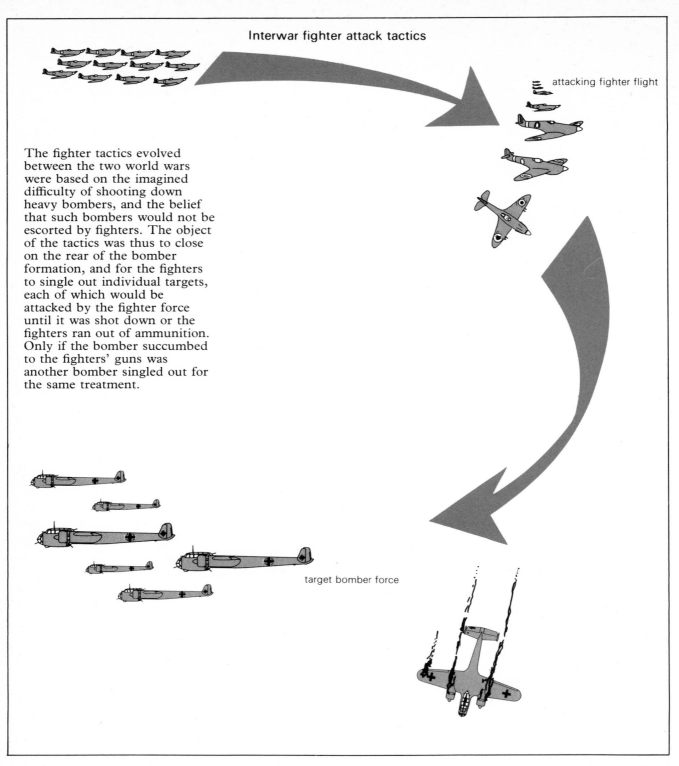

The fighter tactics evolved between the two world wars were based on the imagined difficulty of shooting down heavy bombers, and the belief that such bombers would not be escorted by fighters. The object of the tactics was thus to close on the rear of the bomber formation, and for the fighters to single out individual targets, each of which would be attacked by the fighter force until it was shot down or the fighters ran out of ammunition. Only if the bomber succumbed to the fighters' guns was another bomber singled out for the same treatment.

attacking fighter flight

target bomber force

attacker to single out a two-seater for individual attack: if the attacker came in at a tangent, he could be engaged by the rear gunner of the aircraft under attack, and also by the fixed gun of the aircraft next astern in the circle; if he tried an attack from above, several gunners could engage him; and if he tried to attack from below, the gunners on the far side of the circle could engage him. It was, of course, possible to get into the circle and shoot down several aircraft, but this took considerable skill and great courage, and was not attempted by many pilots.

The skills of single-seat fighter pilots were of a different nature, and can perhaps best be summed up by accounts of two classic actions: the engagement in which *Leutnant* Werner Voss, commander of *Jagdstaffel Nr* 10 and victor of 48 aerial combats was killed; and the battle fought by Major W. G. Barker in

which he took on more than 60 German fighters.

A mercurial man and brilliant individual tactical pilot, Voss took off late in the afternoon of 23 September 1917 in a Fokker Dr.I triplane, painted in his own colour scheme of silvery blue, and set course for the lines. Over Ypres he spotted a formation of six Bristol Fighters and six SE 5as, below his own altitude of 16,404 ft (5,000 m). Despite the odds (or perhaps because of them, which would give Voss the tactical advantage of knowing that all other aircraft involved were hostile, while the British fighters would have to be careful lest they shoot down one of their own number) Voss decided to attack, relying on the supreme agility of the Fokker triplane and his own flying skills to keep him out of trouble. Selecting the rear SE 5a as his victim, Voss plummeted down and caught the British aircraft completely un-

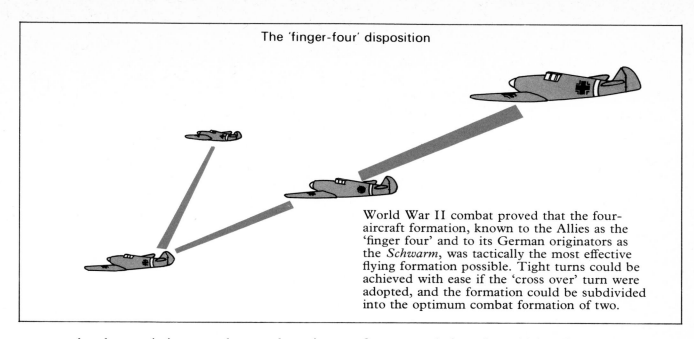

The 'finger-four' disposition

World War II combat proved that the four-aircraft formation, known to the Allies as the 'finger four' and to its German originators as the *Schwarm*, was tactically the most effective flying formation possible. Tight turns could be achieved with ease if the 'cross over' turn were adopted, and the formation could be subdivided into the optimum combat formation of two.

awares; the chosen victim started to go down in a steep spiral dive, with Voss still on its tail putting in further quick bursts of fire. As he dived Voss had spotted two flights of RE 8 reconnaissance/artillery-spotter and two flights of Sopwith Camel fighter aircraft off to the south-west, at lower altitude and too far away to be significant in the short battle planned by Voss. But then Voss suddenly became aware of more aircraft on his tail: these were the six 5as of B Flight, No 56 Squadron, led by Captain James McCudden, who finally scored 57 victories, with 2nd Lieutenant A. P. F. Rhys Davids (22 victories), Lieutenant R. A. Mayberry (25 victories), Lieutenant C. A. Lewis (eight victories), Lieutenant G. H. Bowman (32 victories) and Lieutenant R. T. C. Hoidge (27 victories). Voss could hardly have fallen in with worse company so far as his own survival was concerned. B Flight had many claims to being the most successful British flight of the war, and had earlier been commanded by Ball.

B Flight was just forming up again after dispatching a D.F.W. two-seater, and was about to attack a flight of six Albatros fighters when McCudden 'saw ahead of us . . . an SE-5 half spinning down . . . pursued by a silvery blue German triplane at very close range. The SE-5 certainly looked very unhappy, so we changed our minds about attacking the six V-strutters (Albatros fighters), and went to the rescue of the unfortunate SE-5. The Hun triplane was practically underneath our formation now, and so we dived down at a colossal speed. I went to the right, Rhys-Davids to the left, and we got behind the triplane together.' Voss's escape seemed impossible, for he had SE 5as to each side of him, Sopwith Camels below him, and Bristol Fighters and more SE 5as above him. Then Voss came up with something entirely new: in McCudden's words . . . 'he turned in a most disconcertingly quick manner, not in a climbing or an Immelmann turn, but a sort of half-flat spin. By now the German triplane was in the middle of our formation, and its handling was wonderful to behold. The pilot seemed to be firing at all of us simultaneously, and although I got behind

for a second time, I could hardly stay there for a second. His movements were so quick and uncertain that none of us could hold him in sight at all for any decisive time.'

The situation now was that Voss was engaged by seven SE 5as (the original victim and the six B Flight aircraft), while six Bristol Fighters and 17 Sopwith Camels and SE 5as circled above and below to prevent Voss escaping or other German fighters from intervening. Also in the area were the two flights of RE 8 aircraft earlier spotted by Voss. For minutes Voss fought on, evading each attack with a display of unparalleled aerial agility of an entirely novel nature, and getting off numerous quick bursts of fire towards his attackers. McCudden 'again got a good opportunity, as he was coming towards me nose on, and slightly underneath, and apparently not seen me. I dropped my nose, got him well in my sight and pressed both triggers. As soon as I fired, up came his nose at me, and I heard clack-clack-clack-clack, as his bullets passed close to me and through my wings. I distinctly noticed the red-yellow flashes from his parallel Spndau guns . . . By this time a red-nosed Albatros had arrived and was apparently doing its best to guard the triplane's tail, and it was well handled, too. The formation of six Albatroses which we were going to attack at first stayed above us and were prevented from diving on us by the arrival of a formation of Spads, whose leader apparently appreciated our position and kept the six Albatroses otherwise engaged . . . The triplane was still circling round in the midst of seven SE-5's, who were all firing at it as opportunity offered, and at one time I noticed the triplane in the apex of a cone of tracer bullets from at least five machines simultaneously, and each machine had two guns.'

Several times Voss broke out of the circle of attackers, but each time returned to the fray. The Albatros was shot down, and by now the combat had lost most of its altitude. Then the triplane's flight became erratic, and Rhys-Davids finished off the clearly wounded Voss. He emptied several drums of Lewis gun ammunition into the still fighting triplane, and then fired his fixed Vickers gun into the cockpit. The triplane lost height and then went into a dive, hitting the ground and disappearing into 'a thousand fragments, for it seemed to me that it literally went to powder.' Only McCudden saw this last stage, and Voss, probably dead or very close to death, stalled and dived into the ground from 1,000 ft (305 m). The fight had lasted about 10 minutes, and McCudden summed it up thus: 'It was now quite late, so we flew home to the aerodrome, and as long as I live I shall never forget my admiration for that German pilot who singlehandedly fought seven of us for ten minutes, and also put some bullets through all of our machines. His flying was wonderful, his courage magnificent, and in my opinion he is the bravest German airman whom it has been my privilege to fight.' Only next day was it revealed that Rhys-Davids' victim was Voss, at the time second only to Manfred von Richthofen in the German list.

Major William G. Barker was a Canadian, and had commanded No 139 Squadron in northern Italy. Posted to the command of a school of aerial fighting in September 1918, Barker argued that he needed recent combat experience over France before taking up his new appointment. This subterfuge to get back into action over France worked, and Barker was given one of the latest Sopwith Snipe fighters and a roving commission in France. It was while he was temporarily attached to No 201 Squadron, Royal Air Force, that Barker fought his celebrated action against enormous odds on 27 October 1918.

Barker had, in fact, been ordered home to England, and had set off from No 201 Squadron's airfield with full tanks. About 20 minutes after taking off, he noticed a Rumpler two-seater flying at about 21,000 ft (6,400 m), and could not resist the urge to take one last crack at the opposition. Closing in rapidly, Barker sent the Rumpler down in flames, following to see where it crashed. But then, with his attention wrongly focussed on the Rumpler, Barker felt the impact of machine-gun bullets on his aircraft, and then an agonizing pain in his right leg: an incendiary bullet had ploughed through his right thigh, shattering the bone. This restricted him to left rudder only, which he immediately applied with all the strength he could muster. Swinging round, the Snipe now presented Barker with the intimidating visual evidence that he had fallen foul of one of the oldest tricks in the book: the two-seater had merely been bait in a German trap, the teeth of which were now closing in on him, in the form of *Jagdgeschwader Nr 3*, whose *Jagdstaffeln Nr* 2, 26, 27 and 36 mustered about 60 of Germany's latest fighter, the redoubtable Fokker D.VII, reckoned by many to have been the finest fighter of the war. The Germans were stepped up in four *Jasta*-strength groups from 8,202 ft (2,500 m) upwards.

Unlike Voss, who might have managed to escape, Barker realized that there was no way out for him, and only the surprise of an immediate attack seems to have prevented the Germans finishing off Barker

immediately. Almost immediately Barker shot down the aircraft which had first attacked him, and then turned his attention to another D.VII, which caught fire and crashed after two bursts. By this time, though, the Germans had recovered from their surprise, and realized that the remaining number of them were pitted against a single Briton. Clearly there were too many aircraft for attacks by all of them at once, so while the rest guarded the approaches to the arena, flights of five aircraft attacked from each side, while others stationed themselves above and below Barker to cut him to pieces if he tried to climb or dive out of trouble. In the next few minutes the Snipe was hit by more than 300 machine-gun bullets, and then Barker was again wounded, this time in the left leg. It was now virtually impossible for Barker to operate the rudder bar at all, and all his evasive manoeuvres had to be flown with the ailerons and elevators, operated by the control column, and the engine throttle. Blood was pouring from the original wound in his right thigh, and Barker finally fainted. The Snipe immediately fell into a spin, though the rush of air and the motion of the aircraft roused Barker after the machine had fallen some 6,000 ft (1,829 m). The fight had by now descended to about 8,000 ft (2,438 m), and all four Staffeln were now involved as Barker brought the Snipe out of its spin. Realizing that he had no hope of escape, Barker decided to use all his ammunition and then try to ram one of his opponents. One of the D.VIIs again fell to his guns, but then another German bullet hit him, shattering his left elbow. Again Barker fell unconscious, and again the Snipe went into a spin. It was perhaps this which saved Barker's life, for the Germans could not consciously follow what Barker did unconsciously. Recovering from his second bout of unconsciousness, Barker found himself spinning, and dangerously close to the ground. He managed to come out of the spin and level out, despite being able to use only his right forearm. Barker decided to put the aircraft down though he was travelling at almost 100 mph (160 kph): the undercarriage was ripped right off, and the airframe sailed on for some 200 yards (183 m), losing its wings and much else in the process, before coming to a halt upside down. British troops in the area rushed over to haul out the body and were amazed to find Barker still alive, his legs held to his torso by little more than sinews. Barker was unconscious for 10 days, but when managed a full recovery in time to receive his Victoria Cross from King George V on 30 November 1918.

Between the world wars there was little initial modification of tactics, but rather a refinement of the lessons of World War I. Throughout the 1920s and early 1930s, however, the threat of the bomber came to assume paramount importance, and the tactics of World War I were modified slowly in an effort to provide some means of defeating the threat that many politicians, civilians and even military figures who should have been better informed, believed could not be countered. The concept is enshrined in the words of Stanley Baldwin: 'The bomber will always get through'.

It was therefore accepted in the 1930s that the fighter's primary task would be the engagement of enemy bombers. To what extent there would also be combat against enemy fighters was uncertain, despite the clear lessons of the Spanish Civil War and the air war in China. As late as 1938, the RAF manual on air tactics claimed that dogfighting was no longer possible as a result of the detrimental effect that the g forces inherent in high-speed manoeuvring would have on the pilots.

Most of World War I's tactical formations had survived with little modification into the 1930s, and the formation adopted by most air forces for their bomber forces was a standard V of three aircraft. It appeared logical, therefore, to oppose this bomber formation with a similar fighter formation, and this fitted well with current unit strengths, a standard 12-fighter squadron being neatly divided into four sections each of three aircraft. Approaching combat, the squadron would fly in four Vs, each of one section, the leader of each section flying in the middle of the V, with the squadron leader at the apex of the whole formation of four Vs one behind the other. Arriving hopefully on the flank of the enemy bomber formation, each section would be ordered into echelon port or starboard and then move in to attack the bombers. The first section would tackle the last three bombers and continue their attacks until the bomber was shot down, the pilots ran out of ammunition, or the aircraft were shot down or disabled. Only then would the next section of three move in to the attack.

The tactics above are typical for the Royal Air Force in the last years of peace before the beginning of World War II, but also of battle dispositions envisaged by the theoretical tacticians of the decade in most countries. There were of course variations on the basic theme, but all were marked by a monolithic attitude to the tasks faced by pilots, with every movement controlled to the last degree, and possible in theory only if the bombers behaved exactly as anticipated, and were without fighter escort. The possibility of fighter *versus* fighter combat was not considered except by Germany, Japan and Russia, all of whom had recent combat experience; and of these three Russia failed to develop the right tactics for fast, modern aerial warfare.

The originator of the new German fighter tactics was *Leutnant* Werner Mölders, Germany's highest scoring ace in the Spanish Civil War with 14 victories. In retrospect it is possible to see that Mölders occupies the same position in World War II as did Boelcke in World War I: both men were the supreme air tacticians of their day, in terms of combat success and constructive tactical thinking. Seeing the general inefficiency of the basically linear tactics used in the Spanish Civil War and realizing that, quite contrary to the expectation of most air war theoreticians, air combat between fighters was going to play a decisive part in future air campaigns, Mölders put his incisive mind to the problem of devising tactics to suit the modern fighters coming into widespread service in 1937 and 1938. The basis of Mölders' tactics was the *Rotte* (unit) of two aircraft. Where Mölders' tactics differed so radically from those generally accepted was not so much in the reduction of the number of aircraft in the basic unit from three to two, but in the spacing of the aircraft within that unit. Conventional tactics emphasized the importance of tight formation flying (for better control in cloud typical of European conditions), with aircraft about 40 ft (12.2 m) apart. Mölders' tactics called for the two aircraft of the *Rotte* to be about 191 yards (175 m) apart, with the leader slightly ahead of his wingman. Each of the pilots concentrated his attention inwards, and so watched the other's blind spots under the tail and dead astern. In combat, Mölders decided, the wingman's function was to protect his leader's tail in engagements with enemy fighters, and to engage the bomber next to that tackled by his leader in actions against unescorted bombers.

Next up the unit ladder was the *Schwarm* (flight) of four aircraft, made up of two *Rotten* and disposed with one *Rotte* flying slightly ahead of and to the side of the other, so that the four aircraft were in the relative positions of the nails on the four fingers of a hand. The whole *Schwarm* was some 574 yards (525 m) in breadth, and this meant that it was almost impossible for the formation to turn in the right order. Mölders solved the problem by originating the 'crossover' turn, in which the man on the outside of the turn became the inside man of the formation after the turn, so that the formation became a mirror image of itself before the turn. Three *Schwärme* made up the basic 12-fighter *Jagdstaffel* (fighter squadron), the three *Schwärme* flying in line abreast or line astern.

Simple in all its basic elements, the Mölders tactical disposition met all the requirements that could be expected of it: the aircraft of a *Staffel* or smaller formation all covered each others' blind spots visually; assistance could easily be given to any aircraft attacked; and the whole formation could be manoeuvred as an entity with greater ease than the tighter, but less flexible formations of other air forces. The open position of the German fighters' cruising formation allowed each pilot to keep up a continual search for the enemy, whereas in tight formations all the pilots other than the leader had to concentrate more on keeping in formation and avoiding collision than on watching for the opposition. The wide dispersion of the formation also meant that if an aircraft were attacked, a simple turn by the formation would lead to the attacker being trapped between the aircraft under attack and the aircraft previously on the outside of him in the turn, whereas in a tight formation any of the three rearmost aircraft could be attacked and shot down before the rest of the formation could break, and then turn back to engage the attacker. And so far as manoeuvrability was concerned, the basic rate of turn of anything up to a *Staffel* of fighters was limited only by the rate of turn

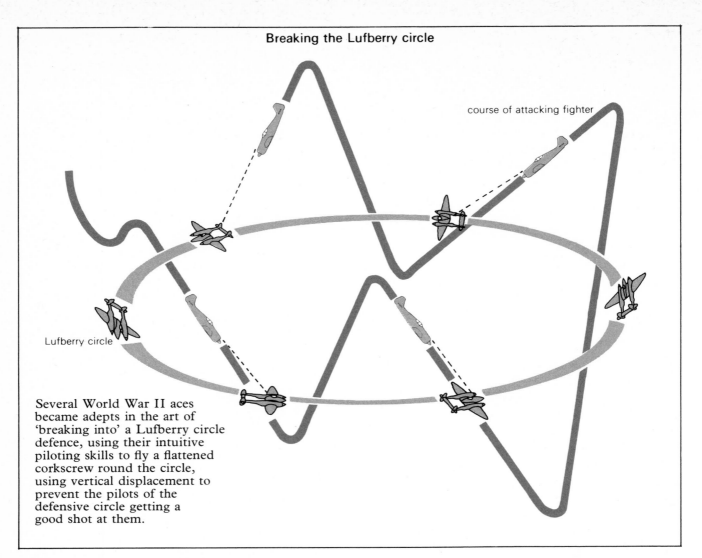

Breaking the Lufberry circle

course of attacking fighter

Lufberry circle

Several World War II aces became adepts in the art of 'breaking into' a Lufberry circle defence, using their intuitive piloting skills to fly a flattened corkscrew round the circle, using vertical displacement to prevent the pilots of the defensive circle getting a good shot at them.

of the aircraft, whereas the tight formations of other nations, which had to bank round as an entire formation, were relatively unwieldy, and maximum rate turns were impossible, or the outside file would have collided with the middle file, and the middle with the inside file.

It should be emphasized, though, that the 'looseness' of the German formation was apparent rather than real, and that though all the benefits of a loose formation were provided, the formation was still under the effective control of one man using radiotelephony, and could close up rapidly if the situation warranted, such as for an attack on bombers.

The inefficiency of the Allied fighter tactics was quickly revealed by operations over France. Although Allied pilots lacked the combat experience of a number of their opponents, once a dogfight had developed they generally proved the equal of the Germans in individual combat, though wingmen picked off a number of Allied pilots engaging *Rotte* leaders. But large numbers of Allied pilots were lost even before combat was properly joined, the more flexibly disposed Germans getting in to the attack while the Allied fighters were still turning to meet them. It was conservatively estimated that a force of Allied fighters meeting a German fighter unit of perhaps only one-third of the Allied strength would suffer the losses that parity of numbers might have suggested.

Indications of the inadequacy of Allied tactics for

fighter *versus* fighter combat appeared first in the later weeks of 1939, but were confirmed only in the Germans' campaign against France, Belgium and Holland unleashed on 10 May 1940. Allied commanders soon came to appreciate the virtues of the German system, but also that any attempt to change the tactics to which their pilots were accustomed would merely cause extra confusion. The only thing which could be done, therefore, was a loosening of the Allied formations. The V was still retained, but spread out to a very considerable extent compared with the previous close formation, so that the three pilots involved could devote more of their attention to searching the skies for opposition than on merely keeping station. The sections of the squadron were also spread out more, and the last section was stepped 1,000 ft (305 m) higher than the other three and flew a zig-zag course to protect the tail of the formation, and to intervene if the rearmost section below were attacked. But the rate of turn of the formation was still slow, and could not be altered without a fundamental reorganization of the standard fighter formation. This would have to wait until the RAF was not so hard pressed, for only with considerable practice could the full benefits of Mölders' formation be attained.

During the Battle of Britain (July–October 1940), no official alterations to the RAF's formations were made, but local commanders and perceptive leaders frequently experimented with altered formations in an effort to come up with a means of worsting the German fighters and getting through to the bombers. Among these experiments were the single weaving section used in France; the separation of the squadron into two flights of six aircraft, each with one weaving aircraft; six loose pairs of aircraft; and two aircraft on separate weaving courses to cover the rear of the rest of the squadron.

Towards the end of the battle there appeared the tactics devised by Squadron Leader A. G. Malan, the commander of No 74 Squadron. Malan had come to the entirely valid conclusion that the basic RAF flight of three aircraft was wrong, for although in combat one man could stick to his leader's tail, two could not. And as it was natural for combats to break down larger formations, the British inevitably ended with a number of individual 'strays' in the combat zone. Malan therefore reasoned that the subdivision of the squadron should be into three flights each of four aircraft in place of the current four flights each with three aircraft. In this way, the flights would naturally break up into effective combat units of two aircraft each, leaving no 'strays' for the Germans to pick off. Malan's squadron was thus disposed in a loose V with the three sections at the apex and on each flank, each section disposed in line astern with its four aircraft. This formation allowed all the pilots to devote considerable attention to the sky round them, because flying in line astern required little concentration compared with flying in tight Vs, and the spacing of the sections some 250 yards (229 m) apart allowed the sections to watch each other's blind spots fairly easily. At the same time the rendering of mutual support was made easier, and the crossover turn by complete line-astern section became the norm.

Malan's formation was adopted universally in the RAF by the end of 1941, and remained the standard formation until the middle of 1943. It was found to be most useful in the 'Rhubarb' fighter and 'Circus' fighter-escorted bomber sweeps into northern Europe during 1941 and 1942. These operations were designed to goad the *Luftwaffe* fighters in the area up into combat, where the large numbers of British fighters would shoot them down in decisive numbers. Though the concept did not work, the tactics of using large numbers of fighters flexibly and under the control of one man was fully vindicated.

But such tactics were not applicable in other theatres where the British were involved, notably over Malta. Here the Germans and Italians could operate in vast numerical superiority, and the British fighters had to scramble in small numbers to try to intercept before the island was forced to undergo yet another heavy raid. The pilots of Malta and North Africa therefore adopted the German *Rotte* and *Schwarm*, with the difference that the line of four fighters was disposed almost abreast: this meant that as each man looked inwards, he covered the blind spots of at least two other aircraft.

This Malta adaptation of the *Rotte* and *Schwarm* spread to the metropolitan RAF during 1943, so that by the end of the year all the world's major air forces were using the basic tactical disposition for fighters evolved by Werner Mölders, who had become the German *General der Jagdflieger* and was killed in a flying accident on 22 November 1941 (his score standing at 115 victories, 33 on the Eastern Front, 68 on the Western Front and 14 in Spain). To the Germans, the units were still the *Rotte* and *Schwarm*, to the British and Americans the pair and finger-four, to the Russians the *para* and *zveno*, and to the Japanese as the *buntai* and *shotai*.

The standard Allied formation for a squadron flying the finger-four section was a shallow V: at the apex was one section, its aircraft in line almost abreast, about 200 yards (183 m) apart, with the squadron commander flying centre-left or centre-right, his wingman outside him, and the other pair leader beside but slightly behind the squadron commander, also with his wingman outside him. This was repeated in the other sections, which trailed the lead section by between 500 and 700 yards (457 and 640 m), the inner wingmen of the trailing sections just outside the wingmen of the lead section. The two trailing sections also flew at slightly higher altitude than the lead section.

Once in combat, fighters generally followed the tactical rules worked out in World War I, adapted to take account of the higher performance of the fighters of World War II, and with a few variations. Superior altitude was still of paramount importance, and so too was the ability to see the enemy before he saw you. This meant that the attacking pilot could usually enter combat on his own terms, taking advantage of the sun if possible. It was always essential to remember that the enemy was probably operating in pairs or fours, and that one aircraft on its own was automatically suspect. All fighter manuals emphasized the constant need to check behind every few seconds, to make sure that an adversary had not got on one's tail, and also the foolhardiness of flying straight and level for more than a few seconds while in the combat zone. As in World War I, it was desirable to score with the first firing pass, which could then be followed by a climb. But if a prolonged combat became inevitable, then the only real method was a turning battle, with each pilot trying to turn just a little tighter than his adversary and so make up enough ground round the circumference of the circle to get into a firing position. Pilots kept a constant watch 'up sun' for opponents waiting to 'bounce' the unwary, and if such an attack was seen coming down, the standard practice was to turn into the attack, climbing slightly in the process, to present the attackers with a difficult deflection shot, and to place the flight being attacked with the height advantage if the attackers continued their diving pass. But what happened once combat had been joined, depended largely on the ability of the aircraft involved to turn tightly without losing altitude. In general British, Japanese and Russian aircraft turned more tightly than German and American aircraft, though there were exceptions depending on the mark of model involved. Basically, if the pilot thought his aircraft could out-turn his opponent's, he was prepared to enter a circling battle; if, on the other hand, he felt that he could not match his adversary in a turning battle, but had better acceleration in a dive, he broke off immediately. This latter tactic quickly became the norm for Allied pilots operating against the Japanese, whose aircraft could almost invariably out-turn Allied fighters. The best way of entering a dive, even with aircraft whose fuel-injected engines did not suffer the negative-g problems of engines with float carburettors, was a quick thrust to open the throttle wide, followed by a roll until the aircraft was inverted, and then a pull back on the control column to send the fighter diving down with maximum acceleration in a positive-g manoeuvre. The manoeuvre was known in the Luftwaffe as the *Abschwung*, the RAF as the half-roll and dive, and in the American air services as the split-S. The dive could only be undertaken at medium and high altitude, as 10,000 ft (3,050 m) could be lost very quickly, but few of the light and highly manoeuvrable Russian and Japanese fighters could match the diving performance of American, British and German aircraft.

As a variation on the circling fight, the Lufberry Circle of World War I also found favour in World War II, though pilots had to be careful in their decision to use the tactic: on one occasion RAF single-engined fighters managed to get inside a circle of Messerschmitt Bf 110 twin-engined fighters, and by circling in the opposite direction to the German aircraft, were able to down a number of them with hardly a shot fired in return by the Bf 110s, whose forward firing guns could not be brought to bear, and whose single flexible machine-guns had little more than nuisance value. So it was essential in a Lufberry Circle to ensure that one's adversary could not insinuate himself into the circle, or disaster was almost inevitable, as was proved by *Oberleutnant* Hans-Joachim Marseille, possibly the *Luftwaffe*'s ablest ace, who shot down 158 Allied aircraft in western theatres (151 in North Africa and seven over north-western Europe) before his death in an accident on 30 September 1942. One of Marseille's greatest missions was flown on 6 June 1942, during the course of an escort mission for a Junkers Ju 87 dive-bombing raid against Bir Hakeim. Marseille was flying a Messerschmitt Bf 109 of

The special tactics adopted for the Ju 87 dive-bomber enabled Germans to release their weapons with unexcelled accuracy. Approaching the target at high altitude, the Ju 87 bunted over into an 80° dive, soon reaching a speed of 350 mph (560 kph) attainable after the dive-brakes had been extended. After a dive of about 30 seconds, the altimeter would indicate the preset pull-out altitude, and the pilot would press the control on his stick to initiate the automatic pull-out. The bomb would be released automatically to drop on or near the target the pilot had kept centred in his reflector sight. With the release of the bomb, the pilot would resume manual control and climb away.

3./JG27, operating from Martuba airfield. Just as the Stukas started their attack, the Germans were 'bounced' by about 15 Curtiss P-40 Tomahawk fighters of No 5 Squadron, South African Air Force. As the Tomahawks came down, the six German fighters countered with the standard manoeuvre, turning into the South Africans in a slight climb, and splitting into *Rotten*, Marseille being accompanied by his wingman, *Feldwebel* Reiner Pöttgen. Apparently surprised by the presence of the six Bf 109 fighters, the Tomahawks pulled into a Lufberry Circle at about 5,000 ft (1,524 m), turning to the right and with about 200 ft (61 m) between aircraft so that each aircraft could cover the tail of the aircraft in front of it.

But Marseille was an excellent shot, especially in deflection shooting, and had magnificent co-ordination. Selecting his moment absolutely correctly, Marseille dived towards the circle, continued past it and then pulled the nose up and round to the right. There, at a range of only 150 ft (45.7 m) was a Tomahawk: Marseille fired his full battery, only one 20-mm cannon and two 7.92-mm machine-guns, his fire striking the engine and then moving back along the belly of the target. Marseille continued his climb, and as he passed through the circle at high speed saw the target aircraft fall away in clouds of smoke, to fall straight into the ground and explode. But already Marseille was closing in again, diving past the circle, pulling the nose up and to the right, and firing as the target aircraft disappeared from his sight below the nose of his own aircraft. Again the shells and bullets hit the engine and 'walked' back towards the cockpit, and again the aircraft fell out of the formation streaming smoke, to tumble to the earth now only 3,500 ft (1,067 m) below. On his third pass Marseille varied his technique slightly, to take advantage of the gaps beginning to appear in the circle: he appeared immediately behind his target, but again dispatched it with a short burst from his whole armament. And even as this victim began to fall out of formation, Marseille had quickly climbed, beginning his fourth attack in a high-speed sideslipping turn to the right. Again Marseille waited until the target disappeared from sight before firing, but despite the fact that his cannon had jammed, the fire of a mere two light machine-guns punched into the Tomahawk's engine and ruined it. Pöttgen, watching with an eagle eye, saw that the fourth victim began to go down even before the third had hit the ground.

Most other pilots would have retired gracefully at this stage, reckoning that a victory with only two light machine-guns could not be repeated. But Marseille was into the rhythm of the action now, and not inclined to ignore further prey. He was already closing in on the fifth Tomahawk in a diving right-hand turn that would take him into the circle behind his victim's tail: again a short burst of machine-gun fire raked the aircraft from engine to cockpit, and within six minutes of the first victim's death, the fifth was hurtling towards the

ground. Marseille had once more regained altitude, checked that he had fuel, and seen that all was still running smoothly. Again he dived, then pulled out into a steep right hand turn behind and outside the sixth Tomahawk. Marseille then eased back the stick to tighten his turn and fired. Again the bullets struck home in the engine, and the Tomahawk lurched out of the formation with a crippled engine as Marseille decided that enough had been achieved and broke off. The sixth victim crash-landed a little way off: Marseille's six 'kills' had all fallen in the space of 11 minutes, to some of the best deflection shooting ever seen. Other Bf 109s had engaged, but none of them had scored, though the South Africans not unnaturally thought it highly improbable that one man could have shot down the six aircraft lost on the mission. When the armourers went to work on Marseille's aircraft, they made the extraordinary discovery that the cannon had jammed after only 10 rounds, and that there was still a fair amount of machine-gun ammunition left. Not one hit was found on the aircraft.

The action exemplifies several of the factors that went towards making a great air ace: absolute precision of flying, magnificent shooting, especially in very difficult deflection shots, the virtues of closing in to very short range, the use of superior altitude, a cool head, and the ability to look ahead of the immediate factors to see how one's current actions will affect the whole pattern one is caught up in. It is also interesting to note that Marseille used his reflector sight only to line himself up, generally closing in to a range below the reflector sight's minimum in order to increase his chances of striking accurately with very short bursts. Some of these attributes were possessed by most fighter pilots who scored more than a few victories, but it was only the great pilots (most of them German, with a smattering of the better Allied ones) who possessed all these attributes of flying skill, courage, tactical ingenuity, a calculating mind and a natural shooting 'eye'.

It was the Germans who set the early pattern for the use of medium bombers in the tactical role during World War II. The initial form-up of the bomber force depended on the type of airfield being used: if it was grass, the bombers could take off in Vs of three aircraft, but if a concrete runway had to be used, the bombers took off singly and joined up into Vs once airborne. Either way, the leading Vs headed straight away from the airfield for a given time, then reversed course, picking up later Vs as they moved back towards the airfield. Once over their starting point, the formation's main elements were all in formation and the whole force turned on to its track towards the target, climbing slowly as it moved. The one main problem with such an evolution was that the bomber force frequently had to climb through cloud, and this was extremely risky, not only for the general formation-keeping of the force as a whole, but also for the dangers of mid-air collission in cloud. Assuming that the force got through the cloud in good order, it then made for the target in close formation. It was realized that such a formation paid dividends in two ways: the weight of defensive fire that the bombers could put up against marauding fighters was that much more dense, and a close-packed formation passed over the AA gun lines quickly, saturating the defences and making losses that much smaller by giving the guns little time to engage the whole mass of attackers.

Once over the target, the Germans adopted either of two bombing methods depending on whether or not there were defending fighters in the area. If there were not, and AA gunfire was ineffective, the bombers attacked individually at low to medium level, often making several dummy runs before releasing their bombs; if there were no fighters, but the AA fire was severe, the bombers were forced to higher altitude, but could still bomb in the same leisurely way. But if there were fighters about, the bombers operated in tight formations to provide each other with heavy covering fire. The Germans were firm believers in the individual type of bombing, for only thus could each crew make sure that their bombs were dropped as accurately as possible. Occasionally, though, pattern bombing was desirable for special targets, and the formation was designed for the task, flying in tight formation and releasing all the bombs on the radioed word of the mission commander.

The *Luftwaffe*'s preferred bombing time was naturally during the day, for only daylight could ensure a modicum of accuracy against the small targets the *Luftwaffe* was basically designed to attack. At times, though, the bombers were forced by the strength of the day fighter defences to operate at night. Such an instance occurred in the closing stages of the Battle of Britain, when the bombers attacking London by day received such a mauling that their effort was called off, and a night '*Blitz*' substituted. For such attacks the Germans used *Krokodil* (crocodile) tactics. As the name suggests, the tactics consisted of a long stream of bombers, the machines of any one *Kampfgruppe* or *Kampfgeschwader* being dispatched along the same route at intervals of four minutes. The aircraft were allowed to fly at between 9,842 ft (3,000 m) and 19,685 ft (6,000 m), with a lateral tolerance of up to 6.2 miles (10 km) on either side of the designated flight path. Different units attacked along different paths and at different times, the object being as much to disrupt the British as to cause damage. Of course, considerable damage was done as bombers arriving later were able to bomb the fires started by earlier arrivals or the pathfinder force (as in the devastating raid on Coventry on 14 November 1940, which was largely attributable to the accurate target-marking of *Kampfgruppe* 100 using the *X-Gerät* radio navigation aid).

With the improvement in the British night defences, especially after the introduction of aircraft fitted with AI (airborne interception) radar late in 1940, the Germans had to abandon the *Krokodil* tactic in favour of what later became known as a 'bomber stream': all the bombers concentrated into as tight a formation as possible to saturate the defences by passing through a large number of aircraft in as short a time as possible. Thus whereas *Krokodil* attacks had lasted perhaps 10 hours in all, the later attacks were notable for one short (about 20-minute) attack of considerable intensity.

With the exception of the Japanese and US naval air forces, the *Luftwaffe* was the chief exponent in World War II of dive-bombing: in this, the object was for the bomber to dive at its targets and release its bombs at low level while still in the dive, so that the bombs followed a relatively flat trajectory over the short distance to the target, while the bomber climbed away to safety; it was expected that the speed of the dive, the small target presented by the head-on aircraft, and the natural nervousness induced in the AA defence personnel by the plummeting aircraft would all render AA fire relatively impotent.

The basic aircraft used for dive-bombing by the Germans was the Junkers Ju 87, which had been specifically designed for the task. Other German bombers, notably the Junkers Ju 88, had been designed as medium bombers with a limited dive-bomber capability, but such types were only rarely used for dive-bombing, their diving angles being limited to about 50°. The approach to the target was normally at 14,764 ft (4,500 m), the Ju 87s flying in *Ketten* (flights) of three aircraft, disposed in a V. Other *Ketten* followed the first at a distance of about 273 yards (250 m), up to a *Gruppe* (wing) of 30 dive-bombers being the maximum. Fighter protection was frequently needed and supplied, most of the escort operating slightly above the approaching bombers, but some descending to 3,208 ft (1,000 m) to support the bombers as they emerged from their stooping dives.

As he approached the starting point of his dive, the pilot of each dive-bomber turned on the reflector sight at the front of his cockpit, set the contact altimeter for the designated pull-out height, opened the windscreen ventilator to prevent misting up, closed the radiator flaps, throttled back the engine, turned on the 'Jericho trumpets' (devices on the undercarriage legs whose banshee scream was designed to terrify those below), and opened the dive-brakes just before peeling off into his dive (if attacking a small target) from the echeloned line the V had previously assumed, or merely nosing into his dive (if a large target were being bombed) in company with the other two members of his V. The dive angle was normally 80°, and in the first 8,202 ft (2,500 m) the Ju 87 picked up speed until a constant 354 mph (220 kph) was reached. A constant dive angle was essential for accuracy, and during the 30 seconds of the dive the pilot watched the target grow right in the middle of his reflector sight, and checked his angle against the horizon by means of lines cut in the cockpit glazing. Four seconds before reaching the preset height on the contact altimeter, normally 3,208 ft (1,000 m), a horn

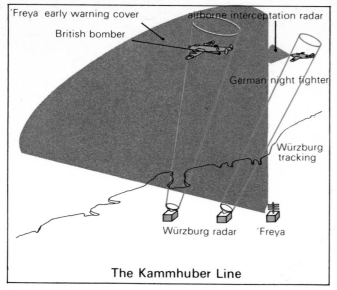

The night-fighter defence of Germany depended on large numbers of radar sets. Each box, one of a number running round the perimeter of Germany, had one 'Freya' early warning set and two Würzburg tracking sets. The single night-fighter was watched by one Würzburg, and when the arrival of 'trade' was signalled by the 'Freya' apparatus, an individual bomber was selected for the other Würzburg to track. The relative positions of the two aircraft being tracked by the Würzburgs could then be established, and the German night-fighter vectored into the area of the British bomber, so that the fighter's own short-range interception radar could pick up the target.

sounded until the preset altitude was reached. As the horn cut off, the pilot operated a button to return the elevator trim tab (automatically lowered as the dive-brakes opened) to neutral, so that the now tail-heavy aircraft automatically pulled out of its dive. As this happened, a timing mechanism released the bombs at the right angle as the aircraft pulled out of its dive and started to climb.

Because its heavy bombers operated by day, and thus met the most concentrated AA and fighter opposition, the USAAF developed the most sophisticated tactical formations seen in World War II, though RAF Bomber Command's tactical organization also reached a high peak of complexity in the search for the optimum means of concentrating bombers over the target area in maximum numbers but in minimum time. This involved an extraordinary administrative effort as the routes and timings of all the components of the bomber stream were worked out, and diversions arranged to draw off the German night-fighters as the pathfinders marked the target just before the main heavy bomber force arrived.

The start of any major American bomber effort was marked by the assembly of the various bomber units. This presented little problem if there was no cloud. But if there was cloud, the bombers took off individually and climbed through the cloud on their own, to avoid collisions, and formed up above the cloud cover over a radio beacon. Good though the arrangement was for safety, it had two major disadvantages: the Germans could pick up the orbiting formation and so deduce that a raid was coming, and also how large it was likely to be. It took about

60 minutes to form up the 36 aircraft of a typical bombardment group, which meant that the bomb-load carried for a long-range mission had to be reduced to allow for the extra fuel needed for the wasted hour, or that a mission of shorter radius had to be flown.

In the early days of its heavy bomber effort over northern Europe, the US 8th Army Air Force used a standard tactical formation based on the six-bomber squadron. Each aircraft flew about 100 ft (30.5 m) from the closest point of the aircraft in front of it, so that the formation resembled a finger-four with the two extra aircraft located just in front of and outside the outer two aircraft of the finger-four. The clearance between the tail of one aircraft and the wingtip of the machine behind was thus about 70 ft (21.33 m). The object of the formation was to keep the squadron well closed-up so that the aircraft could cover each other, but spaced out just sufficiently that formation flying was not too difficult, and that an AA shell exploding between two aircraft would not seriously damage either. The concept at this level was good, but the overall design of the whole formation was deficient. The firepower of six bombers was not enough to deter German fighters and the squadrons were not close enough to support each other. Relative to the lead squadron, the rear squadron was some 3 miles (4.83 km) further back and 1,000 ft (305 m) higher, while the two flanking squadrons were each 2 miles (3.2 km) out from the lead squadron and 1½ miles (2.4 km) back, and about 1,000 ft (305 m) lower. Only a month after the introduction of the formation the Americans realized its inadequacies, and in September 1942 replaced the squadron with the group as the basic 'building-block' of the bomber box.

Each group consisted of two nine-bomber squadrons, each squadron disposed in an elongated version of the six-bomber squadron's deployment across a frontage of some 390 yards (357 m). The squadron on the left led, with the right-hand squadron slightly behind it (the whole depth of the group from front to back was only 160 yards (146 m) and 500 ft (152 m) higher). The new formation met the requirements of concentrated firepower, but was hopelessly unwieldy, especially in turns.

Yet another modification was introduced in December 1942: the strength of the group remained unaltered at 18 bombers, broken down into three squadrons each with six aircraft. Seen from in front, the aircraft were staggered upwards towards the sun from one end to the other, across a frontage of 780 yards (713 m), the same frontage as that of the September group box. From above, the formation was again in a sort of lopsided V, the lead bomber of the lead squadron just to the sunward of the groups' frontage, with the up-sun squadron echeloned back deep, and the down-sun squadron lying back not so deeply. The depth of the formation from front to back was 210 yards (192 m), and the height of the formation some 900 ft (274 m). The up- and down-sun squadrons were designated the

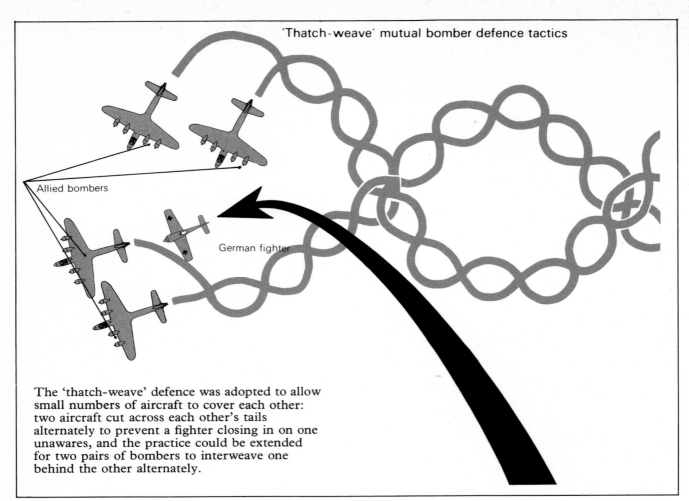

Allied bombers

German fighter

The 'thatch-weave' defence was adopted to allow
small numbers of aircraft to cover each other:
two aircraft cut across each other's tails
alternately to prevent a fighter closing in on one
unawares, and the practice could be extended
for two pairs of bombers to interweave one
behind the other alternately.

high and low squadrons. This new formation was a
distinct improvement, many of the guns hitherto
severely restricted in their fields of fire by friendly
aircraft now being able to play a more flexible role
in the battle. By the beginning of 1943, the 8th AAF
could muster four such groups for most raids, and
these were dispatched in a formation called Javelin:
each group followed the one in front at a distance of
1½ miles (2.4 km), stepped up slightly and echeloned
into the sun. The virtue of the Javelin was that it
made head-on attacks on the rear groups very
hazardous, but the vices of the formation more than
counterbalanced this, for straggling was easy, and
such aircraft provided the defending fighters with
easy pickings.

In February 1943, therefore, the 8th AAF
planners replaced the Javelin with the Wedge: the
18-bomber group remained unaltered, but the lead
group was located in the centre of the formation,
with the other groups echeloned up and down on
each side. This meant that the high group found it
easier to keep up with the rest of the formation in
turns.

A month later there was yet another change,
forced on the 8th AAF by the increasing success of the
German fighters. The object of the change was to
improve the formation's firepower, but still keep
the basic 18-bomber group. The new Combat Wing
formation placed the lead group in the centre, with
the second group just to one side, above and behind,
and the third group just to the other side, below and
behind. From the point of view of firepower the
Combat Wing was useful: only 2,340 yards (2,140 m)

across its frontage, 600 yards (549 m) deep from front
to back and 2,900 ft (884 m) high, the Combat
Wing of 54 bombers could throw up a concentrated
and, at times, effective weight of fire. Unfortunately,
though, it was most difficult to control effectively,
especially in turns. The various Combat Wings of a
raid were divided by a gap of about 6 miles (9.7 km).

April 1943 saw yet another change designed to
improve fire-power and increase controllability in
turns, by compacting the bombers of the Combat
Wing further, with the high and low groups moved
in closer to the lead group, and the three-bomber Vs
echeloned up one way, and the flights (elements) and
squadrons the other way, for greater spatial com-
pression. The result seemed to be what the Americans
were looking for, and the revised Combat Wing
remained the norm for the rest of 1943.

The final change was introduced in January 1944,
and proved so successful that it was retained for the
rest of the war. The change was the result of supplies
of radar-bombing aids, and the availability of long-
range escort fighters. The Combat Wing of 54 aircraft, which had occupied a box of 950-yards
(869-m) frontage, 425-yards (389-m) depth and
2,700-ft (823-m) height, was replaced by the Group
of 36 aircraft, which formed a box 520 yards (475 m)
across, 270 yards (247 m) deep and 600 ft (183 m)
high. Each Group had three squadrons each with
12 aircraft, flying closely packed in four levels. The
lead squadron again occupied the lead position in
the centre, with one squadron echeloned to the side,
back and up-sun, and the other in line with the
second but down-sun and lower than the lead squad-

ron. The compactness of the new formation made the task of the escort fighters easier, and also improved bombing accuracy with the radar aids, which were in short supply and fitted only to the lead aircraft of each squadron. The revised Group was itself revised in February 1945 to take account of the virtual non-existence of the German fighter force, but the increased strength of the *Flak* arm. Instead of three 12-aircraft squadrons, the Group now had four 9-aircraft squadrons, the box being extended in height to accommodate the extra unit and make the height-finding task of the German gunners that much more difficult. The other dimensions of the box remained unaltered, the extra volume now available being used to open up the squadrons, many of whose aircraft now had radar bombing aids. The gap between Groups remained unaltered at 4 miles (6.4 km).

Such then were the main tactical formations evolved by the 8th AAF in the light of its combat experience with the German fighter arm and *Flak* defences. But what tactics had the Germans evolved in their efforts to stop the day bombers? At first, the well-proven attacks by *Rotten* or *Schwärme* from astern or on the beam proved useful, but the tightening of the American formations made the cost of such attacks prohibitively high by the end of 1942. The Germans therefore decided to adopt head-on attacks. The American bombers' armament (before the advent of the chin-turreted B-17G) was weakest in this quarter, and the crew protection was generally disposed to protect against fire coming from the rear. The method adopted by the Germans was to cruise

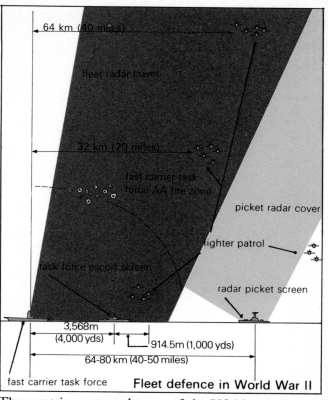

Fleet defence in World War II

The most important element of the US Navy's fast strike forces in World War II was the aircraft-carriers, and elaborate defence schemes for their protection against Japanese aircraft were tried. The standard scheme evolved by the end of the war is shown here, with the carriers to the left, their screen of escorting ships about 4000 yards (3658 m) distant, and a circle of radar pickets between 40 and 50 miles (64 and 80 km) away. Over the pickets, at about 5000 ft (1524 m) operated the 'Tomcap' patrol of defensive fighters, with the 'Hicap' (CAP stands for Combat Air Patrol) at above 25,000 ft (7620 m) and slightly farther in towards the carriers, at about 40 miles (64 km) range. Slightly lower (between 10,000 and 15,000 ft/3050 and 4572 m) and closer in (about 20 miles/32 km) was the 'Medcap' patrol. At about 1000 ft (305 m) and only perhaps 10,000 yards (3050 m) from the carriers was the last-ditch 'Jackcap' fighter patrol, operating just on the edge of the close-in defence zone reserved for the guns.

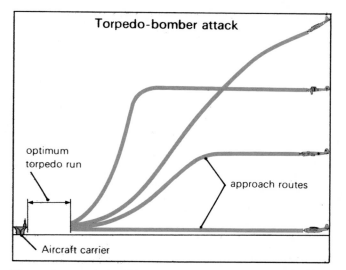

Torpedo-bomber attack

optimum torpedo run

approach routes

Aircraft carrier

Torpedo attacks in World War II varied. The Royal Navy, using elderly Fairey Swordfish bombers, favoured a medium-altitude approach, followed by a steep dive at about 175 mph (280 kph) to the torpedo-release altitude of 150 ft (46 m); the Japanese navy, using the Aichi D3A 'Val', also favoured a slightly higher approach before a shallow dive at 286 mph (460 kph) to the release altitude of 197 ft (60 m); the US Navy, using Grumman TBF Avenger bombers, used a low-level approach at 140 mph (225 kph) for a dropping altitude of between 100 and 200 ft (30 and 61 m); the Germans, using the Heinkel He 111 bomber modified for torpedo-bombing, used a medium-altitude approach before a shallow dive at 171 mph (275 kph) to the release height of 164 ft (50 m).

beside the bombers to make sure of their course and numbers, then to pull ahead for about 1.85 miles (3 km) before turning in towards the bombers. The combined closing speeds of the formations meant that the fighter pilots had only about 2 seconds in which to fire, placing a great premium on accuracy. However, even if a bomber were not shot down in this pass, there was every possibility that it had been damaged, and might thus fall to later attacks with greater ease. Such conventional tactics continued up to the spring of 1944, when the arrival of large numbers of American fighter escorts, mostly the North American P-51 Mustang, placed the Germans in great difficulty. The armament of the German fighter had been specially strengthened to allow thems to tackle the American bombers, and this heavy armament, all essential for the primary tasks, meant that the heavy fighters were relatively easy prey for the agile American escort fighters. The answer was found to lie in a new type of formation, the *Gefechtsverband* (combat formation) with two *Gruppen* of ordinary fighters to engage the escort fighters while the single *Sturmgruppe* of heavy fighters went through to tackle the bombers. When it worked, the *Gefechtsverband* of 100 or more fighters was highly effective. The trouble was that it took the formation a long time to muster, and this time allowed the Mustang escort fighters to intercept it before it reached the bombers, and go on to cut down the *Sturmgruppe* and its bomber-destroying weapons. But from the middle of 1944 onwards the *Luftwaffe* gradually declined as a fighting force, and although German industry and designers produced new weapons and new aircraft, the fuel shortage caused by the Allies' heavy bombing slowly grounded the *Luftwaffe*, and even the pilots who did manage to get into the air in their Messerschmitt Me 262 jet

fighters were not equal to the superb pilots of 1939–1942, and could do nothing against the Allies' massive air superiority.

Night bomber formations had nothing like the concentration of the day bomber masses, but were designed to produce the maximum possible density of aircraft over the German night-fighter radar network, so as to make its task more difficult, and over the target area, where it was considered essential that the bomber squadrons arrive in the right order from the right direction and at the right time to ensure that the cumulative effect of the bombing produced a general conflagration rather than a series of small fires the Germans could cope with easily. RAF Bomber Command initiated its bomber

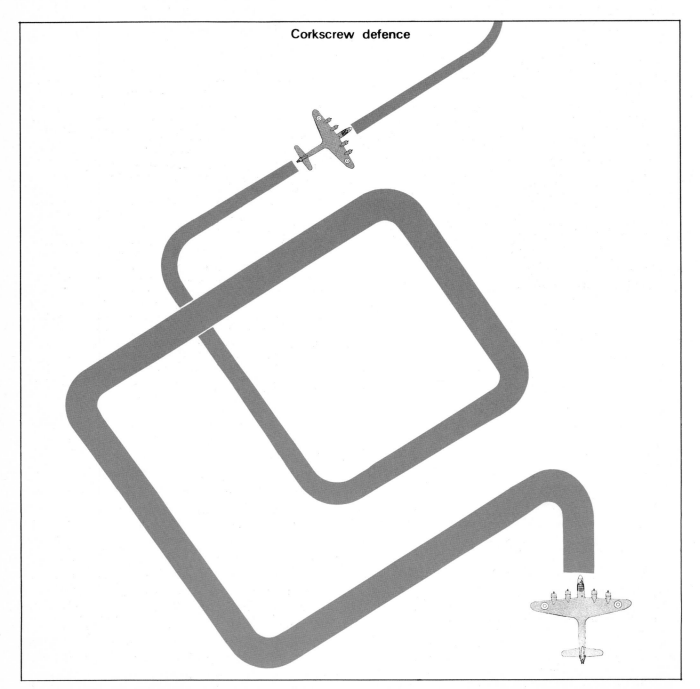

Corkscrew defence

By far the most effective defensive tactic for night bombers in World War II was the 'Corkscrew'. On sighting an enemy fighter, the bomber immediately dived sharply and turned to port or starboard (in this instance port), losing 1000 ft (305 m) in altitude and increasing speed from about 225 mph (362 kph) to 300 mph (483 kph). Still in its port turn, the bomber was then pulled up into a climb, half way up which the direction of the turn was reversed, so that by the time the original altitude and course had been regained the bomber was down to about 185 mph (298 kph), which often caused the pursuing fighter to overshoot. If the fighter was still present, the pilot continued to turn, but again pushed the stick forward to increase speed and dive 500 ft (152 m).

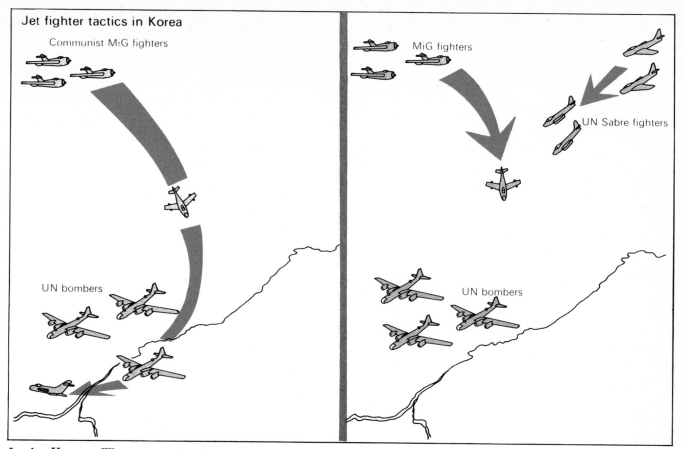

In the Korean War communist fighters could operate without hindrance to the north of the Yalu river, which UN aircraft were prohibited from crossing. MiG-15s could thus climb to high altitude on their side of the river, and then dive down to attack UN aircraft to the south before breaking away, still in a dive, to recross the river at low altitude. UN pilots evolved the tactics of waiting close to the river and diving down to 'bounce' the MiGs as the latter made their diving attacks and retreats.

stream tactics in the '1,000-Bomber Raid' against Cologne at the end of May 1942.

Up to May 1940, the defence of Germany against night bombing was the responsibility of the *Flak* artillery, a branch of the *Luftwaffe*, and a small number of single-engined fighters using *helle Nachtjagd* (illuminated night-fighting) tactics. The aircraft were mostly Bf 109 fighters, generally unsuitable for the task, flown by volunteers with special training. The tactic consisted of waiting over the main target areas for the searchlight to illuminate an Allied bomber which could then be attacked conventionally. As may be imagined, the successes of the fledgling night-fighter arm were few: there were not many night bombers for them to engage, the searchlights found it difficult to pick up and hold a target for sufficient time to allow the German pilot to make his kill, and the Bf 109 was for a variety of reasons wholly unsuited for the night-fighting role.

With the start of the RAF's major effort against German industry starting in May 1940, the German authorities quickly realized that the night-fighter defences would have to be upgraded, and under the energetic command of *Oberst* (later *Generalleutnant*) Josef Kammhuber, the night-fighter arm soon blossomed into an effective weapon against British night bombers. A year after Kammhuber took over, the force had grown to some 250 aircraft, all of them twin-engined machines specially modified for the task. The most important were the Dornier Do 17, the Junkers Ju 88 and the Messerschmitt Bf 110.

Kammhuber had decided that the *helle Nachtjagd* tactics he inherited were not up to the task facing them, and devised the new *Himmelbett* (four-poster bed) tactics: rather than waiting over the likely target areas, where in the event no 'trade' might reach them, and there was a good chance of the AA guns engaging them, the fighters were switched to the approach routes the bombers had to use. Kammhuber therefore built up a line of interception 'boxes' running from Liège north-east to Schleswig-Holstein, astride the routes Bomber Command were bound to use. In each of the boxes of the 'Kammhuber Line' were three radar sets: one 'Freya' general surveillance radar, and two 'Würzburg' precision tracking radars. The 'Freya' was used to detect the arrival of the British bombers, and to direct one of the 'Würzburg' sets onto an individual bomber. The other 'Würzburg' was locked onto an orbiting night-fighter, and a ground controller could thus direct the night-fighter onto an interception until the night-fighter could pick up the bomber visually and come in for the kill. One such control box, each with its three radar sets, was positioned every 18.6 miles (30 km) across the bombers' main approach routes to industrial Germany.

Kammhuber also decided that the air war should be taken to the bombers while they were still over friendly territory, and the *Fernnachtjagd* (long-range night-fighting) or night intruder tactics were devised. Only one *Gruppe*, I/NJG2, was available, but the unit's Do 17s and Ju 88s caused considerable disruption as they operated over British bomber bases. But in the autumn of 1941 these effective tactics, later copied widely by the British with considerable success, were abandoned because of the general shortage of purely defensive night-fighters over Germany, which for political reasons had first priority.

In 1941 and 1942 the 'Kammhuber Line' was extended up to the north of Denmark and south to the Swiss border, to protect all possible night bomber approach routes to Germany. The first response of Bomber Command to the formation of the 'Kammhuber Line' had been the introduction of the bomber stream, to pass the maximum number of bombers over a given defence box in the minimum time, and so capitalize on the ground radars' inability to control more than one interception at a time. Kammhuber responded in turn by increasing the depth of his line in the most likely areas, so that instead of passing over merely one box, the bomber stream would have to run the gauntlet of perhaps three boxes in depth, supported by the three boxes on each side, so that nine night-fighters in all were in place to intercept.

The success rate of the night-fighters began to improve considerably in the early part of 1942 thanks to the introduction of new radar: 'Würzburg Reise' (Giant Würzburg) ground-control sets, and 'Lichtenstein BC' lightweight airborne interception radar, gradually fitted into all the night-fighter arm's aircraft.

During the first half of 1943, therefore, the losses of Bomber Command reached considerable proportions, and the solution to the problem, though known for some time, was applied for the first time during the offensive against Hamburg at the end of July and beginning of August 1943. This was 'Window', bundles of metallized foil dropped by the thousand during the raid. Each of the millions of foil strips was matched to the radar wavelengths used by the Germans, and sent back an echo to saturate the defence's radar screens with myriad false 'echoes'. The result was the virtual destruction of Hamburg for minimal losses. And though the Germans were able to evolve methods for obviating some of the worst effects of 'Window', in the short term two new tactics, the *wilde Sau* (wild boar) and *zahme Sau* (tame boar) were evolved.

The *wilde Sau* tactics were designed to be independent of the radar control network. On the news of an impending raid the fighters massed over the target, above the prearranged ceiling of the German *Flak* shells, to pick off British bombers silhouetted by the bombs and marker flares below, or caught by the searchlights of the target defences. For this purpose the large radar-equipped night-fighters were unnecessary, and a special single-engined formation, *Jagdgeschwader 300*, was formed with Messerschmitt Bf 109 and Focke-Wulf Fw 190 fighters.

The *zahme Sau* tactics were designed to make use of the radar-equipped twin-engined night fighters: reasoning that the thickest concentrations of 'Win-

dow' echoes must hide substantial quantities of bombers, the *Fliegerdivision* would order in all available twin-engined night-fighters to the areas of densest echoes. Once they arrived, and upwards of 20 machines might respond to the order, the fighters searched visually for the bombers, and by means of constant updating on 'Window' density from the ground, the fighters were able to maintain a running battle with the bomber stream, picking off substantial numbers of the British aircraft. The task of the *zahme Sau* fighters was facilitated during the last quarter of 1943 by the introduction of new radar: '*Lichtenstein SN-2*' airborne interception radar, operating on frequencies lower than those being saturated by 'Window'; '*Naxos*' homing radar, operating on the radiations of the British H_2S navigation radar; and '*Flensburg*' homing radar, operating on the radiations of the British 'Monica' tail-warning radar.

The standard procedure when a raid was seen developing was for all available fighters to rendezvous over a designated radio beacon, circling at about 19,685 ft (6,000 m) as they waited for the raid to materialize, and for the ground controllers to assess the likely target and dispatch them to intercept. Once an interception had been made, the individual fighters were prohibited from attacking until they had informed the ground-control station of the whereabouts of the stream so that other fighters could be vectored in. Then free to attack, the fighters usually descended below the chosen target to reduce the bomber crew's chances of spotting the fighter against the dark earth, and to improve the fighter crew's chance of keeping visual contact with the bomber by having the latter silhouetted against the dark sky. The fighter then closed in to firing range, and pulled up the nose to sweep the bomber with cannon and machine-gun fire, unless the aircraft was fitted with the special '*schräge Musik*' (shrill music, or jazz) armament installation. This consisted of a pair of 20-mm cannon arranged in the fuselage behind the cockpit to fire obliquely forward and upward: with this armament fixture the pilot of the night-fighter could destroy the bomber without having to pull up the nose and so slow down.

The most effective tactic to throw off a German night-fighter was found to be the corkscrew, and if this manoeuvre were executed vigorously, there was little chance of the night fighter matching the bomber and appearing in a firing position at the end of the manoeuvre. Faced with a corkscrewing bomber, most night-fighter pilots sheered off to look for other aircraft. The difficulty with such a manoeuvre for the bomber pilot was timing it, for the night-fighters were difficult to spot against the dark ground below. Here the thatch-weave co-operative manoeuvre by two or four aircraft proved useful, for the two aircraft operating closely together could watch each other's tails and vulnerable under-surfaces, and the addition of an extra pair of bombers added to the number of eyes available. The co-operation of four bombers also increased the chance of fighting off a would-be attacker.

The *zahme Sau* tactics remained the *Luftwaffe*'s operational norm for the rest of the war, occasionally gaining notable successes, but generally being ground down by shortage of fuel, the inexperience of replacement aircrews, and the growing number of Allied bombers in the sky, together with large numbers of de Havilland Mosquito night-fighters operating in the intruder role. These took an increasingly heavy toll of the night-fighters operating not only near the bombers, but as they formed up round radio beacons along the bomber stream's route, and even as they took off and landed at their airfields. The last was a favourite hunting ground for many crews, for although the AA fire could be intense in the area, the German night-fighters were committed to a straight course and relatively slow speeds, making them ideal targets.

In general, the tactics adopted in the Korean War were closely modelled on those of World War II with alterations to take account of the political limitations imposed upon the UN air forces and the higher performance of the aircraft involved. In essence, however, they remained true to those of World War II. The same may be said of fighter *versus* fighter combat in succeeding wars, though the guided air-to-air missile has come to play an important part. In general, though, the air-to-air missile has been a medium-range weapon, and if the target was not knocked down by the missile, a classic dogfight usually ensued, to the extent that the Americans, who had come to rely almost exclusively on missile armament in the second half of the 1950s, found themselves forced to re-adopt the fixed gun as part of the fighter's primary armament. The resurgence of fighter *versus* fighter combat is attested by the fact that several nations are building or planning specialized dogfighting aircraft armed with special short-range and highly manoeuvrable missiles and cannon armament. The major difference in fighters since World War II is not obvious change such as turbojet power and vastly increased performance, which are merely logical developments, but in the widespread use of electronic devices not only for the aiming and control of armament, but for the constant 'up-education' of the crew as the tactical situation alters, and for the provision of electronic countermeasures such as chaff (based on the 'Window' concept of World War II), jamming of the enemy's electronics (both airborne and on the ground), and a number of

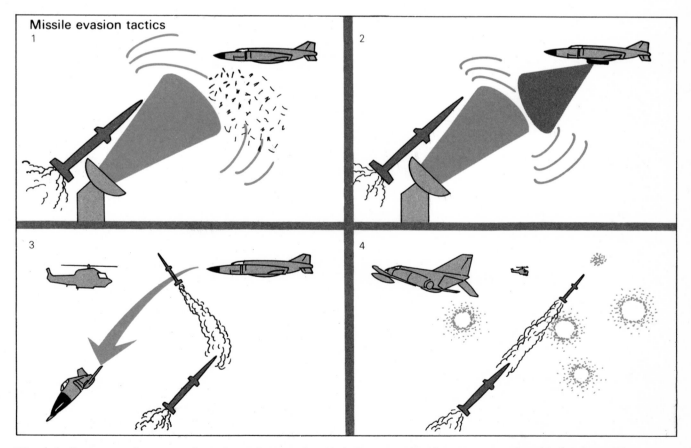

Missile evasion tactics

The missiles so much a part of modern air war played their most significant part to date in the 1973 'Yom Kippur' war between Israel and the Arab states, the latter (particularly Egypt and Syria, the main protagonists) making extensive use of the Russian SA-2 and SA-3 radar-guided missiles, and the SA-6 infra-red homing missile. The main defences against the SA-2 and SA-3 proved to be the use of chaff, metalized strips dropped in large numbers to try to produce a vast number of radar echoes which could confuse the missile-guidance system (1), and the use of electronic countermeasures (ECM) when the receiver on an Israeli aircraft indicated that a missile radar had been locked on to the aircraft. In this a special pod carried under the wing was switched on to produce radar-frequency 'noise' to jam or overload the missile-guidance system (2). Against the SA-6 two methods were used. If the missile was still on its launcher, the aircraft made a steep diving attack (necessary to keep out of the way of the SA-6 as it was fired at its normal low launch trajectory) to destroy the launch complex (3). If the missile had been fired, the pilot of the attacked aircraft could drop flares to try to decoy the missile away from him, or alternatively take violent evasive manoeuvres (4).

decoy devices. It is in this electronic field that the greatest advances have been made since World War II, and this is a highly technical, virtually separate topic.

The sophistication of the electronic warfare system current today is reflected in the lessening importance of the manned bomber, which is considered to be highly vulnerable to detection and missile/fighter interception at high altitude unless it uses extensive decoy missiles such as the Americans' ADM-20 Quail and stand-off missiles such as the AGM-28B Hound Dog or the AGM-69A Short-Range Attack Missile. Most modern bombers are therefore seen as low-level delivery systems, intended to get into position as close to their targets as possible by the massive use of electronic countermeasures and a low-level approach under the enemy's radar cover using the terrain to help its concealment. However, the increasing use of Airborne Warning and Control System (AWACS) aircraft such as the Russian Tupolev Tu-126 'Moss', the American Boeing E-3A Sentry and the British Aerospace (Hawker Siddeley) Nimrod AEW.3, makes even this tactic limited in effectiveness as such aircraft are provided with the special radar necessary for looking downwards and picking out the moving aircraft from the clutter of ground-returned echoes. For strategic purposes, therefore, the surface-to-surface missile, in the form of the intercontinental and submarine-launched ballistic missile, seems the inevitable choice.

For tactical and operational purposes, though, the aircraft which has emerged as the most potent

weapon is the fighter-bomber/attack/interdiction type such as the American McDonnell Douglas A-4 and Republic F-105, the European Panavia Tornado and the Russian Mikoyan-Gurevich MiG-23 'Flogger'. For these aircraft a whole new generation of tactics have been evolved, based on differing approaches to the battlefield, the attack itself, and the return flight: hi-lo-hi missions involve a high-level approach, a low-level attack and a high-level return; hi-lo-lo missions entail a high-level approach, low-level attack and low-level return; lo-lo-lo missions are flown entirely 'on the deck'; and lo-lo-hi missions are flown at low level until the weapons have been dropped, and then the aircraft climbs as it returns home.

The NATO air forces have also evolved a number of complex attack patterns to deliver their low-level attacks. Most of these are designed for the ubiquitous fighter-bomber, and involve the use of two or more aircraft attacking simultaneously from different directions to make the AA defences' task harder. In the 'pop-up' attack, for example, a flight of four fighter-bombers approaches the target area, at low level, at about 500 mph (805 kph), flying at about 30° off its shortest course to the target. This puts the flight about 2½ miles (4 km) to the side of the target. Flying well spaced out, the four fighter-bombers then zoom-climb to about 4,000 ft (1,219 m) and turn left or right for a simultaneous flank attack on the target. The spacing out of the aircraft means that the leader attacks the target from the rear, in a course taking him back towards his own lines, the two middle pilots attack on converging courses just forward and aft of the target's flank, and the last man attacks on the target's front quarter on a course still taking him into enemy territory. Each aircraft attacks in a dive, the aircraft all passing over the target at the same moment but at different altitudes to avoid collision, and then heading for home at maximum speed at low level.

A variation on this theme is the radial attack by a flight of four fighter-bombers, which approach the target in line-ahead formation, with about 385 yds (350 m) between aircraft. The approach is made at about 5,000 ft (1,524 m), and when the lead aircraft reaches a position some 4,000 yds (3,658 m) to one flank of the target, he pulls round into a turn with a radius of 4,000 yds (3,658 m) which will take him behind the target. As he reaches a position on the other flank opposite his original turning point, the four aircraft of the flight will be evenly spaced round the half-circle. All four aircraft then tighten their turns, simultaneously to close the target, with an angle of 60° separating each approach course. The aircraft dive at slightly different angles so that the firing passes are made at low level and high speed.

There are many variations on the ground-attack theme, but all are designed to apply the maximum weight of weapons on the target in the minimum time and from the minimum altitude and range to ensure accuracy.

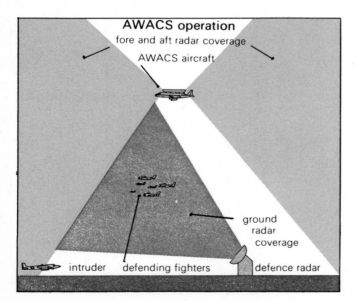

One of the most important aircraft in modern air war is the AWACS (airborne warning and control system) platform, exemplified by the American Boeing E-3A Sentry, the British Aerospace Nimrod AEW.3 and the Russian Tupolev Tu-126 'Moss'. These have special radar that can look towards the ground without the problem of 'clutter' that made such radar all but impossible for high-definition work until recently. The tactical team of the AWACS aircraft can assess the priority of several such threats, and direct fighters with 'snap-down' missiles into a position to eliminate the threats.

Air-to-Surface Armament
World War II

Damage to St Thomas's
Hospital in London is typical of
the heavy material damage
which could be caused by
high-explosive bombs.

The Germans were characteristically meticulous in their bomb designations in World War II, and the weapons are typical of the type in service during the first half of the war, with some notable exceptions. German free-fall bombs fell into three main categories: *Spreng Cylindrische* (SC) or general-purpose high-explosive; *Spreng Dickwand* (SD) or thick-walled high-explosive (semi-armour piercing); *Panzerbombe Cylindrische* (PC) or armour-piercing. Other categories were the *Brandbombe* or incendiary bomb, the type developed at the end of World War I, filled with 17.64 lb (0.2 kg) of a mixture of 10% *Elektron* aluminium and 90% magnesium, to produce an effective thermite combination; the *Sprengbombe* (SB) or demolition bomb, little being known of the SB-1000; and the *Splitterbombe* (a sub-category of the SC series) or splinter bomb, designed for anti-personnel use and for attacks on soft-skinned vehicles.

The *Luftwaffe* did consider larger bombs when four-engined bombers were again being considered in World War II, but nothing came of the bomber or bomb projects, leaving the Germans with the 5,401-lb (2,450-kg) SC-2500 as their largest weapon. Perhaps the most effective of the Germans bombs was one of the smallest, the SD-2 fragmentation or splinter bomb, which proved devastating on the Eastern Front. Special containers were designed for the SD-2, so that the Dornier Do 17 and Junkers Ju 88 could carry up to 360 of the type, and the Messerschmitt Bf 109 and Junkers Ju 87 up to 96. The bombs were dropped individually at a fast rate and, on release, the casing of the bomb sprang open to form winglets, helping to scatter the bombs as they spun to the ground. Each bomb could be fused for impact, delay or disturbance detonation.

The British and Americans started the war with basically similar weapons, which were used in large numbers by Allied twin-engined medium bombers, and by the American heavy bombers. But the Allies developed some unusual weapons, perhaps the most notable being the British 4,000-, 8,000- and 12,000-lb (1,814-, 3,629- and 5,443-kg) high-capacity bombs, with thin casings to allow the maximum weight of explosive to be carried; and the 12,000-lb (5,443-kg) Tallboy and 22,000-lb (9,979-kg) Grand Slam deep-penetration bombs designed by Barnes Wallis, developer also of the rotating cylindrical bomb used in the celebrated 'dams raid'. The Americans developed some interesting weapons, the most important being the 'Little Boy' and 'Fat Man' atomic weapons, and the AN-M26A2 fragmentation bomb cluster (consisting of 20 AN-M41A1 fragmentation bombs) and the AN-M47 incendiary bomb.

'Little Boy', which was dropped on Hiroshima on 6 August 1945, was 120 in (3,048 mm) long, 28 in (711.2 mm) in diameter, and weighed 9,000 lb (4,082 kg). Its explosive power was in the order of 20,000 tons of TNT. 'Fat Man' was the weapon dropped on Nagasaki on 9 August 1945, and used as its 'fuel' plutonium, 'Little Boy' having used uranium. 'Fat Man' was 128 in (3,251.2 mm) long, 60 in (1,524 mm) in diameter, and weighed 10,000 lb

(4,536 kg). Its explosive power was also equivalent to that of 20,000 tons of TNT.

Free-fall ordnance continues to play an important part in military planning, and development of the basic types has continued since World War II, the Americans having produced a bewildering array of such weapons with HE, chemical, gas, canister, incendiary and other fillings. At the same time napalm, a jellied solution of petrol, has been fully developed into an effective, but horrific weapon: released at low level, the napalm tank tumbles into the ground and splits open; on ignition, the jellified petrol melts and spreads in a sheet of flame in the direction the tank was travelling as it hit the ground.

Effective as some of the American bombs of World War II were, they were rapidly found unsuitable for modern fighter-bombers because the bombs had not been designed for external carriage. In the 1950s the American bomb family was therefore redesigned by Ed Heinemann of the Douglas company: the bombs were given elongated shapes reminiscent of the German P.u.W. bombs of World War I to reduce their drag when carried externally. This has resulted in the MK (or Mark) series of bombs, to replace the older M series. The most important of the new series are the MK-81 250-lb (113-kg), the MK-82 500-lb (227-kg), the MK-83 1,000-lb (454-kg) and the MK-84 2,000-lb (907-kg) general-purpose bombs.

Among the older bombs still in service until used up, are the AN-M51, -M57, -M58, -M59, -M63, -M64 and -M65 weapons, most of them specialized semi-armour piercing and armour-piercing bombs.

The function of other American underwing stores for free-fall delivery is indicated by the prefix part of the designation: BLU-weapons are fire or napalm bombs, the largest being 860-lb (390-kg) BLU-27 and -28. CBU- designation indicates a dispenser for small weapons: the CBU-1 to -30 series dispensers bombs, the CBU-46 dispensing *flechette* bomblets and the CBU-34 mine dispenser; LAU- designation indicates a pod for unguided rockets such as the FFAR; and SUU- designation indicates a rocket pack (SUU-20), flare dispenser (SUU-21 and -25), fragmentation bomb dispenser (SUU-30) or XM41 gravel mine dispenser (SUU-41). Amongst other free-fall weapons designations are B and BDU, indicating nuclear stores such as the B61 free-fall bomb used on the B-52 and F-111, and the BDU-38 carried by the F-111.

Among the interesting weapons currently carried by American aircraft is the Rockeye Cluster Bomb Mark 20. This consists of a bomb dispenser loaded with 247 bomblets. These are released by the dispenser after the 500-lb (227-kg) weapon has left the launch aircraft, to land in a comprehensive pattern of small weapons designed to incapacitate vehicles such as tanks and towed artillery. Current research is seeking to develop fuel-air explosive weapons for use in both guided and unguided packages. Such weapons are based on the principle of creating an aerosol cloud of fuel/air mixture, which can then be detonated explosively despite the lack of containment. Two such systems already in limited use are the CBU-55B and the CBU-72.

The bomblet concept has found favour with a number of other nations, especially for the simple strewing of anti-tank weapons. In the French Thomson-Brandt *Giboulée* system, for example, the launcher pod carried under the wing of an aircraft contains 12 or 24 tubes of 1.97-in (50-mm) diameter. Each tube carries five bomblets, launched out of the rear of the pod by a timing mechanism. The tubes are angled outwards from the pod centreline slightly, and combined with the forward speed of the aircraft, this combines to produce a pattern of 21.9-yards (20-m) width and 109.4-yards (100-m) length, strewn evenly with 120 bomblets when one 24-tube pod has been used. Each bomblet weighs 1.54 lb (0.7 kg) and contains 3.53 ounces (100 grams) of HE. The hollow-charge warheads of the anti-tank bomblets are capable of penetrating 9.84 in (250 mm) of steel armour.

Other interesting French weapons are the Matra Type 200 bomb-retarding system, and the Matra *Durandal* penetration bomb. The Type 200 system consists of a small parachute attached to the tail of the bomb, to slow the bomb after low-level, high-speed release by the attacking aircraft. If the bomb is dropped from 100 ft (30.5 m) at a speed of up to 690 mph (1,110 kph), the bomb will be slowed enough for the aircraft to be 1,500 ft (457 m) away before the bomb hits its target and explodes. The *Durandel* is a more sophisticated device, designed for the destruction of concrete runways. After release, the 430-lb (195-kg) weapon is virtually halted by a large parachute, then, as the nose of the bomb drops and the weapon assumes the right angle to penetrate the runway, the parachute is released and a booster motor ignites to accelerate the bomb through 164 ft (50 m) to smash through the runway.

The most ambitious weapon of the bomblet type currently undergoing trials is the West German *Streuwaffe*: this consists of a pod with 19 launching tubes, containing 409 1.1-lb (0.5-kg) anti-tank bomblets. These are fin established, the fins opening after launch through the agency of spring-loaded mechanisms. The bomblets are fired very rapidly to ensure a dense ground coverage.

Such then are some of the free-fall unpowered (except in the case of the *Durandal*) weapons used by aircraft so far this century. From simple beginnings as finned artillery shells, the type has developed rapidly and with enormous ingenuity of concept and design, so that modern free-fall weapons have the utmost destructive power at the upper end of the scale, and the small, highly sophisticated weapons are vital battlefield adjuncts for the ground forces.

Unguided missiles have also come a long way from their simple beginnings as anti-balloon weapons in World War I. During World War II the rocket was most widely used by fighter-bombers in the ground-attack and anti-shipping roles, it being reckoned that the punch of eight 60-lb (27.2-kg) British rockets striking a target together was the equivalent of a salvo of shells from a 6-in (152-mm) gunned cruiser. There were two main types of British air-to-surface rocket projectile: both were based on the same motor and cylindrical body and cruciform fins, but the 3.44-in (87.4-mm) solid armour-piercing head weighed 25 lb (11.33 kg), while the 6-in (152-mm) semi-armour piercing head weighed 60 lb (27.2 kg). In general, the armour-piercing head was used for anti-shipping purposes, while the semi-armour piercing head was reserved for land use against fortifications and armoured vehicles. The American equivalent to this British rocket projectile was the 5-in (127-mm) rocket, carried by aircraft such as the Lockheed P-38 Lightning (10 missiles on two 'Christmas tree' launchers

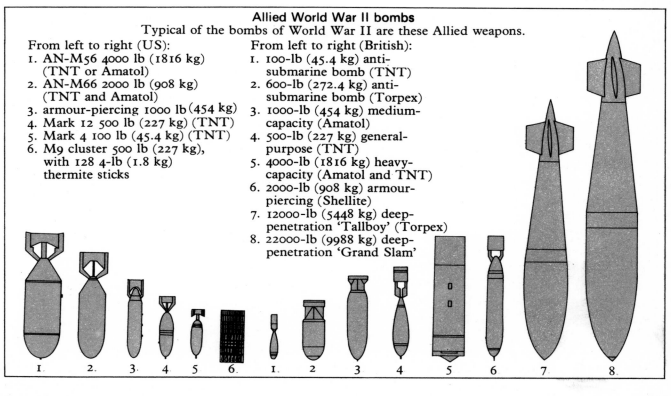

Allied World War II bombs
Typical of the bombs of World War II are these Allied weapons.

From left to right (US):
1. AN-M56 4000 lb (1816 kg) (TNT or Amatol)
2. AN-M66 2000 lb (908 kg) (TNT and Amatol)
3. armour-piercing 1000 lb (454 kg)
4. Mark 12 500 lb (227 kg) (TNT)
5. Mark 4 100 lb (45.4 kg) (TNT)
6. M9 cluster 500 lb (227 kg), with 128 4-lb (1.8 kg) thermite sticks

From left to right (British):
1. 100-lb (45.4 kg) anti-submarine bomb (TNT)
2. 600-lb (272.4 kg) anti-submarine bomb (Torpex)
3. 1000-lb (454 kg) medium-capacity (Amatol)
4. 500-lb (227 kg) general-purpose (TNT)
5. 4000-lb (1816 kg) heavy-capacity (Amatol and TNT)
6. 2000-lb (908 kg) armour-piercing (Shellite)
7. 12000-lb (5448 kg) deep-penetration 'Tallboy' (Torpex)
8. 22000-lb (9988 kg) deep-penetration 'Grand Slam'

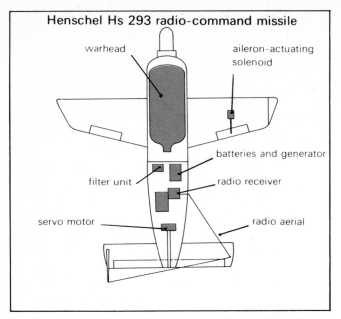

Henschel Hs 293 radio-command missile

warhead

aileron-actuating solenoid

batteries and generator

filter unit

radio receiver

servo motor

radio aerial

Radio-command guided weapons in World War II were relatively unsophisticated, as indicated by the general layout of the Henschel Hs 293. Occupying most of the nose section, and close to the centre of gravity, is the 330-kg (728-lb) HE warhead, while the projection on the nose of this rocket-powered weapon is the fuse. On the wing (complemented by a similar unit on the other wing) is the aileron-actuating solenoid. Immediately behind the warhead are (left) the filter unit for incoming signals and (right) the batteries and generator. Behind these is the radio receiver; and behind this the servo motor for the tail control surfaces. The radio aerial stretches from the fuselage out to the tailplane and across the tail.

under the wings) whereas the standard British installation was eight missiles.

The Germans, too, used rockets in the ground-attack role during World War II, having first concentrated on the use of guns and bombs for anti-tank purposes. The main gun-carrying aircraft were the Junkers Ju 87, which carried two 37-mm Rheinmetall-Borsig *Flak* 18 or *Flak* 43 guns in pods under the wings, and the Henschel Hs 129 anti-tank aircraft, which was fitted at times with a 50-mm BK 5 or 75-mm BK 7.5 gun, the former derived from the KWK 39 tank gun and the latter from the PaK 43 anti-tank gun. Other anti-tank weapons included the SD-2 and SD-4 bombs, the latter being a shaped-charge weapon specifically designed for anti-tank use. With the armour thickness of Russian tanks becoming ever greater, and therefore more difficult to penetrate with weapons relying for their effect on kinetic energy, the Germans turned to chemical weapons, such as the shaped-charge warhead, capable of burning its way through thick armour. The two chief chemical weapons used by the *Luftwaffe* were the infantry's *Panzerschreck*, modified for aircraft launching, and the *Panzerblitz*. The *Panzerschreck* of 3.07-in (78-mm) calibre was adapted as the *Panzerblitz* 1. Effective as an anti-tank weapon, though, the *Pb* 1 had the major disadvantage that it could be fired only at speeds below 298 mph (480 kph), making the launch aircraft with its underwing rails all too vulnerable to AA fire. Therefore the *Pb* 2 was developed from the R4M air-to-air missile: the HE warhead was replaced by a hollow-

charge warhead capable of defeating 7.09 in (180 mm) of armour. This proved highly effective, and the *Pb* 3 with even better performance was under final development at the end of the war. Another anti-tank device tried by the Germans was the SG113A recoilless gun of 2.95-in (75-mm) calibre, designed to fire vertically downward.

Unguided rockets are now widely used as part of the standard armament of fighter-bombers and ground-attack aircraft, mounted in pods carried on external pylons. The Russians have developed such rockets in a number of calibres, several of them large, but most countries use unguided missiles of the $2\frac{3}{4}$-in (69.85-mm) calibre or similar. Such rockets have a considerable punch (the Americans even desisting from using them in the Vietnam war at times because the damage caused was too great), and large numbers can be carried with ease. The most common such rockets in service today are the Matra 68-mm SNEB and American $2\frac{3}{4}$-in FFAR weapons, whose air-to-air use has been discussed in another section. For ground-attack work the SNEB rocket appears in two main forms: the Type 253 anti-tank and anti-personnel model, with a 3.97-lb (1.8-kg) hollow-charge and fragmentation warhead, and a velocity of 1,968 ft (600 m) per second; and the Type 256P general-purpose model, with a 6.6-lb (3-kg) fragmentation warhead and a velocity of 1,476 ft (450 m) per second. Among rockets of a larger calibre are the French Thomson-Brandt 3.94-in (100-mm) rocket currently under development in a variety of forms (general-purpose fragmentation, hollow-charge armour-piercing, semi-armour piercing, demolition and flare), the Swedish Bofors 5.3-in (135-mm) general-purpose and armour-piercing rocket, the Swiss Oerlikon SURA 3.15-in (80-mm) and SNORA 3.19-in (81-mm) ground-attack rockets, various Russian projectiles, and the American 5-in (127-mm) ZUNI rocket.

The other main category of air-to-surface weapon

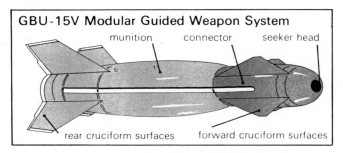

GBU-15V Modular Guided Weapon System

munition   connector   seeker head

rear cruciform surfaces   forward cruciform surfaces

Modern versions of the glide-bomb concept are very considerably more advanced than their World War II progenitors. Seen here, for example, is the GBU-15V Modular Guided Weapon System, in its cruciform-wing version. In essence, the concept of modular weapons allows one of several possible weapons (MK 84 'iron' bomb, SUU-54 dispenser or Hard-Structure Munition) to become the fuselage/payload of the missile. To this basic core are added (at the rear) a data-link module, a control module and the main cruciform wings; while at the nose are added an adaptor to connect the bomb/dispenser/munition with the guidance module and small cruciform wings. Four guidance modules are available: electro-optical (EO), laser, imaging infra-red (IIR) and distance-measuring equipment (DME).

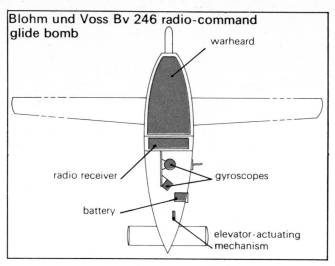

Blohm und Voss Bv 246 radio-command glide bomb

warhead

radio receiver

gyroscopes

battery

elevator-actuating
mechanism

Glider bombs were used relatively freely in the
second half of World War II, and one of the more
promising conventional types was the Blohm und
Voss Bv 246, seen here in diagrammatic form
(fuselage side on). The *Hagelhorn's* clean lines and
sailplane wing bestowed a range of up to 62 miles
(100 km), and the warhead weighed 435 kg (959 lb).
On the centre of gravity is the HE warhead, with the
radio receiver behind it. Behind this, in spherical and
cuboid containers, are the gyroscopes to hold the
missile stable.

is the guided missile, of which there are two main
sub-species, the unpowered and powered missiles.
Again it was the Germans who pioneered the practical use of unpowered guided missiles in combat,
having used the Henschel Hs 293 glider bomb and
the '*Fritz-X*' or FX-1400 guided bomb from 1943
onwards. The Hs 293 resembled a small aircraft,
with a span of 11 ft 9 in (3.98 m). After launch from
its parent bomber, the Hs 293 was accelerated by a
small liquid-propellant rocket for the first 12 seconds
of its flight, thereafter gliding towards its target
under the radio command of the operator in the
launch aircraft, who had only to keep the flare on
the missile's tail on his line of sight to the target to
ensure a hit. As the missile struck at only about
450 mph (725 kph), the anti-shipping Hs 293 was
used mainly against merchant ships, and scored some
useful successes after its introduction in August 1943.
The FX-1400 was basically a controllable version
of the SD-1400 bomb, with stub cruciform wings
and a relatively complex tail. Aimed quite conventionally at first, the FX-1400 was controlled by
radio as it fell free towards the target, normally a
heavily armoured warship. The aircraft which
launched the bomb had to fly slowly in the area so
that the operator could see and correct the flight of
his weapon as it accelerated to about Mach 1 in
its drop from 21,325 ft (6,500 m). Despite the relative
crudeness of the concept, the weapon worked well,
sinking the Italian battleship *Roma* as she steamed
towards Malta to surrender to the British after the
capitulation of Italy in September 1943. The weakness of the two German missile systems was not in
the missiles themselves, but in the fact that once the
novelty of the weapons had been appreciated, the
Allies so strengthened their fighter defences that the
launch aircraft could rarely approach close enough

to drop their missiles. Several other more advanced
air-to-surface weapons were under development by
the Germans towards the end of the war, including
the Blohm und Voss BV 246 and Kramer X-1
unpowered missiles, but no other types entered
operational service.

The Americans also used unpowered guided
weapons in World War II, notably the VB-1 Azon.
This was basically a standard AN-M65 1,000-lb
(454-kg) general purpose bomb fitted with a new
nose cap and guidance controls in the fins. The
bomb was controlled in azimuth only (hence the
name) by the bombardier of a B-17 or B-24 launch
aircraft by means of a radio link. The bombardier
tracked the missile by a flare in its tail. Also used
was the VB-2 2,000-lb (907-kg) version, both models
entering service in 1944. The Americans developed
other similar weapons, but these were used for the
first time in the Korean War: the VB-3 Razon
1,000-lb (454-kg) and VB-4 2,000-lb (907-kg)
bombs, controllable in range and azimuth only
(hence the name again); the VB-6 Felix version of
the former, with an infra-red seeker coupled to the
controls, and the VB-13 Tarzon, basically a British
12,000-lb (5,443-kg) 'Tallboy' fitted with a lift
shroud and radio-controlled surfaces in the fins for
both range and azimuth corrections.

At this stage there seemed to be little further point
in developing glide-bombs, as guided missiles could
apparently do the job just as well. But during the
Vietnam War there was a resurgence of interest in
both the controlled bomb and glide bomb, the controlled bomb concept looking to the Azon/Razon/
Tarzon series, and the glide bomb concept looking
to the GB (glide bomb) series of the early 1940s: the
GB-1 of 1944, a 2,000-lb (907-kg) M34 general-
purpose bomb in an Aeronca-made airframe span-
ning 12 ft (3.66 m) and with a twin-boom tail
assembly and controls preset before launch, and the
GB-4, also of 1944 and the only other member of
the family used operationally, with a similar airframe
to the GB-1 but commanded by means of radio/tele-
vision. The GB series was very far-sighted, and
models were tested with a light-contrast seeker
(GB-5), radar-homing seeker (GB-7), radio/tele-
vision remote control (GB-8), and low-level approach
(GB-9).

Current weapons with similar characteristics are
the GBU-15 HOBOS (Homing Bomb System), with
an electro-optical seeker head and associated control
system attached to an otherwise standard MK-84
2,000-lb (907-kg) or M118E1 3,000-lb (1,361-kg)
general-purpose bomb. Once the seeker head has
been locked onto the target and the weapon has
been dropped, the HOBOS weapon homes in automatically. Derivatives of the concept under development include a planar configured model with wings
to increase range, and also a version with cruciform
wings, designated GBU-15 Pave Strike. And already
in widespread service is the AGM-62 Walleye: this
is a glide bomb with TV guidance, capable of delivering its warhead with very great accuracy over a

range of some 10 miles (16 km). The wings of this model are of cruciform delta configuration.

Finally, there are the air-to-surface powered guided missiles. Here the Germans failed to take the lead with early developments, and it was left to the Japanese to develop a few non-operational missiles during World War II. The Imperial Army planned the *Igo*-1-A, with a 1,764-lb (800-kg) warhead, monoplane wings and radio guidance (flown in prototype form). The *Igo*-1-B was a smaller version with a 661-lb (300-kg) warhead, and the *Igo*-1-C used the conceptually interesting homing device of shock waves from heavy gunfire. All three army missiles proved promising in tests, but were not used operationally. The Imperial Navy produced only the *Funryu* 2 gyro-stabilized air-to-surface missile prototype with a 110-lb (50-kg) warhead.

Modern air-to-surface guided missiles fall into two main categories: strategic and tactical. The strategic type falls into two sub-types: stand-off missile (Boeing AGM-69A SRAM, Boeing AGM-28A Hound Dog and Russian AS-6 'Kingfish') and subsonic cruise missile (Boeing AGM-86A ALCM). And in the field of tactical missiles there are a number of sub-types, such as wire-guided anti-tank missiles, laser-homing missiles, TV-guided missiles and radio-command missiles. The following are typical of some of the latest weapons.

In the cruise missile class, the air-launched leader is the AGM-86A, which carries a nuclear warhead of about 200-kiloton yield. The flying surfaces deploy after the missile has been fired, and the guidance is assumed by a pre-programmed inertial platform, which brings the missile right down towards sea level, and then causes it to cruise at high subsonic speed 'on the deck' while taking evasive manoeuvres. That the course is correct is checked by the terrain contour matching unit, which checks that the radar picture of the ground underneath the missile corresponds with the prerecorded radar picture provided by earlier reconnaissance, altering course as necessary to make the two pictures tally. Speed is about Mach 0.8 and range, with a belly tank and at high altitude, 760 miles (1,200 km). In the field of stand-off missiles, possibly the best weapon deployed by the United States is the AGM-69A Short-Range Attack Missile. This has a 200-kiloton nuclear warhead, and is launched from the B-52 or FB-111A bombers. Speed is in the region of Mach 3, and after a high-altitude launch the missile has a range of about 105 miles (170 km). Whereas the AGM-86A is powered by a small turbojet, delivering only 600-lb (272-kg) thrust, the AGM-69A has a solid-propellant rocket motor of considerable thrust. Guidance is effected by an inertial platform with radar terrain-avoidance capability. It is interesting to note that similar Russian missiles are winged, and require midcourse correction to ensure accurate navigation. However, the range of the Russian missiles is somewhat greater than those of the American stand-off missiles.

Tactical guided missiles are normally capable of two functions, and a typical example is the Anglo-French Hawker Siddeley Dynamics-Matra Martel. In its AS.37 version, built by Matra, the Martel is intended for passive homing on radar antennae in all weathers, its 331-lb (150-kg) warhead being capable of causing considerable damage. In its AJ.168 version, built by HSD, the Martel is designed for ordinary battlefield tasks, and is guided on to its target by the operator in the launch aircraft, who watches an image of the scene in front of the missile produced by a small TV camera in the missile's nose. All the operator is required to do is keep the target right in the middle of the picture. The Martel missile is typical of its class in weights and performance, weighing about 1,200 lb (544 kg), and having speed/range figures of subsonic/18½ miles (30 km).

For general battlefield duties, the Americans have the various members of the AGM-65 Maverick and AGM-12 Bullpup families, with a wide variety of command systems and performance/payload alternatives. The Americans also use large numbers of anti-radiation missiles such as the AGM-45 Shrike and AGM-88A HARM.

Wire-guided air-launched missiles are used almost exclusively for anti-tank and anti-fortification work, the slow speed of such missiles not mattering over short range and when a hollow-charge warhead is used. (The hollow-charge warhead works best when its impact speed with the target is relatively low.) Typical of the older generation of wire-guided missiles is the Aérospatiale AS.11, the air-launched version of the SS.11 battlefield missile. The AS.11 cruises at some 360 mph (580 kph), and has a range of up to 9,840 ft (3,000 m). The operator uses command to line-of-sight guidance techniques, and the hollow-charge Type 140AC warhead will penetrate 23.62 in (600 m) of steel armour. An equivalent missile of the latest generation is the BGM-71A TOW missile. While range is about the same as that of the AS.11, speed is about double that of the French missile, and all the operator has to do is keep the target centred in his sight, the computer in the sight generating signals to bring the missile into the centre of the sighting image. Third-generation missiles currently entering service are of the 'launch and forget' concept: all the operator has to do is lock the missile onto the target and fire, the missile homing automatically on the image locked in its memory.

The last type of air-launched missile is the anti-shipping missile, typified by a number of now obsolescent but powerful Russian types and two modern missiles, the German Messerschmitt-Bölkow-Blohm *Kormoran*, and the American AGM-84A Harpoon. Both missiles fly an inertial/radar altimeter preprogrammed course, with the possibility of mid-course correction, at very low level. For the terminal homing phase the missiles each switch on an active radar seeker which steers the missile finally into the target ship. Range of the *Kormoran* is 23 miles (37 km), and speed Mach 0.95, while the warhead weighs 352 lb (160 kg).

Pacific Theatre
World War II

The Pacific campaign was started by an air attack, and thereafter air power played an all-important part in operations. Early in the morning of 7 December 1941, two Japanese strikes were launched at the US Pacific Fleet in Pearl Harbor, the aircraft being launched from six aircraft-carriers under the command of Vice Admiral Chuichi Nagumo. The idea for such a strike had its origins in the raid by Fleet Air Arm Fairey Swordfish torpedo-bombers against the Italian fleet in Taranto harbour on 27 November 1940. Some 167 Nakajima B5N 'Kate' torpedo-bombers and Aichi D3A 'Val' dive-bombers sank four US battleships and damaged three others, as well as hitting many other ships, while 105 other strike aircraft, supported by 78 Mitsubishi A6M 'Zero' fighters destroyed or seriously damaged 310 of the 400 US military aircraft on Oahu island in the Hawaiian islands. Only 29 Japanese aircraft were lost.

On the same day (8 December on the other side of the international date line) Japanese bombers from Indo-China struck at British airfields in Malaya, destroying or damaging 60 of the 110 British and Australian aircraft in the country, and making an air attack on Singapore city. Again on the same day, Japanese aircraft from Formosa struck at American air power in the Philippines, 108 bombers attacking American airfields, escorted by 34 fighters. The US had recently made efforts to upgrade its air forces in the Philippines, and these new aircraft were the Japanese primary targets. 18 of 35 Boeing B-17 Flying Fortress and 56 Curtiss P-40 fighters were destroyed, for the loss of only seven Japanese aircraft. Many older aircraft were also lost by the Americans.

Following up their initial advantage, the Japanese flattened Cavite Navy Yard in the Philippines, thus destroying the United States' chance of making an air or sea comeback at the Japanese, while land-based bombers of the Imperial Navy ended British naval hopes in Malaya on 10 December by sinking Britain's only two capital ships in the theatre, the battleship *Prince of Wales* and the battle-cruiser *Repulse*. Thereafter, Japanese aircraft and ships were able to operate almost unhindered in support of the main operations in the Philippines and Malaya, leading in 1942 to the capture of both, and the Japanese invasions of Burma and the Dutch East Indies. The British sent out over 100 additional aircraft, 51 of them modern Hawker Hurricane fighters, but even these failed to stop the Japanese onslaught, being too few in number and technically inferior to the Japanese aircraft, which were flown with considerably more skill. Singapore, the bastion of Malaya, fell on 15 February 1942; the Dutch East Indies were in Japanese hands by 9 March; the last organized resistance

in the Philippines ceased on 18 May; and by the end of May the last British had left Burma. Finally, between January and July 1942 the Japanese descended on New Guinea, the Bismarck islands and the Solomon islands to complete the occupation of their planned defensive perimeter.

Yet what could be achieved against the Japanese, whose aircraft were lightly built and devoid of armour protection and self-sealing fuel tanks, is illustrated by the losses of the Japanese raid on Rangoon on 23 and 25 December 1941: out of 160 bombers and escorting fighters, the Allies shot down 27, for the loss of two AVG P-40s and four RAF Brewster Buffaloes. Most of the Japanese aircraft fell to the AVG pilots, who had evolved the right tactics to defeat the Japanese during the fighting over southern China: the avoidance at all costs of turning dogfights with the more manoeuvrable Japanese fighters, and the use of diving attacks to use the Allied aircraft's higher speed. Several raids on Rangoon by the Japanese were

The Mitsubishi Ki-46 'Dinah' reconnaissance aircraft had the unusual distinction of being the only purpose-built reconnaissance aircraft to serve widely in World War II.

similarly treated, the most decisive defeat inflicted by the British occurring on 25 February 1942, when Hawker Hurricanes made the major contribution in the shooting down of 37 out of 170 Japanese aircraft, a loss rate of just over 21.75%.

The loss of Rangoon and the fall of Burma effectively cut China's last land communications with the outside world, and until such communications were reopened on 27 January 1945, all supplies had to be flown in 'over the hump' of the eastern Himalayas, in by far the largest airlift operation of World War II, the most important aircraft involved being the Consolidated B-24 Liberator, the Curtiss C-46 Commando and the Douglas C-47 Skytrain.

Apart from tactical surprise, manoeuvrability had been the Japanese pilots' main tactical advantage during the first campaigns of the war. By the middle of 1942 the Allied pilots, following the example of the AVG pilots (who had become the China Air Task Force in July 1942 after the end of their contract with the Chinese), realized that the weight and strength of their aircraft was a positive advantage so long as they avoided dogfights with the more nimble Japanese, and so the Allies finally began to take the air war back to the Japanese. Confident that

their 1941 generation of aircraft would meet all needs in the immediate future, the Japanese had failed to press ahead with the development of more advanced types. Now they began to feel the pressure.

The first Allied air offensive was launched in April 1942 against Rabaul in New Britain, linchpin of Japan's defence position in the south-west Pacific, with Australian attacks by night and US raids during the day. Losses were heavy and successes few, but the Japanese were forced to keep in the Rabaul area fighters that could more profitably have been used elsewhere, possibly in the New Guinea operations. During April the first USAAF Bell P-39 Airacobra fighters arrived in the area via Port Moresby, and the growing Allied strength in the theatre decided the Japanese on the capture of Port Moresby.

This led directly to the Battle of the Coral Sea between 4 and 8 May 1942. Tactically inconclusive (the Japanese and Americans each lost one aircraft-carrier), the battle had the vital result of checking Japan's expansion for the first time, and persuading the Japanese to undertake an overland attack on Port Moresby, with disastrous results for the Japanese land forces involved.

The Imperial Navy had meanwhile decided to lure the American carrier

forces, which had escaped destruction at Pearl Harbor by being absent, into a decisive battle by invading the key US outpost island of Midway. The battle was fought between 4 and 6 June 1942, and resulted in an overwhelming US victory, the Japanese losing four carriers and the Americans only one, thanks to the strategic and tactical genius of the US commanders. The Douglas TBD Devastator ended its career in the battle with terrible losses, but three other US types (the Douglas SBD Dauntless dive-bomber, the Grumman F4F Wildcat fighter and the Grumman TBF Avenger torpedo-bomber) all enhanced or created reputations for themselves. The Battle of Midway ranks as one of the decisive battles of all time, and had the effect in 1942 of wresting the strategic initiative away from Japan.

The pace of air operations over the eastern Solomons now speeded up considerably with the development of the Battle of Guadalcanal, as American Marines tried to expel the Japanese force garrisoning this most south-easterly of imperial outposts. The Marines finally prevailed in February 1943, but only after a campaign of the utmost savageness. Forced to operate from distant bases, Japanese aircraft fought over the Solomons in the most difficult of circumstances,

losing 1,960 aircraft in combat. More importantly, perhaps, the loss of these aircraft also meant the loss of most of Japan's surviving prewar pilots, whose experience and skill was far superior to that of wartime pilots.

During 1943, the British in Burma and the Americans in China (where the China Air Task Force became the 14th Army Air Force under the command of Major General Claire Chennault on 11 March) began to take the air war to the Japanese with some considerable effect. In Burma this effort was largely tactical, but in China the 14th AAF started a strategic campaign whose main object was Japan-

Above: *The spirit which allowed the Japanese to develop their* kamikaze *suicide tactics is clearly evident in this Japanese painting of newly qualified pilots setting out for the front.* Left: *Grumman F4F Wildcat fighters, that did much to redress the balance against the Mitsubishi A6M Zero, on the British carrier* Formidable. *Below left: The North American B-25 Mitchell was one of the war's best medium bombers and ground-attack aircraft.* Below: *Lockheed P-38 fighters escort Consolidated B-24 bombers over Rabaul.*

ese shipping and port facilities in the China region. So successful was this campaign that the Japanese, in April 1944, attempted to destroy the 14th AAF's base areas. Despite heavy losses, the Japanese made good progress in their efforts against the base areas and in securing a corridor towards French Indo-China, their object being to open a rail link with south-east Asia and so do away with large portions of the shipping that was so tempting a target for the 14th AAF. As a result of their technical superiority, the units of the 14th AAF were moved to new airfields alongside the corridor being driven south, and wrought havoc with the Japanese forces by the widespread use of tactical air power. Eventually, though, the object of

the 14th AAF was to build up the bases for strategic bomber operations against Japan. Beset by the most difficult logistical problems, the 20th Bomber Command was at first forced to operate against targets in south-east Asia from the Calcutta region of India, the force's first Boeing B-29 Super-fortress raid being made against Bangkok on 5 June 1944. Later the bombers were able to stage through China *en route* to targets in Japan and Manchuria, Japan being raided for the first time on 15 June 1944. The 14th AAF's strategic campaign was a failure, however.

In the Pacific area, the Allies were counterattacking strongly in the New Guinea theatre; bombing raids on Japanese rear areas and shipping becoming increasingly effective during early 1943. The key action in this campaign was the Battle of the Bismarck Sea, in which eight Japanese transports escorted by eight destroyers, covered by fighters, attempted at the beginning of March to ferry reinforcements to Lae. The force was attacked by US and Australian aircraft using low-level tactics: on 2 March one transport was sunk, on 3 March six transports and four destroyers were lost, and the last transport was sunk by a motor torpedo-boat. The Japanese lost 20 fighters while shooting down four US aircraft. This set the pattern for the rest of the south-west Pacific campaign, where US and Australian aircraft dominated the skies, allowing the ground forces to operate with great freedom and all the support possible from Lieutenant General George C. Kenney's 5th AAF. During the period between June and December 1943, Kenney developed a pattern of tactical operations that became standard for land campaigns in the Pacific. First, the securing of air superiority over the forthcoming battlefield by fighters and attack aircraft, while long-range bombers attacked the airfields from which the Japanese might be able to intervene; secondly, the battlefield was isolated from reinforcement by fighters and attack aircraft; thirdly, tactical support of great flexibility was provided during the actual battle; and fourthly, air reinforcements and supplies were flown in, if necessary, to allow the ground forces to maintain the impetus of their attacks.

Further to the east, in the Solomons, the Americans were waging an air battle of attrition with the Japanese between January and April 1943, the main objective being the Japanese bases in the Rabaul area. In an effort to halt the growing losses of his forces, Admiral Isoroku

Yamamoto, commander-in-chief of the Combined Fleet, moved into the theatre the remaining carrier aircraft from the fleet lying at Truk. However, the air offensive between 7 and 12 April was a total disaster for the Japanese, culminating on 18 April with the death of Yamamoto in an 'air ambush' over Bougainville. For the rest of the year the Americans whittled away Japanese air strength, and by the end of 1943 the Solomons had cost Japan some 3,000 aircraft and crews.

In the central Pacific, the Americans were beginning to fight their way back across the ocean, with powerful ground forces transported to island objectives by the amphibious warfare units of Admiral Chester W. Nimitz's Pacific Ocean Areas forces, escorted by powerful surface fleets with strong carrier elements. Landings were provided with the tactical air support of the US Navy's and US Marine Corps' air arms, and once the forces ashore had cleared sufficient of the target area, tactical aircraft operated from shore strips built by special engineer detachments. At the same time, fast carrier task forces roamed adjacent areas to engage any Japanese naval forces attempting to interfere, and to bomb any airfields from which Japanese aircraft might operate against the invasion forces. The first of these island campaigns was in the Gilbert Islands, where Tarawa and Makin were assaulted on 20 November 1943. The capture of Tarawa proved one of the bloodiest campaigns in American history, and set the scene for the other island battles of the central Pacific campaign, with the Japanese fighting to the last man, and the Americans having to use overwhelming force to clear tiny islands. After the Gilberts the next objective was the Marshall Islands, with Kwajalein atoll as the main objective. This was reduced between 29 January and 7 February 1944, and shortly afterwards the US fast carrier task force struck at the Imperial Navy's main anchorage at Truk. On 17–18 February the Japanese lost 200,000 tons of merchant shipping and 275 of the 365 aircraft at Truk. Yet they were preparing for a naval counterstroke they hoped would restore Japan's former ascendancy. The carrier force had been built up again, though the aircraft were obsolete (especially in fighters, where the A6M was hopelessly outclassed by the Grumann F6F Hellcat) and the aircrew vastly in-

Although it was rejected by the RAF for lack of manoeuvrability, the Bell P-39 Airacobra was used by the Americans.

The Republic P-47 Thunderbolt, with its heavy armament and good range, proved a useful fighter in the Pacific theatre so long as its pilots avoided more agile Japanese fighters.

ferior in quality to their American counterparts.

Then, on 15 June 1944, the Americans struck at the Marianas group of islands, Saipan being taken between 15 June and 13 July, Guam between 21 July and 10 August, and Tinian between 25 July and 2 August. These were key islands, for they were large enough for a vast complex of strategic bomber bases to be built for the decimation of Japan's industries and cities.

On receiving news of the Saipan landings, the Japanese carrier force moved up to engage the Americans according to a long-planned scheme. Amongst the forces under the command of Vice Admiral Jisaburo Ozawa were five fleet and four light carriers, with 473 aircraft. Admiral Raymond A. Spruance's 5th Fleet included seven fleet and eight light carriers, with 956 aircraft. The result of the Battle of the Philippine Sea on 19–21 June 1944 was inevitably a foregone conclusion once the Americans had learned of the Japanese movement. In a series of air strikes, the 'Great Marianas Turkey Shoot' cost the Japanese 346 aircraft and two fleet carriers, the Americans losing only 30 aircraft. In further strikes the Japanese lost another fleet carrier and 65 aircraft. The Americans lost 20 more aircraft in combat, though another 80 had to ditch for lack of fuel, most of their crews being rescued. The Battle of the Philippine Sea marked the effective end of the Imperial Navy's air arm.

Almost as soon as they had been captured, the airfields in the Marianas were occupied by B-17 and B-24 heavy bombers, and the engineer corps set about building up facilities for the B-29s, the first of which arrived on 12 October, the controlling formation being the 21st Bomber Command, the partner of the 20th Bomber Command in the 20th AAF. On 24 November 111 B-29s were dispatched on the first raid against the Japanese mainland from the Marianas. This was followed by seven more raids during 1944, but success was negligible. Then, on 19 January 1945, 62 B-29s severely damaged the Kawasaki aircraft engine factory.

On 20 January, Major General Curtis LeMay arrived to assume command of the Marianas bombers, and to improve their combat efficiency, which he did by altering tactics from day high-altitude raids with HE bombs to night low- and medium-altitude raids with a mixture of incendiaries and HE. This led to the war's most destructive raid when 334 B-29s dropped 1,667 tons of bombs on Tokyo on the night of 9–10 March 1945; 16 square miles of the city were destroyed, 83,000 people were killed in the firestorm, another 100,000 were injured and one million were left homeless. From this time on the B-29s roamed virtually at will over Japan, destroying cities, industries, power systems, transportation and even food supplies. There was nothing the Japanese could do to halt the bombers, even aerial *kamikaze* tactics failing, and the performance of Japanese fighters being inadequate to tackle the high-performance B-29s.

The strategic bombers brought the war with Japan to a close in August 1945 with the A bombs dropped on Hiroshima and Nagasaki.

The Boeing B-29 Superfortress was the best heavy bomber of World War II, and took the war to Japan in a decisive way from the middle of 1944. B-29s dropped the A-bombs on Hiroshima and Nagasaki. Bomb load was normally about 12,000 lb (5,448 kg).

Korea, Indo-China, Suez

The end of World War II in Europe had seen the strategic bomber at last appear as a decisive weapon, a fact confirmed by the impact of American strategic bombing of Japan, and the destruction of Hiroshima and Nagasaki, each by a single atomic bomb, on 6 and 9 August 1945 respectively. That air power had at last reached decisive proportions as an individual weapon of war was recognized in the United States by the formation of the Strategic Air Command in March 1946 and the subsequent formal separation of the air force from the army. The Russian response was to build up a force of long-range bombers as quickly as possible, for use by the Long-Range Aviation arm, once again given autonomy within the Soviet Air Force in 1946. The importance of these Russian moves may have been seen in comparison with the overwhelming emphasis placed on tactical aviation during World War II.

Combined with the elements of a new hostility between the USA and its partners of the North Atlantic Treaty Organization and the USSR and its satellites in the Warsaw Treaty Organization, the real threat of total war during the late 1940s and early 1950s helped to ensure that the reduction in the world's armed forces did not approach that of the early 1920s. Large resources were devoted to the development of new aircraft, both tactical and strategic, and to further development of jet propulsion whose importance had been fully appreciated at the end of World War II.

Though aircraft played a small part in the various 'wars of liberation' of the period, as people such as the Indonesians attempted to shuck off 'recolonization' by the prewar imperial powers, the first major use of aircraft in the Cold War was during the Berlin airlift of June 1948 to

The useful life of the North American Mustang appeared to be virtually over at the end of World War II, but the start of the Korean War in 1950 found the type in widespread use as the F-51 ground-attack fighter, loaded with bombs, rocket projectiles and machine-guns.

September 1949, when the Russians cut off the city from all land access. During the course of the airlift, Allied aircraft flew 277,264 sorties to fly in 2,343,313 tons of supplies to the city.

The state of Israel was formed on 14 May 1948 after a United Nations' decision of 29 November 1947. Immediately after Israel's formation, her Arab League neighbours attacked the new state with total superiority of forces. In the air this took the form of 300 aircraft against a mere 35 Israeli aircraft. Despite their inferiority, the Israelis were able to repulse the Arab attacks and launch several counteroffensives, achieving some success before the campaign halted on 5 January 1949. Only very limited engagements took place in

the air, however, despite the fact that the Israeli air force grew by 223 aircraft during the war. Israeli fighters claimed 15 victories.

The first major air war after World War II, therefore, started with the Korean War (25 June 1950–27 July 1953), in which the North Koreans, supported by the Russians and then the Chinese, tried to invade and conquer South Korea, which was supported by the United States and other countries, operating under the flag of the United Nations. The North Korean air force had about 180 aircraft, most of them Ilyushin Il-10 ground-attack and Yakovlev Yak-9 fighter aircraft, while the South Koreans had no modern combat aircraft.

The initial advance of the North Koreans was accompanied by widespread air activity of a tactical nature, the arrival of US heavy bombers leading subsequently to an intensive air war against North Korea's lines of communication and supply dumps. However, threatened intervention by Communist China led to the adoption by the UN forces of political restraints on air and surface operations, by which the crossing of the Yalu river under any circumstances was forbidden. This effectively gave the North Koreans and their allies a safe haven close to the battlefield. In this they could stockpile supplies and build up air bases for an air force making increased use of modern Russian aircraft, notably the Mikoyan-Gurevich MiG-15 jet fighter. Allied aircraft continued to arrive in the south, and the South Koreans and UN forces operated under friendly air cover.

Initially the UN air forces, mostly American, were equipped with aircraft such as the North American F-82 Twin Mustang, the Lockheed F-80 Shooting Star and the Douglas A-26 Invader, and these proved adequate to cope with the tasks allocated them, and to deal with the Russian piston-engined aircraft in the theatre. The tables were turned, however, when the first MiG-15 was spotted on 1 November 1950. Clearly the piston-engined UN types, which by this time included North American F-51 Mustang fighters and Boeing B-29 bombers, could not hope to operate with small losses when faced by such a fighter. And at this time the UN air presence was highly effective, most aircraft being used tactically for battlefield support with bombs, napalm and rockets, and even the B-29s being used for interdiction.

The world's first combat between jet fighters (the German Messerschmitt Me 262 and the British Gloster Meteor having failed to meet in World War II) occurred on 1 November 1950 when a MiG-15 was shot down by an F-80C Shooting Star. Despite this success, it was clear that the Russian fighter was far superior to all current UN types in Korea, and that once the communists started to use pilots of a skill matching the technical advantages of the MiG-15, the UN air forces would be in trouble. Accordingly, a wing of the latest North American F-86A Sabre fighters was rushed to Korea. The Sabre met the MiG-15 for the first time on 17 December 1950,

The Douglas B-26 Invader (left), *proved invaluable in Korea, and served also in the Vietnam War up to the early 1970s.*

in the world's first combat between swept-wing aircraft, and the result was another MiG-15 shot down. This was highly encouraging, but it was realized that the MiG-15 was marginally superior to the Sabre in most fighter attributes such as armament, speed, climb and turn rate, and that the Americans would have to rely on the superiority of their pilots to best the Russian fighters. This factor continued to hold true even after the arrival of more advanced versions of the Sabre, such as the F-86F, and was especially true of jet types such as the F-94 Starfire and the Republic F-84 Thunderjet.

At the end of 1950, therefore, the MiG-15s can be credited with having reduced the efficiency of the UN fighter-bomber

and other tactical aircraft. But then a communist offensive starting on 25 November defeated the tactical efforts of the MiGs. Pushing the UN forces back south through all the territory they had taken in their own offensive, the communists forced the abandonment of the Sabre airfields, compelling the Sabres to pull back to Japan. However, the communists based most of their MiGs north of the Yalu, where the fighters' range allowed them only to protect North Korean installations, not to range over the battlefield, so allowing the UN forces to use their tactical air power more effectively again.

This established the basic pattern of air war over Korea, with the UN forces generally able to operate at will over the battlefield, but facing severe opposition in their attacks on targets within 'MiG alley', as the area covered by the MiG defence was dubbed. By the end of the war, the UN air forces could claim 959 communist aircraft destroyed in combat, with another 168 probably destroyed in combat, and 973 damaged in combat.

In French Indo-China, a sporadic guerrilla war had been waged since 1945 as the French sought to re-establish control over the country, the north of which was still full of Viet Minh communist guerrilla units formed during the struggle with Japan during World War II. These had proclaimed the People's Republic of Vietnam in September 1945, under the leadership of Ho Chi Minh. The French had few aircraft in the area initially, and had to use captured Japanese types until quantities of Supermarine Spitfire IX fighters, Douglas Dauntless dive-bombers and Junkers Ju 52/3m

Above: *Major James Jabara was the first ace of the Korean War, and ended it with 15 victories.* Below: *Wounded are loaded onto a Sikorsky S-5 helicopter for evacuation.*

transports arrived from France. The French secured some early successes, but the main Viet Minh strength after 1949 was trained in communist China, out of the reach of the French. In the early 1950s the communists gradually seized control of the mountain regions of northern Vietnam, leaving the French the plains and coast.

The Viet Minh gradually pushed into French-controlled areas, and the French presence in northern Vietnam became evidently impossible after the disastrous defeat at Dien Bien Phu between 20 November 1953 and 7 May 1954. Some 15,000 men were parachuted into a small valley to construct and hold a 'honeypot' fortress in a Viet Minh-controlled area, the idea being that the fortress should be air supplied, and inflict a decisive defeat on the communists who would have to attack the fortress to reopen their lines of communication. However, the French had only 100 transports available (most of them Douglas C-47 and Fairchild C-119 types).

Slowly the Viet Minh brought in four divisions of infantry, using two of them to seal off the Dien Bien Phu fortress and the other two to sweep the area around it as massive artillery reinforcements for the Viet Minh arrived. Artillery bombard-ment of the fortress was severe, and 14 air-craft were lost on the ground to artillery fire. The airstrip was overrun on 27 March 1954, and French aircraft then had to run the gamut of Viet Minh AA fire to airdrop supplies: of the 420 aircraft avail-able, 48 were shot down and another 167 damaged. The aircraft had to fly above the range of the AA guns, and the morale of the pilots sagged. These two factors led to increased inaccuracy in the supply drops, and the fortress was forced to sur-render on 7 May 1954 after a 56-day siege – it was clear indication that air power alone could not ensure success on the ground. This factor had been apparent

The de Havilland Vampire (left) *and Gloster Meteor were Britain's two main fighter and trainer types until the advent of the swept-wing Hawker Hunter in the mid-1950s.*

The Lockheed T-33 Seastar was the US Navy's trainer version of the F-80 Shooting Star, typical of the generation of fighters that were in service at the time of the beginning of the Korean War. The basic design originated in World War II, the prototype flying late in 1943.

in Korea too, as the communists had operated with varying degrees of success throughout the war without air support.

In Malaya the British were faced in February 1948 with a revolt by communist guerrillas, most of them Chinese, who had fought the Japanese during World War II. A sporadic campaign was fought until 8 February 1954 until the communist high command pulled out of the country. Throughout the period careful use of air power, with both fixed and rotary wing aircraft, was made. Early successes in strikes against communist camps forced the guerrillas to pull back into the jungle, where air power could not play a very useful role.

Between 1953 and 1955 the RAF also used aircraft in a limited fashion against the Mau Mau rebels in Kenya, and between 1954 and 1962 the French made widespread use of aircraft in fighting Algerian nationalist guerrillas. In this war the limitations of modern jet aircraft became clear, and older piston-engined types were revived for anti-guerrilla work, their slow speed and high endurance making them very useful where the jet aircraft's high speed and low endurance

had been a positive hindrance. At the same time, the French pioneered the use of armed helicopters for these low-intensity operations, missile-armed helicopters proving to have a quick reaction time and excellent terrain-hugging capabilities.

In 1956, war again flared between Israel and her Arab neighbours. When it became clear that Egypt, Jordan and Syria were planning an invasion of Israel, the latter decided on a pre-emptive campaign, which started on 29 October with a large-scale offensive against the Egyptian positions in the Sinai peninsula. For the campaign the Israelis could muster 85 aircraft to the Egyptians' 200. Among the Israeli aircraft were Dassault *Mystère* IVA fighters and SNCASO *Ouragan* fighter-bombers, to balance the Mikoyan-Gurevich MiG-15 and MiG-17 jets of the Egyptian air force.

Egypt had nationalized the Anglo-French Suez Canal on 26 July of the same year, and the British and French had decided to act with Israel in a campaign to seize back the canal. The Israeli offensive came as a surprise to the British, but probably not to the French, who supplied the Israelis with additional *Mystères* and

also landed their own *Mystère* and F-84F Thunderstreak fighters at Israeli bases to protect them, freeing the Israeli aircraft for offensive use. Starting on 31 October, however, the British and French joined in the campaign, both bombing Egyptian air bases, the British from Cyprus and the French from Israel. By 6 November the Egyptians had lost 260 aircraft on the ground, only seven British and French aircraft being shot down, all by ground fire. On 5 November, an Allied airborne operation to retake the Suez Canal started with strong fighter-bomber support from aircraft-carriers. Three Royal Navy fighters were lost to ground fire. In fact, the only air combat loss of the campaign for the British and French was an English Electric Canberra reconnaissance aircraft downed by a Syrian MiG-15 over Syria. The Israelis had occupied most of Sinai by this time, losing 12 aircraft to the Egyptians' 10.

By now world opinion had been mobilized against the 'aggressors', and a UN cease-fire came into effect on 7 November. In the face of world opinion, the British and French left Egypt between 19 November and 22 December 1956.

Modern Air Warfare

After the end of the Suez campaign, peace did not return to the area, for widespread guerrilla activity and still unresolved ideological and ethnic differences remained. However, these did not involve the Israeli and Arab air forces until 1965, when a period of aerial 'sparring' began. The largest battle of this time took place on 7 April 1967, when Israeli fighters claimed the destruction of six Syrian Mikoyan-Gurevich MiG-21 fighters. But while the Israelis and Arabs were girding themselves for another round in their apparently interminable contest, a little known but important war was taking place over the Indian sub-continent.

For some time a dispute had been simmering between India and Pakistan about the Rann of Kutch, and at the end of April and the beginning of May 1965 there occurred a short, sharp campaign that was apparently won by Pakistan. Aircraft were used in the clash, but played no decisive part. Then, in August, the long-standing feud over the ownership of Kashmir and parts of the Punjab flared up, culminating on 24 August in an Indian expedition across the UN-patrolled cease-fire line. This prompted a Pakistani invasion across the cease-fire line in Kashmir on 1 September 1965. Full-scale fighting continued until 25 September, with the Indians gaining a slight advantage on the ground, where their armoured forces proved superior. In the air, though, it seems that the Pakistani air force prevailed, largely as a result of having better pilots and Sabre fighters, compared with the Indian air force's Hawker Hunters. In air combat, the Pakistanis claimed to have shot down 36 aircraft; the Indians 73 for the loss of 35 of their own aircraft. Some food for thought lay in the fact that, though missiles proved important, so too did cannon, especially

since the first engagement frequently proved inconclusive. The aircraft would then start on close-turning dogfights, in which manoeuvrability and guns were decisive, just as they had been in World War I and II. In such combat the Folland Gnat flown by the Indians proved itself a first-class fighter. Such was the belief in missiles launched from supersonic aircraft, however, that the major powers largely ignored this pointer.

More attention was focused on the Middle East, where the growing incidence

of air and land clashes, combined with the increasing strength of the Israelis and their Arab neighbours indicated that another major clash might well be in the offing. By June 1967, the Israelis had some 300 aircraft to the Arabs' 1,000.

The Six-Day War, as the conflict has become known, started on 5 June 1967: the Israelis, seeing the build-up of Arab weapons and military intentions, decided to strike first. A great pre-emptive raid was launched at the Arabs airfields: *Mystères* and *Ouragans* struck at the Egyptian bases in the Sinai; Super *Mystères* and *Mirages* struck at the bases in the Nile delta and around Cairo; and *Vautours* tackled targets in southern Egypt. Correctly estimating that the Egyptian air threat was the most dangerous, the Israelis concentrated most of their air strength in this early morning raid. The aircraft attacked fast and low, having evaded the Egyptian radar cover until the last minute. This last-minute warning gave the Egyptians

Above: *The Dassault* Mystère *series of fighters, introduced in the 1950s, saw the revival of the European aerospace industry as a rival for the US.* Below: *Russia's MiG-21* Fishbed.

just enough time to start up the engines of their aircraft and so provide the Israelis' heat-seeking missiles with ideal targets on the ground. Wave after wave struck, some aircraft using guns and missiles, others 'dibber' bombs designed to break up concrete runways. Once this strike against Egypt was completed, the Israelis turned their attentions to Iraq, Jordan and Syria, causing great damage on their airfields too. By the end of the first day's operations, the Arabs had lost 240 Egyptian, 7 Iraqi, 16 Jordanian and 45 Syrian aircraft – 308 aircraft in all (but only 30 in combat) for an Israeli loss of a mere 20 aircraft (only 1 in combat). It was the

opposition, and the unwieldy SA-2s could be used only for the static defence of areas that were usually avoided.

There followed six years of 'peace' in the area, during the course of which the spasmodic fighting of the so-called 'War of Attrition' cost the Arabs another 114 aircraft and the Israelis about 25. During this time the French and Israelis fell out, and the US became the main supplier of arms to Israel, the Russians again making good the Arabs' material losses.

To the east, though, the Indians and Pakistanis were once again at war with each other as a result of their long-standing border disputes. Since the 1965 war

bat), for the loss of 54 of its own machines; India, on the other hand, claimed 94 victories. Of the admitted Pakistani losses, 10 were in the air and the remaining 44 on the ground. In the air, the main opponents appear to have been F-104A against MiG-21, and Shenyang F-6 against MiG-21 and Su-7. In general, the lesson of these combats appears to have been that unless a missile 'won' the engagement right at the beginning, the result of the ensuing dogfight usually went to the more manoeuvrable and better armed aircraft. During combat speeds slowed drastically to below 500 mph (805 kph) and the MiG-21 was thus able to hold the Starfighter, the F-6

The Dassault Mirage III has been the most successful European military aircraft since World War II. Many hundreds of the type have been exported to several user countries, notably Israel. Under this French aircraft is a single Matra R.530 air-to-air missile.

most successful pre-emptive strike ever flown, and effectively gave Israel command of the air while her army made great strides in the ground operations. For the rest of the war, which ended on 10 June, the Israelis gave excellent support to the ground forces, though suffering some losses to the SA-2 surface-to-air missiles used by the Arabs. Notwithstanding, air superiority was wholly Israeli, and by the end of the war the Arabs had lost 353 aircraft to the Israelis' 31. As can be seen from the figures, losses after the first day were small; the Arabs' because they saw no point in committing the remnants of their air forces in widespread actions that would result in their destruction, and the Israelis' because there was little fighter

both sides had been reinforced considerably: the Pakistani air force now deployed Canadair Sabre Mark 6, Lockheed F-104 Starfighter, Dassault Mirage IIIEP and Shenyang F-6 (Chinese-built MiG-19) fighters, and Martin B-57B (American-built English Electric Canberra) bombers. The Indian air force had large numbers of MiG-21, Hindustan HF-24 *Marut* I and Folland Gnat fighters, Sukhoi Su-7 fighter-bombers, and English Electric Canberra Mark 66 bombers. Border clashes started in November 1971, with full-scale war breaking out on 3 December. Again it is very hard to disentangle propaganda from reality in assessing the nature of the air war: Pakistan claimed to have shot down 104 Indian aircraft (50 of them in com-

proving superior to the MiG-21 and Su-7, though the latter was used mostly with the *Marut* for ground-attack work.

In 1973, the war in the Middle East yet again flared up, this time the Arabs, in the form of Egypt and Syria, managing to surprise Israel with a double attack across the Suez Canal and in the Golan Heights. At the beginning of the Yom Kippur War, Israel had some 130 McDonnell Douglas F-4E Phantom II multi-role fighters, about 55 *Mirage* III fighters, a small number of the IAI *Nesher* derivative of the *Mirage*, and about 120 Douglas A-4D Skyhawk attack aircraft, plus a number of transports, helicopters and trainer/light attack aircraft. Egypt possessed more than 600 fighters, mostly MiG-21, -19 and -17,

Sukhoi Su-7 and a few MiG-25s, the last probably flown by Russians: Syria deployed some 75 Su-7s and a large number of MiG-21s; and other Arab nations, though not directly involved, supplied a number of aircraft and crews.

The Arab attack started with land and air strikes on 6 October 1973, and at first made excellent progress. Attempting to halt the Arab offensives with air power, while the army mobilized, the Israelis suffered heavy losses, mostly to the excellent mix of missiles and guns used by the Arabs. High-level aircraft were hit by SA-2s, medium-altitude aircraft by SA-3s and SA-6s, and low-level aircraft by the ZSU-23-4s or SA-7s. Israeli losses are hard to establish, but were about 40 aircraft (30 Skyhawks and 10 Phantoms), most of them over the more threatening Golan front during the first day of hostilities, which had started at 1400 hours. During the first week of fighting the Israelis seem to have lost about 80 aircraft, most of them to the AA defences as they tried to stem the Arab advances. Various counter-measures were tried, without significant success, and the only Israeli tactic that seemed to work at all depended on outflying the missiles once the launch had been spotted by a helicopterborne observer team. During the first week of the war the Israelis made their main effort in the Golan, and gradually got the better of the Syrians' AA measures to the extent that the Sky-hawk attack aircraft could begin to play a useful part in the land battle without prohibitive losses. On 8/9/10 October the Syrians fired a number of FROG missiles into Israel, and the Israelis responded with a series of devastating raids on Syria's ports, oil facilities and even targets within Damascus. By this time the Israelis

had contained the Syrian advance, and in turn drove a wedge through the Syrian defences and advanced on Damascus, under cover of the customary air support and superiority.

On the Suez front, the missile 'umbrella' over the Egyptians' rear areas effectively prevented Israeli air attacks on dumps and lines of communication until a surprise crossing of the canal broke open a portion of the defence line and allowed Israeli aircraft to play their usual decisive part. During the second week of the war, which ended with a UN armistice on 24 October, Israeli aircraft losses were 38. Of the 118 aircraft lost in two weeks, almost 100 were lost to the AA defences, and only about 20 to Arab fighters. However, the Arab losses were also severe, and by 20 October amounted to 115 of 580 Egyptian, 150 out of 240 Syrian, and 21 out of 200 Iraqi aircraft. Thereafter, Arab losses continued

(about 24 aircraft falling to the few Improved HAWK missiles fired), so that by the end of 1973 the Israelis claimed 248 Egyptian and 221 Syrian aircraft, these figures including Arab losses before the Yom Kippur War, during the war, and some 30 after after it.

Aircraft have played a part in a number of other conflicts during the 1960s and 1970s, the most important being in Katanga in 1961, in Nigeria between 1968 and 1970 and the wars of liberation fought by communist and other guerrillas to free Angola and Mozambique from Portugese rule. There have been various operations against guerrillas in south, central and north Africa, and in central and south America; the Ethiopian civil war and war with Somaliland, and various disputes in the Arabian peninsula. However, by far the most significant war of the period has been the war in Vietnam,

Above: *Russian pilots board their Mikoyan-Gurevich MiG-17 'Farmer' jet fighters, developed from the MiG-15.* Below: *The Sukhoi Su-7 ground-attack fighter.*

A scene typical of carrier operations, in this instance aboard the British Ark Royal. In the foreground are a pair of Fairey Gannet early-warning aircraft, while nearer the bows are four Hawker Siddeley Buccaneer strike aircraft on the left, and three McDonnell Douglas F-4 Phantom II multi-role fighters. The angled flight-deck can just be seen to the left.

which started with sporadic communist attacks against government installations and personnel in 1956, and then escalated until US combat forces became involved, covertly in 1961 and overtly in 1964. The real 'Vietnam War', which led to the loss of Vietnam, Cambodia and Laos to the communists, may perhaps be dated to February 1965, when the army of North Vietnam began to support the Viet Cong communist guerrillas in South Vietnam.

Two squadrons of helicopters arrived in Saigon on 11 December 1961, the first direct US military support for the South Vietnamese regime. Ground 'advisers' were already in the country, and these had already been in action, though the use of weapons was allowed only if these advisers came under fire. The same strictures also applied to AS air units. This set the scene for a gradual growth in direct US involvement in Vietnamese military affairs as the situation in South Vietnam continued to deteriorate as a result of inefficiency, corruption, and the wrong tactics.

Overt military intervention by the US began in August 1964, after an apparent attack by North Vietnamese craft on a US destroyer in the Gulf of Tonkin on 2 August. The same destroyer and a companion were attacked again two days later, and President Lyndon B. Johnson authorized retaliatory action. On 5 August, 64 US carrier aircraft destroyed three attack craft ports and some oil storage tanks, losing two aircraft but sinking eight attack craft. At the same time, the USAF began to build up its fighter and fighter-bomber strength in South Vietnam. This move was approved by the US Congress in the 'Tonkin Resolution' of 7 August, which gave the president power to take 'all necessary measures to repel any armed attack' against the US armed forces, and to take 'all necessary steps, including the use of armed forces' to aid any country asking for help in 'defense of its freedom'. The arrival of US air forces in South Vietnam was signalled by the increase of largely ineffectual attacks on targets in South Vietnam, which the Viet Cong were usually found to have left by the time of the attack.

On 7 February 1965, the US forces began raids into North Vietnam, as a reprisal for continued North Vietnamese involvement in the affairs of South Vietnam despite American warnings. Wholly unexpectedly, despite a previous attack by units of the North Vietnamese army against an American airbase, the attacks of 7 and 11 February on targets in the

'panhandle' of North Vietnam caused considerable damage and losses to the North Vietnamese army. As a result of the North Vietnamese attack on the airbase, Johnson decided to commit US ground forces, a brigade of the US Marine Corps coming ashore at Da Nang on 8 March. Then the build-up of US forces was rapid, and by the end of the year there were 190,000 Americans in South Vietnam.

Keen advocates of the concept of strategic bombing, the US authorities believed that North Vietnam could be brought to the negotiating table by the use of American air power against key targets in North Vietnam. The concept, whether sound or not, was voided by the political

The McDonnell Douglas F-4 (above) *is perhaps the best fighter and multi-role aircraft developed since World War II. Here an F-4B of the US Navy releases iron bombs against suspected Vietcong positions.* Right: *An F-4B Phantom II moves into the attack.*

restrictions placed on the bombing campaign. The campaign started on 18 March 1965, and at first US attack aircraft and fighter-bombers (but not strategic bombers) were allowed to raid only military targets in the 'panhandle' region. If the North Vietnamese still proved recalcitrant, the northern limit line for the bombing would be moved gradually north towards Hanoi until the threat of bombing finally brought the North Vietnamese government to the realization that it could not hope to fight a war with the United States. The restrictions defeated the campaign, for the North Vietnamese were immediately aware that only a limited campaign was being waged, and that even within the permitted bombing zone built-

up areas were safe, and could thus be used for the storage of vital *matériel*. At the same time, it was clear that the line would probably be moved north, and so the North Vietnamese began to prepare effective defences for the region that became known as the 'Iron Triangle': Hanoi-Haiphong-Thanh Hoa.

The North Vietnamese air force was soon in action, a Republic F-105 Thunderchief fighter-bomber being shot down on 4 April 1965 when a US raid was intercepted by four MiG-17 fighters. Realizing the vulnerability of bomb-laden aircraft, the Americans immediately started to escort such raids with missile-armed McDonnell Douglas F-4C Phantom fighters.

At the same time, the deployment of Douglas EF-10B Skynight electronic support measures aircraft to the theatre did much to mitigate losses to AA fire by jamming their radar.

The North Vietnamese, heavily supported by the USSR, were able to deploy SA-2 missiles for the defence of northern areas, and on 24 July 1965 an F-4C Phantom became the first SAM victim of the Vietnamese war. The Americans had known of the missile sites since they were revealed by reconnaissance in April, but the suggestions by the staffs of the US 7th Air Force and the US 7th Fleet for a combined air force/navy offensive to 'take out' the missiles had been vetoed by Washington on political grounds – the

North Vietnamese had cleverly sited the missiles in taboo areas such as villages. The ban was lifted after the loss of the Phantom, but when 55 USAF North American F-100 Super Sabres and F-105 Thunderchiefs attacked the site three days later, four of them were shot down by AA gunfire. The solution to the SAM problem in fact lay with US electronic countermeasures, to jam the missile's radar and control frequencies, SAM suppression sorties using 'Wild Weasel' (USAF) and 'Iron Hand' (USN) technology. For such suppression sorties, the attack aircraft were fitted with anti-radiation missiles, with a homing head attracted to electro-magnetic radiation, such as radar.

There remained the threat of about 75 North Vietnamese fighters, mostly MiG-17, -19 and -21 types. Although relatively small, the threat was countered by the use of airborne early warning aircraft patrolling off the coast: as soon as these detected signs of North Vietnamese air activity, the strike force was warned.

One of the major oddities of the Vietnam campaign, so far as US air power was concerned, was that in the 'strategic' campaign against North Vietnam, the tactical aircraft of the USAF and USN were the main protagonists because of the political constraints imposed by Washington; and that for the tactical operations in South Vietnam, the Boeing B-52 heavy bombers

of the Strategic Air Command were called to play an increasingly important part. This was largely because the generation of aircraft in service with the USAF in 1965 had been designed with a European conflict in mind: they were high-performance aircraft intended for the delivery of nuclear weapons in a short campaign. For operations in Vietnam, however, they needed aircraft capable of intensive and prolonged operations in climatically difficult conditions, carrying heavy loads of conventional ordnance and capable of loitering over the battlefield, bombing when called in by the forward air observer. The latter would use an aircraft such as the Cessna 0-2 or Grumman OV-1 Mohawk

Launch time on board the American carrier Constellation: an LTV A-7 Corsair II attack aircraft, loaded with external stores, is about to be catapult-launched. Note the blast deflector raised behind the aircraft to divert the efflux of its jet engine, and the bar connecting the front undercarriage leg to the catapult traveller in the deck slot.

– a multi-sensor reconnaissance type. Only in the raids over North Vietnam did the USAF fighter-bombers really come into their own, and were there found to be sadly deficient in inbuilt armament. Only in 1972, for example, did Phantoms with a fuselage-mounted 20 mm Vulcan rotary cannon become available.

Far more effective, however, were the tactical aircraft of the US Navy, for they were designed for just such operations, albeit at sea and in coastal regions. Nevertheless, aircraft such as the Douglas A-4 Skyhawk, the Grumman A-6 Intruder and the Ling-Temco-Vought A-7 Corsair II proved to be excellent warplanes. The A-6 Intruder was probably the best attack aircraft of the war, being capable of delivering a heavy load of weapons with devastating accuracy.

And so the bombing campaign against the North continued, with minimal results offset by heavy losses. By the end of 1967, the North Vietnamese were no closer to the negotiating table than in 1965. The pace of their operations in South Vietnam had increased, and the Americans had lost 675 aircraft, although only 15 of these were Boeing B-52 heavy bombers.

The key to North Vietnam's continued success was American failure to close the 'Ho Chi Minh Trail' by which supplies were moved south into South Vietnam, the political restraints on the bombing of the 'Iron Triangle', and further political constraints against the closure of Haiphong harbour, through which nearly all Russian supplies reached North Vietnam. In the middle of 1966 the 'Iron Triangle' was opened to US bombing, and then the American aircraft were allowed to attack the communications systems linking Hanoi and Haiphong with the rest of the country. Haiphong harbour silted up after the dredgers had been sunk and stores were stockpiled in the open for lack of transportation. The incidence of missile firings fell rapidly as stocks fell, oil became a rare commodity, and electricity generating stations in the 'Iron Triangle' were ruined, all seriously affecting North Vietnam's war making capacity.

Then, with the possibility of victory finally in sight, the Americans called the bombers off for the 1967 'holiday stand-down' for Christmas and both the western and Vietnamese new years. The North Vietnamese finally came to the negotiating table in January 1968, but almost immediately afterwards they launched the major Tet Offensive in South Vietnam to divert attention away from the difficulties

in North Vietnam to the success of communist arms in the south. The ploy worked well, though the Americans resumed bombing of the north until 31 March, when a 'pause' was ordered to show that the US was still willing to talk. Targets in the panhandle just north of the demilitarized zone were still bombed, as was the Ho Chi Minh Trail. But then, on 1 November 1968, all bombing of the North was halted. By this time 915 US aircraft, excluding helicopters, had been lost over North Vietnam.

All this time, a steadily growing tactical air war had been developing in South Vietnam: on the one side were the air forces of South Vietnam (RVNAF) and of the USA, and on the other were the AA defences of the communists, aided by inhospitable terrain and poor climate. In its early days the war had been a guerrilla conflict, with the conventional forces of the USA and South Vietnam trying to counter the shapeless advance of ideas, political control, subversion, terrorism and then a gradually increasing tide of military activities. At first, it was thought that the right type of aircraft to aid in suppressing such a movement were counter-insurgency types such as the versatile Douglas A-1 Skyraider and the Douglas B-26 Invader, both of World War II

vintage, capable of operating from semi-prepared strips, of carrying a heavy weight of guns and bombs, and possessed of long loiter times.

Gradually, though, the increasing tempo of the war persuaded the Americans that they should bring in more advanced aircraft, and so, eventually, nearly every combat type in the USAF's inventory found its way to south-east Asia. Without enemy aircraft to worry about, the straight fighter types were quickly converted into fighter-bombers.

To supplement the weight of ordnance that could be dropped by these aircraft, the USAF also used in the tactical role B-52 strategic bombers based in Thailand and Guam. These mighty aircraft operated with virtual impunity at first, dropping up to 70,000 lb (31,752 kg) of bombs from high altitude with great precision using radar. The only other way the USAF could achieve the same concentration of explosive was the use of massed fighter-bombers operating in close formation at medium altitude, and dropping their bombs on the signal of a master bomber in a Douglas EB-66 electronic counter-measures and pathfinder aircraft.

For the accurate delivery of all this ordnance, which came to include large numbers of air-to-surface missiles, the

A McDonnell Douglas A-4E Skyhawk attack bomber returns to its mothership, the American carrier Oriskany. *The A-4 is another classic aircraft of post-World War II.*

A Lockheed F-104G Starfighter of the West German Luftwaffe *on patrol.*

Americans and Vietnamese made great use of the forward air controller concept, such controllers braving intense ground fire at low level to bring the attack aircraft and bombers right in on target. The most commonly used aircraft were the Cessna 0-2, the North American OV-10 Bronco counter-insurgency and FAC aircraft, and the Grumman OV-1 Mohawk STOL observation aircraft.

Reconnaissance naturally played a vital role in the war, and several aircraft could be modified for the role by the addition of external pods, but two specialist reconnaissance types bore the brunt of such operations: the McDonnell RF-101 Voodoo and RF-4C Phantom, which together covered most battlefield reconnaissance. Also used was the North American RA-5C Vigilante, an altogether more sophisticated reconnaissance aircraft that was used mostly to support the strategic campaign in the north ('out-country' operations), though the type was also employed for 'in-country' work over South Vietnam.

Other support for the ground forces was provided by fixed-wing gunships such as the Douglas AC-47, Fairchild AC-119G and -119K, and Lockheed AC-130 con-

versions of transport aircraft. The AC-47 mounted three 7.62 mm Miniguns, each firing 6,000 rounds per minute; the AC-119G had four Miniguns and equipment allowing the aircraft to operate by night; and AC-119K had infra-red sensors, radar and two 20 mm weapons; and the AC-130 four 20 mm Vulcan rotary cannon, four Miniguns, and a large assortment of sensors and other aids. The basic C-130 was widely used for all types of tactical supply, as was the Fairchild C-123 Provider, which was also used for defoliating missions. Strategic supply was handled by the Lockheed C-141 Star-Lifter and the Lockheed C-5A Galaxy.

Tactical as well as strategic air-to-air refuelling became increasingly important in the Vietnam air war, and although some 'buddy' refuelling was undertaken by the US Navy, the most important air tanker was the Boeing KC-135 conversion of the civil 707 airliner. Both fighter-bombers and attack aircraft were almost wholly dependent on the Stratotanker as the war progressed.

These tactical aircraft provided the US and South Vietnamese ground forces with magnificent support, though only at a high

loss rate. It is debatable, however, whether such concentration of 'fire-power' was really necessary in any but the final stage of the war. A clear example of what the aircraft could do, however, was provided during the five-month siege of the US Marine Corps forward base at Khe Sanh starting in January 1968. This was compared with the siege of Dien Bien Phu in 1954. At Khe Sanh, though, the garrison was intrinsically better armed than the French had been, and could call in a massive quantity of aircraft for all types of purposes: transport aircraft and helicopters for supplies, reinforcement and evacuation; fighter-bombers and attack aircraft for close and area support; helicopter gunships for the same purpose; and B-52s for interdiction and area support. For a time, the US Navy used the aircraft from five aircraft-carriers in support of Khe Sanh. Under such circumstances the communists could not prevail, and in June 1968 they called off the siege.

But it was, perhaps, the campaign against the North that could have won the war most effectively for the Americans. After the bombing halt of 1 November

The Boeing B-52 Stratofortress has been the mainstay of the USAF's Strategic Air Command since its introduction in the 1950s, and was used widely for bombing in Vietnam.

Above: *A McDonnell Douglas A-4F attack bomber releases its bombs over North Vietnam.*
Below: *A Grumman A-6 Intruder, one of the most accurate weapons delivery platforms in the world, comes in to land on a US carrier.*

1968, the North Vietnamese almost completely rebuilt their country, and brought in new defences, including the MiG-21 fighter to the exclusion of all earlier types, the more versatile SA-3 surface-to-air missile, and a new network of radar warning and control systems. At the same time, a decision to 'Vietnamize' the war led to the retraining and re-equipping of the South Vietnamese forces to enable them to meet the North Vietnamese on equal terms. Allied forces operated in Cambodia and Laos, where hitherto the communists had been able to train and build-up unmolested, and American tactical air power was used more effectively in the interdiction of the Ho Chi Minh Trail and in the occasional destruction of key targets in North

Vietnam. When this policy was regarded as completed most of the American and other allied forces were pulled out, leaving the South Vietnamese to cope with the situation alone.

But realizing that a purely military victory over the communists was impossible, it was still the intention of the allied governments to try to negotiate a settlement to the war. That this was still not the intention of the North Vietnamese government became clear on 26 December 1971, when communist forces occupied the vital central plain of Laos, and the peace talks in Paris were clearly making no progress. The US government therefore decided to bomb North Vietnam to the conference table by a short, sharp strategic campaign with few restrictions of a political nature.

In view of the North Vietnamese re-equipment with the latest Russian electronic aids, the USAF and USN deployed large numbers of electronic support measures and electronic countermeasures (ESM and ECM) aircraft to the theatre. The most important of these were the Martin RB-57, the Douglas RC-47, the Douglas RA-3B Skywarrior and the Grumman EA-6A Prowler. All of these had been used earlier, but now the latest versions were shipped out to identify, assess and then counter the Russian radar systems.

The resumed campaign against the North was, nonetheless, more costly than the earlier campaign, but to offset against these losses were very real victories in the campaign to decimate the North's ability and willingness to continue the war. Faced again with the prospect of defeat, the North once more resorted to diversionary tactics, launching its army on a massive invasion of South Vietnam on 2 April 1972. There was little that the South Vietnamese army could do to stem the offensive, which was of the type which the USAF in particular had trained to attack large-scale conventional forces in the open, in this case without SAM support except from the shoulder-launched SA-7. This proved effective against helicopter and lightplane types, but it was not effective enough against the larger jet-powered

Despite its somewhat elderly lines, the English Electric Canberra bomber, seen here in its T.7 variant, remains a classic bomber and reconnaissance aircraft, serving with several air forces into the 1980s. Insert: *A Dassault Mirage 2000-01 being loaded.*

fighter-bombers and attack aircraft.

Despairing of North Vietnam's attitude, President Richard Nixon at last authorized the measures that should have been taken right at the beginning of the strategic campaign: on 9 May 1972 A-6 Intruders of the USN laid thousands of mines (acoustic, magnetic and pressure) in and around the port of Haiphong, with the result that effective Russian aid to North Vietnam was halted. North Vietnam was forced to rely on the stockpiles it had built up in the three-year US bombing halt.

At the same time the 'conventional' bombing of targets in the rest of North Vietnam continued, until Nixon responded to a North Vietnamese indication that they were willing to talk by halting the bombing again on 23 October. Having achieved their aim, the North Vietnamese as usual stalled, despite a heavy raid by both tactical and strategic aircraft on 22

Above: *The Bell UN-1 family, seen here in its UH-1N model, is nicknamed 'Huey' and is the most widely used Western helicopter of the 1970s.* Below: *Bell UH-1H Iroquois utility helicopters on a mission over Vietnam. Special armed version of the 'Huey' family mount a variety of powerful weapons, and are generally known as 'Huey Cobras'.* Right: *In the Vietnam War the Boeing CH-47A Chinook proved an invaluable medium-lift helicopter.*

November. By then the Americans had despaired of North Vietnamese recalcitrance, and decided to administer a decisive lesson. With the exception of a short break over the Christmas period, the Americans bombed any and all targets connected with the war effort in North Vietnam, starting on 19 December. The cost to the Americans was high (exact figures have not been released, but it seems that probably 17 and possibly 29 B-52s were lost to North Vietnam's last-ditch air defence effort), but the North Vietnamese at last began to show real willingness in the peace negotiations. Thus strategic bombing, applied properly for the first time, had 'won' the war for the Americans. Eventually, however, in the face of domes-

tic and international opinion, the US was forced to evacuate its troops while making desperate efforts to aid the South Vietnamese with training and additional *matériel*. But the 'hearts and minds' war had already been lost, and ineluctably the tide of the ground war turned in favour of the North.

Perhaps the most important advance in air warfare made during the Vietnam War was in the military use of helicopters, not only as rescue, casualty evacuation and liaison machines, but also as tactical transport, gunship, heavy lift and general-purpose aircraft. Helicopters were able to fly large numbers of ground troops straight into action, escorted by other helicopters, and return to base to pick up more men or

supplies while the landed forces received air support at very close range from gunships. Heavy lift helicopters would be on call the whole time to carry out any helicopter shot down, or to bring in heavy equipment such as artillery, light armoured vehicles or bulldozers – yet more helicopters being available to ferry out casualties and act as flying command posts or as radio links with rear headquarters. This massive use of helicopters has altered the face of war considerably by bringing about a revolution in battlefield mobility and firepower. The most numerous helicopter type in Vietnam, and possibly the most versatile, was the Bell UH-1 Iroquois, better known by its nickname 'Huey'. From this was developed the Bell Model

The Sikorsky CH-53D is one of the most powerful Western helicopters, and is used for heavy troop and equipment movement. Other developments of the type are the CH-53E three-turbine version, which has an increased payload, and the RH-53 specially modified minesweeping variant, which can tow most modern minesweeping gear.

209 AH-1 HueyCobra gunship, with a slimmer fuselage, only two crew, and stub wings – able to carry a useful load of unguided rockets or a pair of 7.62 mm Minigun rotary-barrel machine-guns. But the main armament of the type was contained in a chin turret housing two Miniguns, or two 40 mm grenade launchers, or one of each weapon. Also widely used were the Hughes OH-6 Cayuse observation helicopter; the Boeing-Vertol CH-47 Chinook transport helicopter, widely used for rescuing other downed aircraft; the Sikorsky UH-34 multi-role helicopter; the Sikorsky CH-53 transport, which was used for the lifting of heavy loads to the network of bases established all over South Vietnam by the Americans; the

Sikorsky CH-54 Skycrane or Tarhe heavy-lift helicopter, which could rescue downed fighter-bombers and other heavy helicopters; and the Sikorsky HH-3 'Jolly Green Giant' transport helicopter, also used for ordnance moves, aircraft rescue, and even aircrew rescue deep in North Vietnam, usually escorted by A-1 Sky-raiders or other protecting fixed-wing aircraft.

The most ambitious type developed at this time was the Lockheed AH-56 Cheyenne AAFSS (advanced aerial fire suppression system) helicopter, which cost very nearly as much as the B-52 strategic bomber but then did not enter service. The US authorities preferred to lose relatively large numbers of less expensive aircraft.

The lessons of the Vietnam and Middle Eastern wars have given air forces and aircraft constructors much food for thought in the design of the latest generation of combat aircraft, and these are as yet untried in action. Inevitably, greater emphasis had been placed on the aircraft's sensors, both in range and sensitivity, but also on the 'anachronistic' factors of manoeuvrability and inbuilt cannon armament. Less emphasis had been placed on outright performance, and more on serviceability and ease of handling.

Inevitably, these new aircraft will be used in combat, if not by their countries of origin, then almost certainly by the clients of the main world powers, probably in the Middle East and in Africa.

Surface-to-Air Armament

The American MIM-14B Nike-Hercules second-generation surface-to-air missile is elderly, but still has a useful function in the long-range interception role.

It seems that ground-based anti-aircraft gunnery can be traced back to the wholly inefficient mountings produced by the German firm Krupp for the Prussian army in 1871, when the besieged garrison of Paris was sending out messages by balloon. But it was not until 1908 that the first effective (or potentially effective) AA gun mounting was produced, when the German firm Ehrhardt produced a car-mounted quick-firing 5-cm piece capable of considerable elevation and traverse, and supplied with adequate quantities of ammunition.

As early results of combat operations in World War I revealed the general utility of aircraft in war, and also the very real military threat of the airship, a number of improvised AA gun mountings were produced. The chief requirements for such guns were those met by the Ehrhardt mounting of 1908,

plus a high rate of fire and high muzzle velocity for a straight trajectory and improved accuracy. For such purposes a number of naval guns were found to offer the best capabilities, for they had been designed to deal with the maritime version of aircraft, the torpedo-boats so feared by naval thinkers before 1914. Thus a variety of naval pieces (1-pounder pom-pom, QF 3-in/76.2-mm and QF 4-in/101.6-mm), and some land service weapons which met the requirements found their way on to special mountings designed to allow them large arcs of fire and quick traverse. A number of machine-guns were also fitted on tall tripods and other elevated mountings so that they too could try to bring down the occasional aircraft or two. Luckily for the AA gunners, the performance of the aircraft of the time was so poor in general that they managed to bring

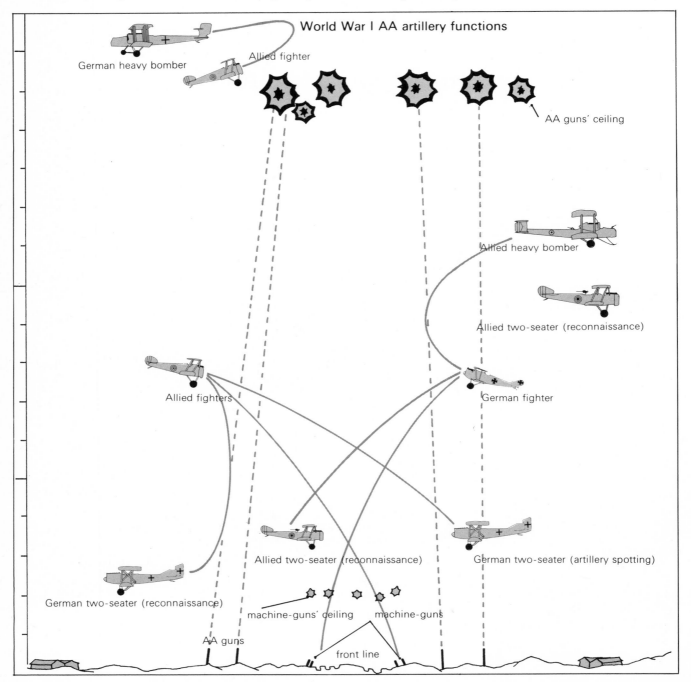

Typical of AA protection over the Western Front in 1918 was the scheme whereby the front line was protected against low level attacks by machine-guns, usually on tripod or pole mountings to allow high angles of elevation. Such fire was effective up to about 2000 ft (610 m). Above this height, up to about 16,000 ft (4877 m), the most effective weapons were AA artillery pieces, with a calibre of between 75- and 105-mm. Such guns were usually sited between 4000 and 8000 yards (3658 and 7315 m) from the front.

Oerlikon have specialized in recent years on the development of powerful AA cannon for ground use, such as this GDF-001 twin 35-mm mounting. The 'cages' in front of the muzzles are associated with the measurement of muzzle velocity, needed to upgrade the fire-control computer's predictions.

down about one aircraft for every 1,000 rounds fired (excluding machine-guns). As aircraft performance increased in 1915 and 1916, however, the success rate of the gunners fell rapidly.

By 1916, the AA arms of the various armies involved on the Western Front had developed adequate AA mountings: the Germans used special modifications of their 7.7-cm field gun, the French of their classic 75-mm Model 1897 field gun, and the British a 3-in (76.2-mm) QF 20-cwt gun. The German gun had a vertical ceiling of about 13,943 ft (4,250 m), and the two Allied guns of 18,044 ft (5,500 m) and 16,500 ft (5,029 m) respectively. Rate of fire was 10, 15 and 15 rounds per minute. The guns were usually mounted on lorries on pedestal mountings giving a traverse of 360°, and were generally adequate for the tasks facing them. Yet their results were poor, largely because of the inherent difficulty of computing the right point at which to aim (even if the gunners had known their target's exact course, speed and altitude), allowing for their shell's loss of velocity, the wind, changing atmospheric pressure and a number of other factors. Part of the solution was found to lie in the control of a number of guns from a central command post, which made it possible for a group of guns to fire a pattern of shells to explode at different heights and in different places, and so perhaps 'box in' the aircraft with fire. Further progress was made with the development by a French officer, Brocq, of a 'Central Post Instrument'. This resolved figures on the target's course, speed and height into a prediction of the target's future position, on which the guns could be laid to fire at the right moment for their shells to

arrive and detonate at the second in which the target aircraft arrived. The principle was excellent in theory, but depended entirely on accurate information, which was hard to come by with the instruments of the time, and on the continued straight course of the target.

More and more AA guns came into service as the war progressed, and improvements were made to the Brocq type of mechanical predictor, but the chances of scoring a hit on a high-flying aircraft continued to be small, and it was low-flying aircraft, which came within range of the massed machine-guns of the trench lines, which suffered the heaviest losses.

The situation did not improve much during the 1920s and 1930s, for although new guns with excellent performance were coming into service, there was still not available an effective method of laying them accurately on anything other than low-flying or very slow and poorly handled aircraft. The biggest change in AA armament during the period was in the number and quality of the light anti-aircraft guns available (20-mm to 40-mm), and the increasing number of heavy anti-aircraft equipments entering service.

The notable guns of the period were the German 2-cm *Flak* 38, the four-barrel 2-cm *Flakvierling* 38, the 3.7-cm *Flak* 36 and 37, and the legendary 8.8-cm *Flak* 18, 36 and 37; the Japanese Navy's 25-mm Type 96 cannon; the Swedish 40-mm Bofors gun; the Swiss 20-mm Oerlikon cannon; the British QF 3.7-in (94-mm) and 4.5-in (113-mm) guns; the US 90-mm M1 gun; and the Russian 85-mm Model 1939 gun. These were all good guns, and were followed in World War II by better guns, and

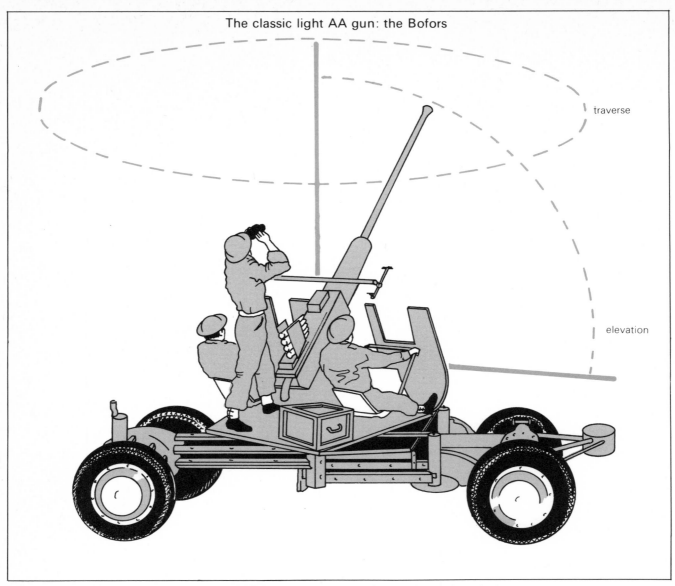

traverse

elevation

In World War II the arbiters of low-level air warfare were the light AA guns, in calibre between 20 and 40 mm. The smaller calibre weapons were often encountered in multiple mountings. The most widely used (up to the present day) of such weapons has been the 40-mm Bofors gun, of Swedish origin. Weighing 5418 lb (2460 kg) on its four-wheeled carriage, the Bofors L/60 gun could be elevated from −5° to +90°, and traversed through 360°. It fired a round weighing just under 2 lb (0.9 kg) at an effective rate of between 60 and 90 rounds per minute. Effective ceiling was 3280 ft (1000 m).

several large-calibre AA guns of prodigious performance, but all still foundered on the problem of accurate laying, with the exception of the weapons below 40-mm in calibre, which were designed to engage low-flying aircraft by eye.

That improvements in the guns and their predictors had been made since 1918 is indicated that British 3.7-in guns, for example, could destroy one aircraft for every 298 rounds of aimed fire, though the number of rounds needed per kill rose to 2,444 if the guns had to fire as part of a barrage at night. Such firing may not have scored large numbers of kills, but it had the effect of rattling the crews of the aircraft engaged, and of forcing them to operate at altitudes higher than they might have deemed best for their purposes.

Gradually, though, the success rate of the AA guns began to rise as the use of radar as part of the predictor system was pioneered, particularly by the Germans as American day and British night bombers roamed over Germany. Most of these aircraft operated at high altitude, and the Germans came to rely increasingly on radar-directed heavy AA guns, such as the 8.8-cm *Flak* 41, the 10.5-cm *Flak* 38 and the 12.8-cm *Flak* 40. This last was an excellent gun, firing a 57.3-lb (26-kg) shell with a muzzle velocity of 2,886 ft (880 m) per second at the rate of 10 rounds per minute up to an altitude of 48,556 ft (14,800 m). The standard radar for use with AA guns in German service was the '*Würzburg-D*' which had a tracking range of 15½ miles (25 km).

As important as the introduction of radar-controlled prediction, was the introduction in 1944 of a decisive Allied weapon, the proximity fuse. Containing a tiny radar set in its nose, the shell exploded as it passed close to a reflector object such as an aircraft.

6-gun battery of 10.5 cm AA guns

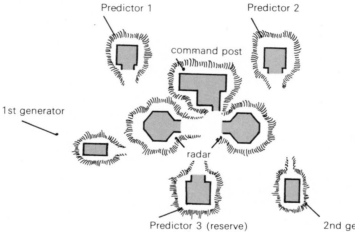

Predictor 1   Predictor 2

command post

1st generator

radar

Predictor 3 (reserve)   2nd generator (reserve)

Seen here is a diagrammatic representation of
the layout of a German *Grossbatterie* of AA
guns, with three batteries sited round a central
command post, in an effort to produce the
maximum possible weight of aimed fire against
British night bomber streams and American day
bomber boxes. The command post was sited
facing the priority arc of fire, with two batteries
of guns in front of it, and one behind it. In the
centre of the command post are two radar sets
and the command post itself, with two
predictors in front of them. To the rear were
another predictor and two power units.

This did away with the difficult task of assessing the right fuse setting, the shell merely detonating when it was at its closest point to a target. The use of proximity-fused shells played a decisive part in Britain's success in defeating the Fieseler Fi 103 (V-1) flying bomb during the summer of 1944, and in the ability of the US Pacific Fleet's ships to fight off overwhelming odds in Japanese suicide attacks with a concentrated barrage of light and medium AA fire, making full use of the advantages of proximity-fused shells.

The most advanced AA guns to emerge from World War II was the American 75-mm 'Skysweeper', which saw service in the Korean War. This exemplifies the height of design in 1945 and 1946, and the final stage of heavy AA gun development before such weapons were replaced by missiles. The operation of the training and elevating mechanism was entirely automatic, controlled by a radar predictor and powered by an inbuilt electric motor; fusing and loading were also automatic, and controlled by the director and its associated computer. Provision was made for manual operation and optical laying, but this was seldom needed.

After the Korean War the heavy AA gun had slowly faded from the scene, except in communist countries, where a variety of Russian-designed weapons is still used. Their place in long-range high-altitude AA engagements has been taken over by guided surface-to-air missiles. But the AA gun is still far from finished, for the light variety has still an important place in the armies of the world, in both mounted and static forms. The use of AA guns on mobile mountings was pioneered by the Ehrhardt car of 1908, but it was only during World War II that AA gun mountings in tracked, armoured chassis came to play an important part in operations. The best of these mountings were probably the German *Flakpanzer* IV *Mübelwagen* (furniture van), a four-barrel 2-cm mounting on the chassis of the PzKpfw IV tank, and the *Flakpanzer* IV *Wirbelwind* (whirlwind), a four-barrel 2-cm mounting in an armoured turret on the chassis of the PzKpfw IV tank.

The concept has been developed in the 1960s and 1970s particularly, and the two best armoured AA vehicles in the world today are probably the Swiss 5 PFZ-B2 *Flakpanzer* 1 *auf Gepard*, mounting a pair of 35-mm cannon, and the Russian ZSU-23-4, mounting four 23-mm cannon. Each vehicle has full cross-country capability as a result of its tracked chassis, and the armoured construction of the vehicles is proof against many weapons except specialized anti-tank weapons. The *Gepard* has two radar systems, one for acquisition of the target, and the other for target tracking once acquired, the maximum range of the system being 9.94 miles (16 km) and the minimum range 328 yards (300 m). The turret mechanism for the twin Oerlikon 35-mm cannon can traverse at 90° per second, and the guns can be elevated at 45° per second. Each barrel has a rate of fire of 1,100 rounds per minute, and 680 rounds are carried. Muzzle velocity is 3,855 ft (1,175 m) per second, and effective range is 4,375 yards (4,000 m).

The ZSU-23-4 is a slightly less sophisticated

The Gepard Flakpanzer 1 used by Belgium is a Swiss system typical of the advanced armoured AA vehicles coming into service in the late 1960s.

vehicle, but is nonetheless highly effective, as the Israeli air force discovered in the Yom Kippur War of 1973. The four NR-23 cannon are water-cooled, and have a cyclic rate of fire of up to 1,000 rounds per minute, though standard practice is to fire in bursts of 50 rounds. Some 500 rounds of ammunition per barrel are carried, the muzzle velocity of the high-explosive incendiary and of the armour-piercing incendiary being 3,182 ft (970 m) per second. Control is effected by the B-76 'Gun Dish' acquisition and tracking radar, which has a range of 12.4 miles (20 km). The turret traverses 360°, and the guns can be elevated from −7° to +80°. Both traverse and elevation are quite rapid.

Light AA guns are also used widely today, small-calibre weapons (up to 35-mm) being mostly of Swiss (Oerlikon and Hispano-Suiza) and West German (Rheinmetall) manufacture, and medium-calibre weapons (40-mm) of Swedish (Bofors) manufacture. Possibly the most advanced 'simple' mounting in service today is the Rheinmetall Rh.202 Mark 20. This is a twin-barrel 20-mm system mounted on a light two-wheel trailer. Sighting is based on a monocular optical device, and the gunner has to estimate the target's speed and range to the engage-ment point, the information being processed by a simple computer to alter the lead marks on the gunner's sights to give the right lead for the target's speed and range. Each barrel has 270 rounds of belted high-explosive incendiary tracer and armour-piercing tracer, which are fired at a cyclic rate of 2,000 rounds per minute with a muzzle velocity of 3,445 ft (1,050 m) per second. The maximum slant range is 2,187 yards (2,000 m).

Of the conventional AA guns, the Bofors 75 system is probably the best. It is based on the L40/70 gun, with the addition of the BOFI (Bofors Optronic Fire-control Instrument) control system. The gun, control system, ammunition supply and power supply are all carried on the four-wheel carriage. The basic gun is derived from the Bofors gun that proved so successful in World War II, with improvements dictated by better materials and user experience, as well as design modifications. Some 122 rounds of 40-mm ammunition are carried, and the gun fires at the rate of 300 rounds per minute with a muzzle velocity of 3,396 ft (1,035 m) per second. The effective slant range of the gun is 3,828 yards (3,500 yards). Three types of ammunition are carried: prefragmented proximity-fused, weighing

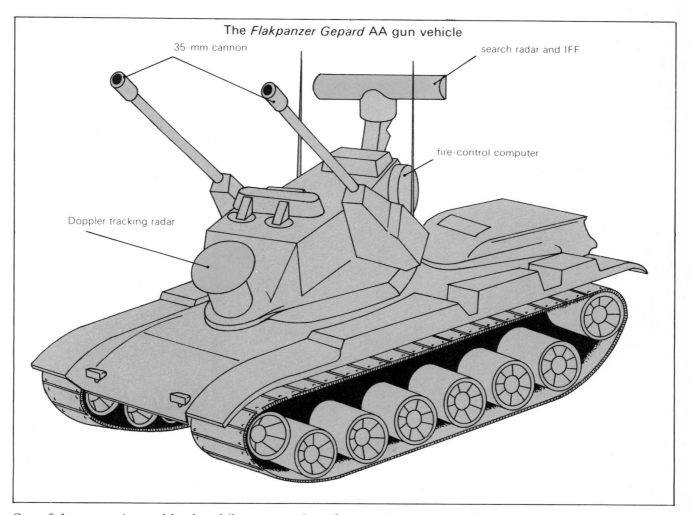

The *Flakpanzer Gepard* AA gun vehicle

35-mm cannon

search radar and IFF

fire-control computer

Doppler tracking radar

One of the most advanced land-mobile, armoured, surface-to-air gun systems is the Swiss *Flakpanzer* 35-mm system, seen here in its 5PFZ-CA1 form on the chassis of the West German Leopard MBT. Heart of the system is the *Hollandse Signaalapparaten* integrated search and tracking radar, which uses a common transmitter. The search component is mounted on the turret rear, and has inbuilt IFF (Identification Friend or Foe) capability. The tracking component is mounted on the turret front, and is of the monopulse-doppler variety with a Cassegrain antenna. The search radar can detect targets at ranges up to 9.3 miles (15 km) distant, and then identify it as friend or foe. If it is the latter, it is then tracked by the tracking radar, and the computer slaves the guns to the tracking radar.

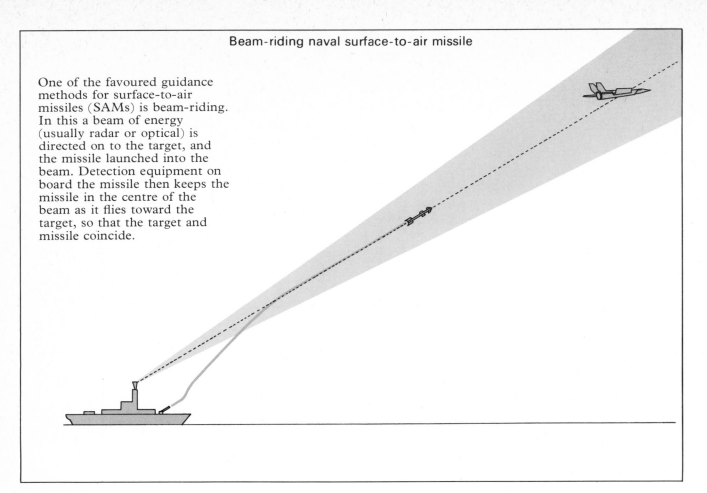

Beam-riding naval surface-to-air missile

One of the favoured guidance methods for surface-to-air missiles (SAMs) is beam-riding. In this a beam of energy (usually radar or optical) is directed on to the target, and the missile launched into the beam. Detection equipment on board the missile then keeps the missile in the centre of the beam as it flies toward the target, so that the target and missile coincide.

30.92 ounces (875 grams); high-explosive tracer, weighing 33.92 ounces (960 grams); and armour-piercing tracer, weighing 32.86 ounces (930 grams).

The gun and its ammunition (especially the pre-fragmented proximity-fused round) are excellent, but what makes the system superior to most other similar systems is the BOFI control system, which the manufacturers claim increases the efficiency of the equipment by a factor of 10. The BOFI consists of a day and a night sight, a laser range-finder, and a computer to work out the right aim-off (deflection) angle. The computer can also accept information from an optical target indicator working in conjunction with the weapon, or from a search radar deployed separately. Power for the electrical part of the system is provided by the petrol generator mounted at the rear of the lower carriage, and this also provides power for the electro-hydraulic laying system. The weight of the whole system is 11,354 lb (5,150 kg).

Also of considerable interest is the American Auto-Track Vulcan Air Defense System (AVADS), based on a 20-mm Vulcan rotary cannon mounted with a radar system on an M113 armoured personnel carrier chassis. The system is under evaluation, but could prove very useful if an armoured turret could be provided. Rate of fire is between 1,000 and 3,000 rounds per minute, the gun can be traversed at 80° and elevated at 60° per second, with the radar ranging out to 5,500 yards (5,029 m). Normally the gunner acquires the target optically in his helmet sight and then passes it to radar tracking.

Surface-to-air missiles were at first seen as a possible alternative to heavy AA guns as a defensive

weapon against high-flying bombers. Operating at more than 30,000 ft (9,114 m), such bombers were virtually immune to conventional and even radar-controlled AA guns, only the proximity-fused shells possessed by the Allies in World War II made the chance of a 'kill' more than remotely possible.

With their characteristic technological resource, therefore, the Germans set about the design and manufacture of a series of surface-to-air missiles of varying design philosophy and performance. None of these was fired operationally, for the technical problems to be overcome were formidable, but the four more promising missiles were the Henschel Hs 117 *Schmetterling*, the Konrad *Enzian* E-4, the Peenemünde C-2 *Wasserfall* and the Rheinmetall *Rheintochter* R.1.

The *Schmetterling* (butterfly) design originated in 1941: the missile was 13 ft 1½ in (4 m) long, 9 ft 2½ in (2.8 m) in span and $39\frac{2}{5}$ in (1 m) in tail span, weighed 992 lb (450 kg) at launch, had a speed of 652 mph (1,050 kph), and could attain a ceiling of 49,212 ft (15,000 m). Power was provided by a 838-lb (380-kg) BMW 109-548 liquid-propellant rocket, with launch boost from two 3,858-lb (1,750-kg) Schmidding 109-553 solid-propellant rockets jettisoned after four seconds. Control was effected by radio, and the missile had a warhead containing 50.7 lb (23 kg) of HE.

The *Enzian* (gentian), was, like the *Schmetterling*, basically a rocket-powered, remotely-controlled aircraft, though of considerably more squat proportions. The missile was 32 ft 2¼ in (9.81 m) long, 33 ft 2⅘ in (10.12 m) in span, and 7 ft $3\frac{3}{5}$ in (2.225 m) in diameter. Power was provided by a 4,409-lb (2,000-kg) Konrad liquid-propellant rocket, but to get the 4,354-lb (1,975-kg) missile off to a high-acceleration start, boost power was provided at launch by four strap-on 3,858-lb (1,750-kg) Schmidding 109-553 solid-propellant rockets. Speed was only 572 mph (920 kph) and ceiling 44,291 ft (13,500 m), and again radio-command guidance was used.

The *Wasserfall* (waterfall) was an altogether more advanced weapon than the previous two, being a genuine missile rather than remotely-controlled aircraft: 25 ft 7 in (7.8 m) long, 6 ft 10¾ in (2.1 m) in span and 34⅔ in (88 cm) in diameter, the *Wasserfall* weighed 7,937 lb (3,600 kg), had a speed of 1,454 mph (2,340 kph), and could reach an altitude of 59,054 ft (18,000 m) and range of 16 miles (26 km), carrying a warhead containing 220 lb (100 kg) of HE. Power was provided by a 17,637-lb (8,000-kg) liquid-propellant rocket, and guidance was by beam-riding. All in all, the *Wasserfall* could have proved an effective missile had faster progress been possible.

Finally, there was the *Rheintochter* (daughter of the Rhine): 18 ft 10⅓ in (5.75 m) long, 8 ft 8¼ in (2.65 m) in span and 1 ft 8 in (50 cm) in diameter. The *Rheintochter* R.1 was a two-stage missile powered by a 35,274-lb (16,000-kg) Rheinmetall solid-propellant rocket for the first stage, and a 16,535-lb (7,500 kg) Rheinmetall solid-propellant rocket for the second stage. The missile's 3,858 lb (1,750 kg) thrust and the two-stage propulsion could lift the warhead to 19,685 ft (6,000 m), a range of 25 miles (40 km) and a speed of 1,087 mph (1,750 kph). The HE warhead weighed 55 lb (25 kg), and guidance was effected by radio command operating with radar tracking.

Almost immediately after the end of World War II, the victors began to capitalize on their captured German scientists and designers to produce new AA missiles, again with high-altitude and long-range bomber interception as the primary role. First into service was the Western Electric Nike Ajax, which entered service in December 1953. Guidance was by radar command, and the two-stage missile proved itself quite effective: 34 ft (10.36 m) long, 4 ft 5 in (1.35 m) in span and 12 in (30.5 cm) in diameter, the Nike Ajax weighed 2,455 lb (1,114 kg), and was powered by a liquid-propellant rocket after solid-propellant boost launch. The HE warhead was proximity-fused, and could be delivered to a range of 50 miles (80 km) at a speed of over 1,500 mph (2,414 kph). The Nike Ajax was replaced by the Nike Hercules in 1958. The design was based on that of the Nike Ajax, but an HE or nuclear warhead could be delivered 75 miles (121 km) or more at a speed in excess of 2,200 mph (3,541 km). Then in 1959 the Nike series was supplemented by the Boeing Bomarc. This was basically a winged vehicle, slightly slower than the Nike Hercules, but having a range in its IM-99B model of 440 miles (708 km). Radio command was used for the first part of the weapon's flight, and active radar homing in the terminal phase. A nuclear or HE warhead was carried, and after launch using a Thiokol solid-propellant rocket, propulsion was by a pair of Marquardt ramjets.

Great Britain had begun to develop surface-to-air missiles in 1949 but, after a number of government models had failed, in 1958 the Bristol Bloodhound was adopted. This is a winged ramjet, with four solid-propellant rocket boosters for launch, an HE warhead with proximity fuse, and semi-active (Mark 1) or continuous-wave (Mark 2) guidance. The RAF's Bloodhound was supplemented in 1960

The Rheinmetall-Borsig Rheintochter R-1 was a German surface-to-air missile of World War II, used mainly for the testing of guidance systems.

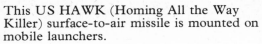
This US HAWK (Homing All the Way Killer) surface-to-air missile is mounted on mobile launchers.

Infra-red homing light surface-to-air missile

Another favoured method of guiding surface-to-air missiles (SAMs), especially where lightness of the ground equipment is important, is infra-red seeking. This has the disadvantage of being limited to pursuit-course engagement as the small, shoulder-launched missile homes on to the hot engine of the aircraft once it has attacked the position.

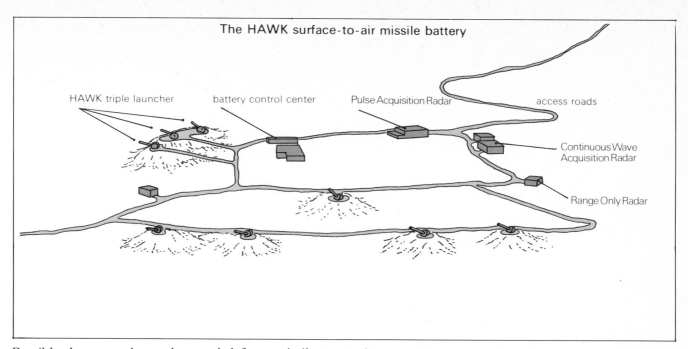

The HAWK surface-to-air missile battery

HAWK triple launcher   battery control center   Pulse Acquisition Radar   access roads

Continuous Wave Acquisition Radar

Range Only Radar

Possibly the most advanced ground-defence missile system in operation today for tactical purposes is the US Army's Improved HAWK system. The battery of HAWK missiles is controlled from the Battery Control Center, where a Battery Control Officer and two assistants (one for detection, identification, evaluation and high-command co-ordination, and the other for low-level target acquisition) select the targets for engagement and pass them to Fire-Control Operators. The Battery Control Center is provided with Pulse Acquisition Radar for general area coverage round the battery, Continuous-Wave Acquisition Radar for the acquisition of low-level targets, and Range-Only Radar for swift and accurate ranging. Each missile is controlled directly by the Guidance Group, which consists of the Continuous-Wave Illuminator Radar and the HAWK semi-active radar homing missile, which homes on to the illuminated target.

by the British Army's English Electric Thunderbird, a missile similar in configuration, but powered by a solid-propellant rocket after a four-booster launch, and using semi-active radar.

Since 1960 the pace of surface-to-air missile development has increased rapidly, technological advances making possible missiles far smaller than their predecessors, but with improved capabilities. This has meant that although long-range high-altitude interception is possible (even of inter-continental ballistic missiles, using the Russian ABM-1 'Galosh' and American Raytheon MIM-23B Improved HAWK), the threat of the missile has forced combat aircraft to operate at lower altitudes. To meet this threat, a variety of missiles for medium- and low-level interception have been produced, some on semi-static launch facilities, others on trailer-borne mountings, and still others on tracked chassis for battlefield mobility and protection. Finally there are also a number of shoulder-launched missiles intended for very short-range, low-level defence against fighter-bombers and armed helicopters. Most of these missiles are operated in conjunction with sophisticated radar and computer adjuncts (especially on board ships), but the shoulder-launched missiles are optically aimed.

Typical of the modern mobile surface-to-air missile is the French Thomson-CSF/Matra *Crotale*, a completely automatic short-range all-weather low-level surface-to-air system, capable of being mounted on all types of vehicle. Normally these are three in number (launch, command and surveillance radar vehicles): the surveillance radar has the primary function of acquiring and tracking the target, and the secondary function of tracking the missile; the

command system computes the interception course, fires the missile, tracks the missile by infra-red gathering, and controls the missile by digital radio link. The launch vehicle has four *Crotale* missiles, all in ready-to-fire transportation/launch container tubes. Optical tracking of the missile is also possible in the event of radar failure. The missile itself weighs about 176.4 lb (80 kg), and has a speed of Mach 2.3, which is reached in 2.3 seconds. Range is 5 miles (8 km). Other important missiles in this category are the Franco-German Roland, the Italian Sistel Indigo, the Russian SA-3 'Goa', SA-4 'Ganef', SA-6 'Gainful' and SA-8 'Gecko', the British BAC Rapier, and the American Aeronutronic Chaparral and Raytheon Improved Hawk, soon to be supplemented by the Raytheon Patriot.

Typical of the portable and shoulder-fired weapons is the Swedish Bofors RBS70 portable system, with a three-man crew (one to carry the missile in its launch tube, one to carry the launch tube's stand, and one to carry the guidance package). The missile in its container weighs 176.4 lb (80 kg), and is capable of engaging targets up to 3.1 miles (5 km) distant. Relatively unusual is the laser-beam-riding guidance used. With this all the operator has to do is keep the target in his sight, to which the missile is automatically gathered after launch, then moving up the laser beam to the impact point. The two fuses of the missile are a percussion and an active optical unit. Similar weapons (though shoulder-fired and some with infra-red homing heads) are the British Short Brothers Blowpipe (with thumb-controlled radio guidance), the American General Dynamics Redeye (infra-red guidance) and the Russian SA-7 'Grail' (infra-red guidance).

Index